American Puritanism and the
Defense of Mourning

American Puritanism and the Defense of Mourning

Religion, Grief, and Ethnology in
Mary White Rowlandson's
Captivity Narrative

Mitchell Robert Breitwieser

The University of Wisconsin Press

The University of Wisconsin Press
114 North Murray Street
Madison, Wisconsin 53715

3 Henrietta Street
London WC2E 8LU, England

Printed in the United States of America

Library of Congress Cataloging-in-Publication Data
Breitwieser, Mitchell Robert, 1953–
   American puritanism and the defense of mourning: religion, grief,
and ethnology in Mary White Rowlandson's captivity narrative /
Mitchell Robert Breitwieser.
      234 pp.   cm.—(Wisconsin project on American writers)
      Includes bibliographical references and index.
      1. Rowlandson, Mary White, ca. 1635–ca. 1678. 2. Indians of North
America—Massachusetts—Captivities. 3. Indians of North America—
Massachusetts—Biography. 4. Indians of North America—
Massachusetts—History—Colonial period, ca. 1600–1676.
5. King Philip's War, 1675–1676. 6. Puritans—Massachusetts—
Religious life. I. Title. II. Series.
E87.R895B74   1991
974.4′302′092—dc20   90-50080
ISBN 0-299-12650-1
ISBN 0-299-12654-4 (pbk.)   CIP

Contents

Acknowledgments

I would like to thank the University of California, for sabbatical leave and for a President's Humanities Research Fellowship, and all of those who contributed to the invention of the Apple Macintosh SE20 computer. I also want to thank friends and colleagues who read and commented on part or all of the final manuscript, or of its earlier avatars: Elizabeth Abel, Rachel Brokken, Joseph Kronick, Kristin Ross, Donald McQuade, Frederick Crews, Michael Cartmell, Anne Lackey, Kathleen Moran, Abdul JanMohamed, Steven Goldsmith, Carol Christ, Anne Middleton, T. Walter Herbert, Alan Sinfield, Neil Schmitz, Carolyn Dinshaw, Susan Schweik, Carolyn Porter, Susan Howe, and Sacvan Bercovitch. Though they were not directly involved in this work, Douglas Crowell, Gregory Jay, and Thomas Schaub are always with me when I think. I owe quite a lot to former and current students of mine who have discussed Rowlandson and Puritanism with me or who have read the manuscript, especially Richard Moreland, Steven Wartofsky, Edward Hutchinson, Jonathan Elmer, Curtis Marez, Jennifer Royal, Valorie Thomas, Shelley Streeby, Leslie Katz, Paul Rajcok, Ellen Walkley, Ellen Lane, Steven Rubio, Arthur Riss, Lawrence Howe, Jeanne Holland, Bruce Burgett, Tina Brooks, Michael Harrawood, Eva Cherniavsky, and Kimberley Drake, the last three of whom were splendid research assistants, as well as superb students. Donald Weber and Cecilia Tichi read the manuscript for the University of Wisconsin Press, read it in a way that was both critical and sympathetic to the manner of my argument. Barbara Hanrahan, Shirley J. Bergen, Margaret A. Walsh, Susan Tarcov, Carol Olsen, and Raphael Kadushin at the press have supervised and enhanced my work in its transit from manuscript to print. Allen Fitchen, director of the press, has been a tireless supporter of my work over the course of several difficult years. Finally, I want to thank my parents, Clyde and Vyrgil Breitwieser, and my brother, Chip Breitwieser, who have not only supported me in my work but who are bound up in more ways than I know in what is for me the mystery of this book, and its composition.

American Puritanism and the Defense of Mourning

Introduction

Mary Rowlandson saw what she did not see said what she did not say.
—Susan Howe

The known events of Mary White Rowlandson's life until the publication of her narrative, *The Sovereignty and Goodness of God,*[1] are succinctly reported by Robert K. Diebold:

Mary Rowlandson was probably born in South Petherton in Somerset, Eng., between 1635 and 1638. Her father, John White (b. 1602), immigrated to Salem, Mass. in 1638 and was followed by the rest of the family a year later. The family soon moved from Salem to Wenham, where, according to a note in the town records, the Whites lived "for a long space of time . . . in ye woods from ye meanes [of grace]." By 1653, the family was in Lancaster, of which her father (identified as the wealthiest landowner in the area) was an incorporator. In 1656 Mary White married Joseph Rowlandson, the town's first minister. She bore four children, one of whom died in infancy. She and the remaining three children were taken captive in Feb. 1676, when Lancaster was besieged by Indians during King Philip's War. The youngest child, a girl aged six, died in her mother's arm in captivity. The other two escaped or were eventually ransomed. Mary herself was ransomed in May, the ransom negotiations themselves signaling the disintegration of the Indian confederacy and the end of the war. During her three months of captivity, she lived mainly with Weetamoo, a squaw sachem of the Pocassets, and her husband, Quanopen, a sachem of the Narragansetts and one of the leaders of the attack on Lancaster. Her narrative records conversations with King Philip among others.

After her ransom, Rowlandson joined her husband in Boston, where they lived for about a year, aided by the generosity of friends. In the spring of 1677, the Rowlandsons moved to Wethersfield, Conn., where Joseph had obtained a position as minister. Internal evidence suggests that Rowlandson's narrative of her captivity was written in Wethersfield in either 1677 or 1678. Her husband died in

November of the latter year. She appears last in the town records of Wethersfield in 1679, when she was granted a sum of money to pay for her husband's funeral. Although Rowlandson was probably still alive in 1682, when her narrative was published, there is no known historical record of her after 1679.[2]

With that aptness to which coincidence aspires at an improbably frequent rate, the historical record as it was available to Diebold has Rowlandson arranging for mourning, and then vanishing. Because this book is about Rowlandson's concern for the remembering of the dead, I want to add some names I have gathered from the notes to Alden T. Vaughan and Edward W. Clark's edition of her narrative: the three-year-old girl who died in 1657/1658 was named after her mother, as was the daughter who at the age of ten survived captivity; the little girl who died during the captivity was named Sarah, and the son, thirteen when he was taken during the attack on Lancaster, was named after his father—Mary, Joseph, Mary, and Sarah, in order of birth, the first and last of whom were "taken in an untimely manner."

Her life is remarkable by virtue of the narrative she brought into existence, not just because it is the only sustained prose work known to have been written by a woman in the seventeenth century New World, but also because it is among the more intense and unremitting representations of experience as a collision between cultural ideology and the real in American literature before Melville, whose writing often echoes hers. She wrote this remarkable narrative because she considered her life to that point to have been remarkable for three reasons that I will discuss in Chapters 3 and 4, after a preliminary discussion of the social context of her narrative in Chapter 2: remarkable for the manifest intrusion of the sacred into what would have been the otherwise decent but nondescript life of a minister's wife, for having been singled out by meaning; remarkable for all the vanishings and for the struggle to which they consigned her; and remarkable for the startling things that appeared to her in the places where the vanished things had been, the denizens of a cultural economy (including the demon Philip) whose bizarre argot she learned to maneuver without transcending the wonder and outrage that emanate from sheer astonishment.

Rowlandson's involvement with the singularity of her experience continues into the composition of the narrative, which fails to annul the power of anomaly, and which, as a result of this emphatic engagement with the mysteries of what happened, is uncoupled from more abstract representational frames, not only from ideological representations of the meaning of the war, but also from the public chronology of onset, major engagements, and conclusion. In part, such public time is absent because she knew it was being recorded in other books and because she considered herself to have been assigned to chronicle only her segment of the event. But I think there is a deeper cause as well, a feeling that her time was dissevered from public time, governed by eccentric and private accelerations and retardations that she shared with no one, and also a feeling that she was not yet, as a writer, resynchronized. Consequently, the reader who has become immersed in her intrinsic temporality will be startled when she interpolates the following remark between two personal anecdotes: "This was about the time that their great captain, Naananto, was killed in the Narragansett country" (338). Such connections between personal and group experience, even at the sparse level of "at the same time as," are almost entirely absent from the narrative, and the effect of this terse note is roughly analogous to awakening briefly from a dream, long enough to become aware that one is dreaming, but then sinking back and forgetting. The effect is similar, if less startling because less abrupt, near the end of the narrative, when she interrupts personal narrative on the verge of her return to the English in order to digress into what I would call a treatise on the broad meanings of the war: "But before I go any further, I would take leave to mention a few remarkable passages of providence, which I took special notice of in my afflicted time . . . But to return again to my going home . . ." (358–60). Though she may not have meant the term to be read this way, hers was an afflicted *time,* in which the public's war was a faint noise at the horizon. If Philip's forces had so completely exterminated the English interlopers and their culture that Rowlandson's narrative were the only surviving record, if it were an MS found in a bottle,[3] we would have an at best cloudy knowledge that a long series of jurisdictional and property disputes during the 1670s, not only between Indians and English but also between the various colonial governments of Connecticut, Rhode Island, Plymouth, and Massachusetts Bay, together with the ascendancy of a newer and less cooperative generation of leaders such as Philip (Metacomet), ignited a violent uprising in June 1675 among the Wampanoags of Mount Hope peninsula in what is now Rhode Island; that the Wampanoags were joined by most of the other major remaining Algonquian tribes, the Nipmucks, the Pocassets, and the Narragansetts (the more northern Abenaki, Pennacook, and Sokoki tribes participated only partially or fitfully, and the eastern Niantics and the Mohegan remnants of the Pequots allied themselves with the English), an unprecedented intertribal coalition that suggests that the real cause of the war was the English encroachment per se, rather than the specific grievances that first triggered the Wampanoag attacks on settlers at the neck of the peninsula; or that the Algonquian attack was swift and successful throughout the rest of 1675 and the spring of 1676, to the point of nearly annihilating English culture outside of centers such as Boston or Plymouth; but that it crumbled in the late spring and summer of 1676 due to English adaptations of Indian techniques of wilderness combat, to the Indians' conceptual unpreparedness for extended and total war, and to the withholding of supply by and the active hostility of the Iroquois Mohicans acting partly under instruction from the colonial government of New York, partly under the influence of economic, political, and ethnic rivalry with the Algonquians.[4] Uninhibited conjecture might recover some of these facts, but not many, and the *large picture* would be quite vague, because for Rowlandson experience came to mean disconnection from enclosing contexts, not only from the life she enjoyed before the war and the Algonquian life amidst which she survived, but also from the social reality constructed in the aftermath of the war, a labor of construction to which her narrative was supposed to be an important contribution.

If winning means outlasting the enemy, then the English won the war, but the victory was hardly magnificent. According to Richard Saunders Webb, the proportion of dead to living may have been higher than in any subsequent American war, many of the settlements, including Providence, Rhode Island, were destroyed, the accumulated capital of the previous generations was consumed, and general prosperity was injured so severely that it would not regain its prewar level for a century. The trauma must have been heavy, a situation that would have generated extreme ideological volatility, provoking the survivors perhaps to turn *toward* the ministerial elite with a certain desperation, to confirm the moral splendor of a victory that seemed so bleak, or perhaps *away* from the ministers with an equal vigor. Webb contends that more than a few colonists shared a view that had been prominent in the London press, that the theocratic elite had both needlessly provoked and badly mismanaged the war. Such criticism, bringing to the fore longstanding dissatisfactions about the conduct of power in the semi-autonomous New England colonies, combined with the increased colonial dependence on English economic support after the war and with the monarchy's pursuit of greater power over the North American colonies, culminated in the constitution of the Dominion of New England Council in 1684, two years after the publication of Rowlandson's narrative, "to unhinge the commonwealth of Massachusetts Bay and, subsequently, to displace the rest of New England's colonial regimes." King Charles's advisors understood, Webb argues, that the success of this project of securing direct control would depend on the willing cooperation of a number of locals whose alienation from the theocratic regime could be counted upon, and who would as a result be willing to serve as administrators and / or informal supporters.[5] A politician as shrewd as Increase Mather, therefore, would have realized that the postwar trauma offered both abundant opportunity and great danger, leading him to desire, like Creon in Hegel's reading of *Antigone,* to *control the meaning of the war,* a desire that may have largely motivated not only his own written histories and explications of the violent past but also his active support for the publication of one woman's apparently contrite acknowledgment of the providential justice and rectitude of her suffering during the war, an acknowledgment he underlined in a preface he supplied to ensure proper interpretation of the work and the war.

Rowlandson probably knew Mather rather well. Her husband was a minister, which would have brought the family into Mather's sphere of acquaintance, an association that led Joseph Rowlandson to seek Mather's assistance in the negotiations for her release; and, as Diebold notes, the surviving members of the family spent time in Boston after she was released, where they were dependent on the financial and emotional support of the community. It may be, therefore, that Mather participated directly or indirectly in the composition of the narrative, making specific or general suggestions, shaping it. Even if he did not play a role in the composition, however, he was during the period after the war preaching and writing extensively about the war and its meaning, and in the ensuing years he was collecting several personal narratives by captives such as Quentin Stockwell, whose story appeared in Mather's *Illustrious Providences* (1684), published by Samuel Green, who had published Rowlandson's narrative a couple of years earlier.[6] Whether Mather involved himself in the primary composition or not, then, Rowlandson could not have failed to perceive what Mather would have wanted from a narrative such as hers, and his support for the publication of the work reveals that she was correct.

Mather was quite deft at apprehending the intentional structure and the consequences of the Puritan ideological formation, and at presenting it in an easily accessible form. I will argue throughout this book, therefore, that, despite his personal power, he was important to her as a spokesman for the attitude toward affliction that she perceived as the general crux of Puritan religion, rather than as an individual with a distinct point of view: similar attitudes, for instance, pervade her husband's last sermon, which was included as an appendix to her narrative. Mather articulated a worldview that she certainly did not encounter for the first time in his voice, and that she would have recognized easily when she heard or read him for the first time, a worldview that was a highly functional cultural machine, not only a set of abstract tenets but also a tradition of application, of bringing those tenets to bear on individual experience with great specificity and consequent power. Mather's innovation was the lead he took in showing how Puritan thinking could explain the new experiential matter of King Philip's War, in all its minute and extravagant horror, as a confirmation of its precepts, rather than allowing it to remain as raw trauma or to bleed off into other exegeses that might imply Puritanism's managerial or hermeneutical ineptitude.

For Mather, the utility of Rowlandson's narrative lay in the assistance it supplied to this task of application: she affirmed that the meaning that Mather sought to establish could illuminate experience not only at the level of large historical events, such as the causes of the war or the outcomes of battles, but all the way down to a level of unsurpassable specificity, such as the utterance of a given Indian to a given captive woman on a given afternoon. With the assistance of narratives such as Rowlandson's, Puritanism could once again govern, by virtue of explanatory cogency, the entire range of human experience: nothing was outside of it; there was nothing that happened that was not a clear *example*. Rowlandson's task was to *complete* Puritanism by affirming that her extraordinary experience was extraordinary because of the clarity with which it typified or exemplified a general meaning that had descended upon the Massachusetts of the late 1670s with renewed force. She was remarkable for having been at the very center of meaning, rather than outside of it in some discursive equivalent to the wilderness: rather than having been exiled or sent out from Puritanism, she had been brought close to its lucid essence.

And the narrative complies, in part: this is its best intention, a term I will use here as an ironic ventriloquiation or allusive citation of a notion of the good that she strove to support, with uneven success. At quite a few points in the narrative, especially at the beginning, she *hands herself over* to Mather's view of the war, searching through the minutiae of her experience for *evidence,* in part perhaps because she knew that this was the only game in town, the only way her thoughts and words could escape from the eventual oblivion of isolated memory. But this desire to share or participate leads down to a deeper layer of motivation, a desire to belong again among the lives of those from whom she had been torn, a desire not only to communicate with them but also to share meaning and thus to have been fully rather than only physically rescued, even though such participation in meaning demands gruesome concessions, such as that her home was destroyed and her daughter killed because she had been inclined to smoking and to rendering insufficient attention to the true purpose of the Sabbath. She desires to affirm, despite the cost, and only a shallow understanding of complicity could lead us to see her desire as an unimaginative or weak capitulation.

But *as she goes along* with the writing, and despite her best intentions, things get loose or come forward that do not reduce entirely to exemplary status without residue, things that therefore adumbrate or signal the vitality of a distinctly non-Puritan view of her experience. Such emergences result from a kind of ideological misfire: having been instructed to deliberate over whatever memories have a feel of significance, Rowlandson *comes across* significances that have teleologies leading, primarily, to mourning, rather than to faith as it was constructed by Mather and the other members of his cadre. This alternate teleology, I argue, was itself opened up by Puritanism, which was in large measure an attempt to sublimate mourning, to block and then redirect its vigor to various social purposes: to sublimate something, one must start by encouraging it to be, to consolidate its vigor, before appropriating it; but such cultivation risks the possibility that the sublimated thing might remain in itself, rather than accept transference to the proffered sublimatory surrogate; and, in the case of mourning, such a failure of sublimation would be antithetical to the ideology that seeks to appropriate it, because mourning is a project of constructing a personally sufficient memory of what has died, and thus tends to show a certain stubbornness when required to view the dead and the death as clear specimens of a general moral type. If such a "personally sufficient" memory is fully social, discursive, and historical, shaped by the complex knotting of cultural inheritances that composed the identities of both the survivor who remembers and the dead who are remembered, rather than an unmediated accession to an unconditioned truth, it is not therefore identical with the coherent, single, and simple representation of the survivor and the dead that Puritanism sought to impose: though the difference between mourning and exemplification is *intramural,* it is nevertheless far from trivial or imaginary.[7] As Rowlandson goes about fulfilling her instructions, then, she comes across intensities of memory that resist rather than aid exemplary reduction, and, as a result, moral clarity becomes forcible clarification, conspicuously coercive with respect to the material it putatively summarizes, and marred by intrusive dissonances. The project of mourning is for Rowlandson incomplete at the time she writes, and the writing becomes a part of the work of mourning, a work that first insinuates itself into the project of providential explication and then replaces it *in fact* if never explicitly: providence remains the narrative's announced argument to the end, but by the end it has dwindled to an extrinsic credo alienated from the intensities of what is going on. But even at the end the argument for providence is not perfunctory: because mourning is undone and the mark that trauma has left is unhealed, the clarity of providence is, though increasingly unpersuasive, still highly desirable. As Rowlandson remarks at a crucial moment, "Oh that we could believe that there is nothing too hard for God!"(356). I want to emphasize at this point that Rowlandson's mourning does not prompt a counter-exemplification, an alternate abstract meaning of the war that Mather's political enemies might find useful or that, in a broader frame, foreshadows the bourgeois view of the world that will in the years ahead slip itself into the place that Puritanism had occupied. Rather, she holds to the ruined world that is still her world despite the fact that she lives among the English again, a ruination of meaning that allows various anomalous glimpses, not only of her own emotions, but also of her captors. The text is itself an interregnum in meaning or an afflicted *time,* an anomalous textual ambience through which move interdicted subjective presences otherwise almost completely absent from the seventeenth-century New England archive, survivals of Puritanism's social unconscious. To use the figure in a different sense than I did above, the narrative *is* an MS found in a bottle.

For these reasons I feel that Rowlandson's narrative is a realistic work, not because it faithfully reports real events, but because it is an account of experience that breaks through or outdistances her own and her culture's dominant means of representation, and because it is itself a continuation of that breakthrough rather than a fully composed and tranquilized recollection. Obviously, I am adopting a concept of realism that suits my purpose, and if it turns out to be tautological or not itself "realistic," not an adequate representation of objective literary value, I am not especially worried, because I am trying to characterize, as a practical critical act, what I experience as the strength of Rowlandson's writing, rather than to adjudicate theoretically a canon of worthy writing based on measurements of relative mimetic success. If the first activity necessarily always entails or tends toward the second, the second, at least at our current moment of radical ideological debate, presents so many problems that it always threatens to invade the first and bring it to a halt. If one must wait for an *immune* criterion to explain his or her experience of a test's veraciousness, he or she will either write only about texts that are historically and sociologically very close to his or her own background (though differences can be introduced into *any* such closeness), or not write at all: certainly a late-twentieth-century former Midwestern now Californian academic man of mixed German and English ancestry, all four of whose grandparents were born on farms, will not attempt to signify conceptually what he finds realistic in the writing of a seventeenth-century English woman whose family relocated to the Massachusetts wilderness and whose adult family was destroyed by the Algonquian attackers who held her captive for a number of months. (Even with this degree of specificity, my list of differences is extremely superficial—the specification of identity spirals down into a deep specificity that is, if not completely known, *best* known in the mournful recollection of the family member.) If, therefore, difference will insert itself into any proximity not based on admiration for the work's *formal* accomplishment (how could I write about *Illinois* writers if I'm from *Wisconsin*? How can I even write about *Wisconsin* writers since I lived my first five years in *Indiana*? How could I write about my *brother,* who cannot remember the Indiana years? How could I write about anyone except myself? What could be more difficult than that? Isn't that what I'm really doing when I write about *Rowlandson*?), then the only outcome for us would seem to be to avoid the question of a text's mimetic worth altogether, and to wait collectively for someone to express his or her notion of worth, so that we can critique it. In this academic equivalent to what Hegel saw in the Reign of Terror, the community maintains its solidarity, its ideological preciseness, in acts of judgment passed against those who venture into positivity, but does not admit that it depends on such victims of judgment in order to maintain its solidarity and to preserve for itself a false sense of having acted. Meanwhile, furtive identifications, recognitions, and appreciations play constantly across the structured heterotopic field of texts and readers (or hearers, listeners, seers, watchers, even touchers, feelers, smellers, and tasters, since, as Rowlandson discovered in her encounters with Algonquian food, texts are not only written things; perhaps even allergy, a sixth mode of sensing, should be included), despite the absence of an adequate theoretical explanation of such anomalous, peculiar, and unbaptized intersubjective flows, and despite the various taboos, prohibitions, and interdictions that seek to control such flows but are themselves nevertheless sites in the general field. The alternative I have chosen is to explain (or confess) what I mean by *realism,* to explain that I find it useful without claiming theoretical immunity for it, and to signify, with a tone of outright speculation rather than of reasonable and judicious surmise, the extent to which my appreciation for Rowlandson's truth arises from my particularity rather than from my successful embodiment of an objective canon of value, and to say, as I do now, that *this* book is, to borrow one of William Carlos Williams' titles, *al (or a ella) que quiere.* My aim throughout is not a bogus humility, but instead a degree of candor about my specific vantage point.

Of all the critical terms that were taken for granted when I was an undergraduate, realism has perhaps suffered most in the theoretical debates of the last fifteen or so years. The terminology of prosody is, if neglected, not incriminated; ambiguity, irony, and point of view survive in new versions . . . only organic form has taken as much of a beating as has realism. Deconstruction has successfully challenged the model of a text affixed to an external reality and thereby validated, arguing instead that textual strategies include reality effects to disguise or attempt to arrest their intrinsic quandaries. In a parallel development, post-Stalinist leftist criticism, arising largely but not entirely from the Frankfurt School, concludes that the idea of the realistic text is either naive or ideologically pernicious because it uses an invention of the real to legitimate particular political interests. We are left with a body of works, largely European and American, largely written in the nineteenth century, that signified themselves as realistic for discernible reasons, but no realistic works. But for both schools of thought, though the idea of a coherent reality distinct from the work that legitimates the work on the basis of a criterion of mimetic adequacy has been discarded, there is nonetheless a largely consistent attention to an X that breaks into or through the work's aspiration to formal and ideological coherence, an aspiration that motivates the work's positing of a guaranteeing or legitimating reality. I feel like I'm trying to pick up a dime with a thick glove here, but I want to suggest that all this attention to a surreptitious getting-through amounts to a different way of seeing literary realism, as a transcription of reality's astonishing and at least discursively hurtful impact on systems of coherent representation. I do not mean that what I call the real at this point has an extradiscursive, extratextual, or extrahistorical authority, all of which propositions ultimately dissolve into logical absurdity, but that it exceeds the specific coherence the writer intends to achieve—even if this exceeding is a contrary intention. The real leaves its mark in the contortions it enacts within the writer's best intentions. If as Derrida argues such contortions cannot not happen in writing, I am interested in Rowlandson's narrative as a work in which the intrusion of the real is a focal trauma. Consequently, I will be arguing not that Rowlandson accurately or adequately depicts Algonquian society, English colonial society, or the conflict between the two, but that her narrative is one of the very few seventeenth-century Massachusetts texts that permit or keep close to a break-in of the real. The narrative is, of course, like all of the other narratives of the war, *about* intrusion, about the intrusion of Algonquian forces through the periphery of white settlement, into her life, into her house, into the *gestalt* which was for her normality. But Puritan representation contained the intrusion discursively by hypostatizing it as diabolism (or, to a lesser degree, as unreason), at which point it ceases to pose a *discursive* danger and in fact becomes a valuable cautionary resource. In Rowlandson's narrative, though, the intrusion is raw, and unremedied by the rehabilitated representation that was the major project of the postwar peacetime. I introduce the term realism, then, to characterize what I find valuable about her work as it stands apart from the general writing of the postwar period, her ethical commitment to staying close to what experience did to comprehension during her travail (perhaps travail should echo here with the French *travaille*). Any use of the concept of realism will necessarily involve some version of the term *close to,* but that does not mean that that to which the writing is close exists independently of the writing, that it transcends representation, or that the writing is good because it has successfully ingested this objectivity as its *content.*

The notion of realism that I am proposing corresponds to what I would call the first movement of Lukács' perception of realism. For Lukács, the realistic work is to be known by the human and historical complexities that cross the grain of its author's explicit view of what is the case in his or her society.

A great realist such as Balzac, if the intrinsic artistic development of situations and characters he has created comes into conflict with his most cherished prejudices or even his most sacred convictions, will, without an instant's hesitation, set aside these his own prejudices and convictions and describe what he really sees, not what he would prefer to see. This ruthlessness toward their own subjective worldpicture is the hall-mark of all the great realists, in sharp contrast to the secondraters, who nearly always succeed in bringing their own *Weltanschauung* into "harmony" with reality, that is forcing a falsified or distorted picture of reality into the shape of their own worldview. This difference in the ethical attitude of the greater and lesser writers is closely linked with the difference between genuine and spurious creation. The characters created by the great realists, once conceived in the vision of their creator, live an independent life of their own; their comings and goings, their development, their destiny is dictated by the inner dialectic of their social and individual existence. No writer is a true realist—or even a truly good writer, if he can direct the evolution of his own character at will.

There is quite a bit more arrogant heroization in this passage than I will invoke in my discussion of Rowlandson, the specific point of difference being Lukács' assertion that the cherished convictions are "set aside without an instant's hesitation," and thereafter absent from the work. Rowlandson's writing seems to me not to fit Lukács' criterion exactly because the assets and limitations of the initial *Weltanschauung* emerge piecemeal in the course of the writing, and therefore remain throughout as one of several centers of gravity. But I find Lukács' sense of the course of writing useful, his emphasis on autonomous perceptions that get loose and develop as the writer's exploration goes along:

> If, therefore, in the process of creation their conscious world-view comes into conflict with the world seen in their vision, what really emerges is that their true conception of the world is only superficially formulated in the consciously held world-view and the real depth of their *Weltanschuuang,* their deep ties with the great issues of their time, their sympathy with the sufferings of the people can find adequate expression only in the being and fate of their characters.

Rowlandson, of course, does not write fiction, but I see a similar development in the course of her writing about her characters—herself, her captors, the members of the society to which she returns—all of whom, "in the process of creation," undergo accretions of complexity that outdistance the typological schematizations she constantly attempts, a process Lukács finds most distinctly present in Balzac:

> It is precisely this discrepancy between intention and performance, between Balzac the political thinker and Balzac the author of *La Comedie Humaine* that constitutes Balzac's historical greatness . . . What makes Balzac a great man is the inexorable veracity with which he depicted reality even if that reality ran counter to his own personal opinions, hopes and wishes. Had he succeeded in deceiving himself, had he been able to take his own Utopian fantasies for facts, had he presented as reality what was merely his wishful thinking, he would now be of interest to none and would be as deservedly forgotten as the innumerable legitimist pamphleteers and glorifiers of feudalism who had been his contemporaries.[8]

Again, the canon of the "great man" is not of use for me, but the account of the "discrepancy" that is allowed to emerge in the work, that the writer has something like what I would call the strength to allow to emerge, bring us toward what I see as Rowlandson's realism.

Lukács' heroizations are linked to phrases such as "their true conception of the world," which point toward the second movement of his realism, toward his premise that this single and freestanding truth is the same for all great realists, who apprehend it with a fullness surpassed only by Soviet Marxist-Leninism, with the prescience that Lenin attributed to his avant-garde in *What Is to Be Done?* If the "central aesthetic problem of realism is the adequate presentation of the complete human personality," then the great realists are all on the right track, forerunners of the USSR as the various Old Testament prophets saw Christ through a glass darkly but at least saw him, unlike the idolators who lived in opacity:

> Marxism searches for the material roots of each phenomenon, regards them in their historical connections and movement, ascertains the law of such movement and demonstrates their development from root to flower, and in so doing lifts every phenomenon out of a merely emotional, irrational, mystic fog and brings it to the bright light of understanding . . . For it is no easy matter to look stark reality in the face and no one succeeds in achieving this at the first attempt. What is required for this is not merely a great deal of hard work, but also a serious moral effort. In the first phase of such a change of heart most people will look back regretfully to the false but "poetic" dreams of reality which they are about to relinquish. Only later does it grow clear how much more genuine humanity—and hence genuine poetry—attaches to the acceptance of truth with all its inexorable reality and to acting in accordance with it.[9]

These passages from the first pages of the book illustrate succinctly both the distinction between and the intermingling of the "two Lukács," the brusque and brutal stipulation of the truth, the psychologically more trenchant summary of both the pain and the necessity of representing what the real has done to what have as a result become *illusions perdues,* the return to commissar aesthetics in the phrases "genuine humanity" and "genuine poetry," the return to the position and positivity of the completed demystification. My point here echoes de Man's contention concerning Lukács' *Theory of the Novel* that the insight of a first movement is contradicted but not negated by the intransigence of a second.[10] Lukács' deep and sensitive insight into the seriousness of the realist writers, into the difficulty and consequent ethical achievement of their resolve to remain with what unfolds during the writing, is not annulled by the decision to sacrifice that insight to a political commitment that might leave many unmoved by the decision to supply its meaning.

A skeptical criticism would suggest that the putative reality that breaks through the best intentions of Lukács' Balzac is in fact a new order of aesthetic, social, and/or political convention as devoid of "reality" as the last, a conclusion that might easily be drawn from an even casual observation of the political order to which Lukács lent his support. Such may have been the motive for Boris Tomashevsky's sardonic reply to those such as Lukács, or, for that matter, Auerbach, who would see realism as anything more than a changing of the guard.

> We demand an element of "illusion" in any work. No matter how convention-filled and artistic it is, our perception of it must be accompanied by a feeling that what happens in it is "real." The naive reader feels this with extraordinary force and may try to verify the authenticity of the statements, perhaps even to make certain that the characters existed . . . For more experienced readers the need for realistic illusion expresses itself as a demand for "lifelikeness." Although firmly aware of the fictitious nature of the work, the experienced reader nevertheless demands some kind of conformity to reality, and finds the value of the work in this conformity. Even readers fully aware of the laws of aesthetic structure may not be psychologically free from the need for such illusion . . . When traditional means of introducing motifs are debunked during the development of new schools of poetry, of the two kinds of motivation used by the old school (the traditional and the realistic) only the realistic remains after the traditional declines. That is why any literary school which opposes an older aesthetic always produces manifestoes in one form or another about "faithfulness to life" or "adherence to reality."[11]

Writing in the Soviet 1920s with the tone of someone who has already had to listen to too much cant, Tomashevsky effectively assaults the positivism of Lukács' second movement, but he seems to me to have become too aloof or Olympian in the process. Announcing that there is nothing real under the sun, only the use of illusions of the real to constitute novelty out of the midst of the familiar—illusions sometimes produced with such sophistication that even literary adepts may not be free of credulity—he *requires too much* of a literary event before he will allow it mimetic consequence, and reduces the writer's experience of a hollowing-out of his or her understanding at the hand of historical experience to a species of naiveté. Tragically, we desire the real, a craving that sometimes leaves us unable to see prestidigitations for what they are: only the "psychologically free" being can inform us that the pea isn't under *any* of the shells, and even then we may not hear. But the fact that the real as it intrudes through the work is always already discursive ("illusion") and that it is susceptible to subsequent development into a dominant paradigm in its own right does not mean that the event of experience as it exists in the work is therefore trivial, or merely an opportunity for a writer seeking to establish himself by means of manifesto. Only someone immune to such shocks, who has seen enough of what there is to see, could say such a thing: and is there such a someone? On the other hand, to grant Tomashevsky his point, the event of experience does not amount to a discovery of an objective and final human totality thereafter impervious to intrusions of the real.

As my comment on Tomashevsky and emergent orders of convention will suggest, I will not in this book investigate the generic conventions of the captivity narrative, which achieves widespread popularity in North America in the eighteenth and nineteenth centuries, and which in many cases seems to draw on Rowlandson's example. I have done an at best cursory reading in these books, and they do not enter my argument for the simple reason that the genre was not present to Rowlandson as a means of representation to be either affirmed or rejected. It may be that these works absorb what I see in Rowlandson's narrative in toto, or they may only select extrinsic and easily reproducible features. The question interests me, but it is outside what I have chosen to investigate here. Rather than looking at a genre that may or may not come out from Rowlandson's writing, I will look at the genres that she faces—conversion narratives, funeral sermons, and scriptural typology, primarily—to describe her narrative as a collision between the costs and potentialities of these genres on the one hand and the perplexing area of history that afflicted her on the other.

2

The Society of the Example

When the Saints die let us mourn: And there is no greater Argument to be found that we should excite ourselves to mourn by, than by the remembrance that they were *Saints:* it should more affect our hearts at the thoughts of this that they were *Saints,* than that they were our Father, or Mother, or Brethren, or nearest or dearest Friends, for this is that which makes their loss to be greater than any other Relation doth or can; others are natural, but these are pious Tears that are shed upon this account. Another man may be a private loss when he is gone, his Family or his Nieghbours, or Consorts may miss him; but a *Saint,* though he be a private Christian, is yet, when he dies a publick loss and deserves the *tears of Israel . . .* we should embalm the memory of the Saints with the sweet smelling Spices that grew in their own Gardens, and pick the chiefest Flowers out of those Beds to strew their Graves withal; we should remember and make mention of them with honourable thoughts and words: and though it be now grown a Nick-name of contempt among wicked and prophane Men, yet count it the most orient jewel in their Crown, the most odoriferous and pleasant Flower in their Garland, that we can say of them that they lived and died Saints; all other Escutcheons will either wear away, or be taken down, every other monument will become old, and grow over with the Moss of time, and their Titles, though cut in Brass, will be Canker-eaten and illegible: this onely will endure and be fresh and Flourishing, when marble it self shall be turned into common dust.

—Samuel Willard

The saints, according to Samuel Willard, *"doe beware of irregular Mourning,"*[1] carefully judging the difference between the remembrance that truly lasts, longer than stone, and other remembrances, natural rather than pious tears, garlands that are as transient as the inconsequential aspects of the dead that they mistake for the truth of the dead. This need for scrupulous discrimination arises because pious and natural remembrances are easily confused in the intensity of grieving, an understandable but nonetheless dangerous confusion of a thing itself with its simulacrum. The long stretch of time will clear up the confusion because natural remembrance will drop away, but the *meanwhile* is too important to be sacrificed, there is too much urgent work at hand. The confusion would be prevented by a wholesale prohibition of mourning, but this would abandon a key aid to faith's efficacy during that meanwhile. So the saints resign themselves to sifting, a labor that is more than fancifully analogous to the attention they devote to women's writing.

Sandra Gilbert and Susan Gubar,[2] as well as Wendy Martin,[3] have cited John Winthrop's attempt to join Anne Hopkins' desire to write to what he called "the loss of her reason and understanding" in order to posit an American Puritan hostility toward women's writing per se, as if the excruciating duet between Silas Weir Mitchell and Charlotte Perkins Gilman had first been composed on the *Arbella*. However, though Winthrop's diagnosis is not based on purely personal opinions, neither is it the only formulation of the general Puritan mistrust of women's writing, a writing that was on other occasions cautiously celebrated when it was scrupulously confined to minor or supplementary genres, not meddling in the major modes of doctrine, theory, or collective history. Anne Bradstreet appeals to this nervous tolerance in her "Prologue," where she disingenuously promises that her modest verse will not venture into the great topics and petitions to be allowed her bare and unenviable discursive ground.[4] Confinement to the minor, rather than complete exclusion, persists in New England culture, in the judgment that the women of the Abolitionist movement, like the ex-slave autobiographers, ought most properly to write narratives conferring appropriate sentiment on the abstract tenets developed by Abolitionist men, or later, in the tendency of women writers toward regional rather than cosmopolitan realism.[5]

"Per Amicum,"[6] probably Increase Mather, writing a preface to defend the composition and publication of Mary White Rowlandson's *The Sovereignty and Goodness of God, together with the Faithfulness of His Promises Displayed,* intimates that a total opposition to women's writing is too tight or precise, and contends that the text at hand is safe because it ventures no more than a concrete and vivid "display" or illustration of principles she has neither devised nor altered: "forasmuch as not the general but particular knowledge of things make deepest impression upon the affections, this narrative particularizing the several passages of this providence will not a little conduce thereunto" (321). Kathryn Zabelle Derounian reports that Rowlandson's publisher, Samuel Green, Jr., printer of one of the editions of the narrative, continued this citation of the narrative's emotionalism in an advertisement he placed in his edition of *The Pilgrim's Progress:*

This advertisement [for Rowlandson's narrative] not only provides facts about the book's publication, but also adds information to whet a prospective reader's appetite: he will learn many details ("particular circumstances") about the experience; he will see how a mere woman and her children tried to survive; and he will read a first-person account written "pathetically," that is, according to seventeenth-century usage in *OED*, "movingly" and "earnestly." The emotionalism underlying the book advertisement should have helped sales, as should its inclusion in Bunyan's masterpiece, which quickly established itself as the single best-selling work in America and England, excluding the Bible and certain other devotional or popular works like Aesop's fables.[7]

Her life having been an especially intense example of God's manner of operation, Rowlandson offers vicarious experience to supplement what Mather and others were declaring to have been the meaning of King Philip's War: "Of the thirty-seven persons who were in this one house, none either escaped present death, or a bitter captivity, save only one, who might say as he, Job 1. 15, *And I only am escaped to tell the news*" (325). She is not referring to herself at this point, because she was among those taken captive, but the captivity made her a storyteller of more profound news, of meaning rather than simple chronicle, of news on the order of Job's knowledge of deep cost rather than of the sole remaining herdman's breathless report of the pillaging of Job's cattle by the Sabeans: "When we are in prosperity, oh the little that we think of such dreadful sights, and to see our dear friends, and relations lie bleeding out their heart's blood upon the ground" (325). If, as she later remarks, Rowlandson *cannot stop* returning to these sights, the Lord's purpose in bestowing this trauma may have been to move her to save others by supplying images that prove as arresting as experience itself and that lead to a more than curious or abstract memory of New England's terror. In both living and writing, Rowlandson seems to have been lifted out of ordinary wifeliness and to have been given a *vocation.*[8]

Though Per Amicum assures us that Rowlandson's book, like her captivity, is a *pure and transparent medium,* displaying God's message without addition, subtraction, or obfuscation, abstraction and the remembrance of experience in general tend not to converge exactly. Illustration, exemplification, and emblematization, for all of their rhetorical utility, are a risky business: the recollection of experience is apt to import a certain extra that a normalizing thematic will have to either discard as dross or confine as nonsignifying ornament, the sugar on the pill, gestures of trivialization that, though more or less conspicuously forcible or tense, are not impossible for ordinary ideological purposes. Captivity narratives are in general rather congenially functional in their social environments, and "practical application" is, according to William Perkins' *The Art of Prophesying,* properly one of the most useful and regular parts of the sermon, as it presumably would not have been if such application were thought to pose too great a danger to the homogeneity of the message. The dispersive potential of exemplification remains just that in most Puritan discourse. Only that, but always that: and in Rowlandson's narrative, a version of "practical application"—the doctrinal parts being presented in other texts, male texts, such as Per Amicum's preface or Increase Mather's writings on the providential meaning of the war—burgeons into a distended or hypertrophied supplement, *precisely because the doctrinal work is left to occur for the most part elsewhere.* If the ways of God are always enigmatic, and especially so to a woman cautious about trifling with major discourse, then the remaining duty would be to present accounts of episodes and experiences that were suggestive, that had the hum or aura of extraordinary significance, leaving it to reader-commentators to render the significances explicit. But the feeling of significance does not confine itself to what is amenable to orthodox signification, even less so for one brought up in a culture where every piece of minutia is thought to bear a possible message, so a resolute commitment to displaying the pretheoretical can say too much, despite best intentions:[9]

> And here I may take occasion to mention one principal ground of my setting forth these lines: even as the Psalmist says, To declare the works of the Lord, and His wonderful power in carrying us along, preserving us in the wilderness, while under the enemy's hand, and returning of us in safety again, and His goodness in bringing to my hand so many comfortable and suitable scriptures in my distress.
> (336)

Rowlandson's diligent, modest, and generous inclusiveness evades ideological filtration, leaving the task of selecting among the recollections to those who come after but in the meanwhile allowing into Puritanism's printed archive various nuances, implications, resistances, grievances, and daydreams whose feel of significance does not tend inevitably or sometimes even at all toward the sort of explanation she accepted as the destiny of her writing. The glorification of God is "one principal ground" of writing, a phrase that implies that there are other grounds, too, grounds that may include the desire to say that the "us" that is returned to normality is a diminished us, us minus (at least) one, the dead daughter Sarah, an us that is therefore not a return to or of what was, but a new thing. The present is a subtraction from rather than/as well as an addition. Seeking to confine herself to serving as a kind of preconscious loam for Puritan theory, she makes available to us some of Puritan theory's social unconscious, by which I mean thoughts, feelings, practical inclinations, and implicitly prin-cipled objections that were in the main purged from public discourse by an alert, imaginative, and scrupulous doctrinal exegesis in virtually full control of the means of textual production and social legitimation.

In this book I will argue that the unredeemed grief of which Willard is so wary is the wound over which dissonance congeals in Rowlandson's narrative, but I want first in this chapter to explain why grief *was* dissonant in the field of Puritan social politics, rather than an ordinary member of the array of permissible feeling. In the seventeenth century, Anglo-American Protestantism was not yet sufficiently genteel to opposite emotional intensities per se, so its injunctions against grieving have to have more to do with grief's content, its intrinsic thought, than with its amplitude. Unfortunately, Puritan writing is for the most part practical and militant, rather than theoretical and multisided, so no Puritan text I know of *explains* the origin of the hostility to mourning or registers mourning as other than a force haunting the periphery of thought, though there are many texts that express or deploy the hostility. Consequently, I will turn to Hegel for a defense of the Protestant objection to grief that is, first, explicit about its needs and axioms and, second, determined to apprehend its opponent as a countervailing form of ethical thought, rather than as an insurgent diabolism.[10]

Hegel's writing differs from Puritan writing on these two related rhetorical grounds, but this is a difference within a larger affinity, a difference that allows us to hear from Hegel what Puritanism does not say about itself. Hegel maintains the Protestant commitment to opposing grief, but opens it to view, especially in his revisionary interpretation of *Antigone* midway through *The Phenomenology of Spirit,* where he represents Creon's contest with Antigone as a tension between ethical orders and Creon's bleak victory as the regrettable but necessary commencement of a spiritually whole human society. In this commitment to the installation of a total Christian society, transparent, permeated in all its parts by a single compository vision, Hegel takes up the quandary that ate away at and thereby defined American Puritanism: the arduous task of reconciling the "abrogation of externality"[11] or extreme hostility toward institutional objectifications of devotion that instigates radical Protestantism, on the one hand, with the legitimation of a sociolegal apparatus on more than merely pragmatic grounds on the other. Puritan and Hegelian thought grow from this common problem: given that Protestantism has defined the negation of socially objectified form as an essential motion of true spirit, how can Protestantism be put to the task of legitimating a sociolegal order, since such legitimation requires specific positive codes, norms, and precepts, rather than a devout contemplation of the evanescence of codes? Despite important historical and theoretical differences—notably the insuperable segregation between the saved and the damned maintained in Puritan predestinarianism[12]—the crucial energy of both Puritan and Hegelian thought is generated by the challenge to Protestantism of entering social politics without losing its intrinsic character, a challenge that will encounter one of its major obstacles and resources in the human experience of grief.

A thread of connection might be traced on this quandary from Cotton Mather and Jonathan Edwards through the early Pietists to Kant and then to Fichte, Schelling, and Hegel. Along this line the crucial moment would perhaps be Hegel's dissatisfaction with Kant's attempt to mediate between the unavailable absolute and social practice by way of the chilly negativity of the categorical imperative (or by way of the aesthetic in *The Critique of Judgment*), a dissatisfaction that led Hegel to seek out the possibilities of actual and embodied morality, thus reprising in theory the New England experiment. Not simply a problem occupying philosophy, this intellectual affinity is grounded in a historical echo between seventeenth-century New England and the society in which Hegel was raised. Mary Fulbrook and Lawrence Dickey have suggested lines of common concern between early British Puritanism and the Pietist Lutheranism of areas such as the Old Württemberg of Hegel's youth, especially on the question of the politicization of the Protestant legacy.[13] According to Dickey, Hegel's philosophy originates in the ideological situation of Old Württemberg, a relatively republican *ecclesia-polis,* dedicated to the practice of both devout inwardness *and* civic piety, driven to fortify and defend itself in the face of a suspicious Roman Catholic regent by developing an ideological reply both to its own doubts and to the doubts of the reigning powers—the notion of a community of saints in exemplary accord with virtue, rather than a heterogeneous aggregate of individuals regulated by custom and common law, and the notion of history as a sequence of exemplary partial prefigurations of the community's contemporary achievement. Such political and historical exemplarism resolves the quandary of Protestant politics with a reassignment of negativity to a preliminary rather than a final position in historical signification: rather than an ultimate dissolution of all forms, iconoclasm is the work of history, clearing the ground of crude and fetish-ridden conceptions of socially embodied morality in order to make way for the *ecclesia-polis.* The dialectic of exemplary historiography thus at one blow answers both those who would call the community a dangerous innovation and those who would call it a betrayal of the genius of Protestantism. I am not arguing that Hegel's Germany and Puritan New England were substantially or essentially identical, only that their responses to their particular tasks of legitimation both took the form of a conception of history as the progressive refinement of the holy community through a series of increasingly perfected avatars. The "delay," as it were, may be attributed to the different rates of national unification, which kept German Protestantism from envisioning extended social administration until the eighteenth century, and then only in certain zones. Thus whereas Anglo-American philosophy during the second half of the century purveys the moderate pragmatic tranquillities of Hutcheson, Hume, and Socttish common sense, German philosophy during the same period grapples with the Calvinist turmoil around

THE SOCIETY OF THE EXAMPLE

the force of the negative: a turmoil to which Hegel, like Puritanism, responded
by attempting to demonstrate the manner in which the Protestant legacy can
pass into an explicit political culture without crucial self-loss, to demonstrate,
he hoped, the inferiority of spirituality that held itself back from articulation
for fear it would lose the purity it enjoyed while remaining in reserve: "But the
absolute Being of faith is essentially not the *abstract* essence that would exist
beyond the consciousness of the believer; on the contrary, it is the Spirit of the
[religious] community, the unity of the abstract essence and self-consciousness.
That it be the Spirit of the community, this requires as a necessary moment the
action of the community."[14]

Without for the most part inquiring into political motivations, American
Puritan studies have for some time now recognized the central importance of
exemplaristic typology, the exercise of perceiving persons and events not in
terms of their singularity but as specimens of abstract spiritual types recurring
through history. Puritanism challenged Augustine's belief that sacred history
stopped with Christ, and asserted the extension of sacred history into the
present: the Protestant critique of Catholic allegorism, in which the concrete
vehicle seemed too easily to evaporate into abstraction, resulted not in what we
would see as a realism but in a historical scheme that searched for abstraction
realized or actualized in present circumstances such as Rowlandson's captivity.
The abstract *was* concrete, it relinquished its nervous celibacy and organized
the world. At its intensest moments, according to Sacvan Bercovitch, American
Puritanism postulated that the present instance of the type was not merely a
recurrence, but the abstraction's purest and least encumbered actualization, so
that prior history amounted to a series of imperfect adumbrations: in the dual
movement that also underlies Hegel's historicism, the past announces and legitimates the present, and the present renders explicit the hidden meaning of the
past.[15]

The sophistication and complexity of the typological connections developed
by Puritan writers, especially Edward Taylor, have been taken as evidence that
the American Puritans did not oppose or fail to feel the power of poetic figurality as such,[16] but instead set bounds within which the operation of figurality
was not only permissible but desirable, although Taylor's concealment of his
verse reveals the anxiety attendant upon setting and maintaining the border of
permissibility. This fear of figurality's slippage into unregulated areas such as
those opened in Rowlandson's narrative reveals that, for the Puritans themselves, there was an *other-to-the-type* that, though it could be labeled sin or
error, was nonetheless a real factor in signification, and had considerable force.
Responding to this Puritan fear of or worry over its other, literary criticism that
moves beyond describing the internal structure of typology seems to encounter
repeatedly the question of segments of experience to which the type (but not

representation as such) is inadequate. Unwilling to avail themselves of the Puritan thesis that such an apparent experience of the real is merely an illusion produced by sin, twentieth-century critics have clustered in three groups. First, an aesthetic historicism has claimed that the type seems *to us* to be a coercive representation of reality because we inhabit a wholly different notion of mimesis that we naively project back, faulting the type for failing to address *our* view of what is real.[17] Second, the post-Coleridgian Christian existentialism of New Criticism admits the existence of a countervailing experience of the real in Puritan society, but sees it as the chaos of physical and social incoherence, which the type opposes with the clarifying redemptiveness of the symbol: the discord between the type and experience is, precisely, the type's intrinsic virtue. Third, a post-sixties social criticism addressing ethnic and gender issues sees the type as a form of ideological slander, deploying images such as those of the diabolical Indian or Licentious Woman, the Virtuous Savage or compliant Domestic Goodwife, to repress the idea that the other can be extratypological and still be a coherent *subject*—conscious, intentional, social, even if not assimilated to Puritanism's restricted view of the nature of subjectivity. Puritanism's uncontained other does not exist, because it is an anachronistic retrojection; or it is redeemed by the type; or it is repressed by the type.[18]

I do not want to adjudicate the relative merits of these critical positions here (because each has descriptive utility according to the text at hand), but rather to point out the regularity with which the question of the type raises the question of the inadequation or antithesis between the type and some X. The recurrence of this question in critical studies of Puritanism indicates the intentional structure of the type, its crucial function as a manner of addressing experience by annulling and then absorbing alternate representations of the real. Typology takes up a concrete experience of a person (including oneself), thing, or event, highlights a trait that reveals the referent's participation in a preordained and historically repetitive category, and then declares the referent's other traits (those that might make the referent's emblematicity seem partial, unimportant, secondary, or derived) to be inconsequential for determining the referent's state of being—at best, pleasantly ornamental, at worst a blurring or obfuscation of the true. Thus typology is antithetical not to experience per se, but to those aspects of represented experience that do not confirm it: representation that concerns itself with the other-than-exemplary is lost in the woods, wilderness being for Puritanism an emblem for what is outside emblematicity; the type annuls wilderness thought in order to edify it, to teach the soul the path for which it has been searching. The discord criticism feels between the type and experience, therefore, results not from the type's unreality or lack of concreteness, its falsehood, but rather from its insistence on exclusivity and totality, on being the whole story, the only path through the forest of memory. The negational abstraction of the type does not accept the status of being one order of mimesis among others in a socially heterogeneous amalgam, but rather insists on its status as representation's final instance, with all the other modes either arrayed in proper subordination below it or improperly straying into forgetfulness, the autonomy of error. Rather than being one way of thinking among others in the seventeenth-century English repertoire, exemplarism and typology are *assaults on* other ways of thinking, tools for negating the autonomy of other paradigms and practices in order to claim that they should be enjoyed in purged versions as vestibules or avenues to the pure. Puritan theory is thus *by design* a hermeneutic violence directed against Puritanism's others, an assertion that would not be in the least shocking to the major Puritan thinkers, who believed that holy aggression was needed to clean the good of the various accretions that had come to encumber it, accretions that were unworthy of notice save in their power to interfere with or obscure that to which they affixed themselves. If the type were *not* intentionally antithetical in this manner, it would subside into being a mere member of a heteroglossic array; *because* it is intentionally antithetical to the other ways of formulating experience, it can bid for the sovereign power to be a Protestant version of Plato's science of sciences, to acquire the capacity to assemble discourse into a centered whole, and thereby to accomplish the dream Puritanism extracted from the Tudors, the Stuarts, and the fledgling British bourgeoisie—the creation of a homogeneous social space—but in the case of Puritanism grounded on manifested spirit rather than on sheer political power, staged personal charisma, or a developed commodity market.

Criticism's inquiry into the dialectical negativity of Puritan typologism follows almost inevitably from the work of Perry Miller, whose allegiance to the negative theology of Barth, Tillich, and Niebuhr led him away from what was in his time the prevailing view of Puritanism as a static body of dogmatic affect and into the dialectical energetics that he called the marrow of Puritan divinity.[19] Whether in praise or blame of Puritanism, the critics with whom he chose to disagree failed to perceive, according to Miller, its essential commitment to Calvin's unknown god. A presence manifested as inscrutable force, known by its turbulent impact on cognition and signification, this god demanded a fealty that in practical consequence resulted in taking all explicit formulations of truth to be flawed and inadequate, however useful for regulating the conduct of ordinary life. God is an interruption of sense, not a form but, according to Karl Barth, an "effulgence, or, rather, the crater made at the percussion point of an exploding shell, the void by which the point in the line of intersection makes itself known in the concrete world of history . . ."[20] Cataclysm rather than code, Miller's unknown god lies beyond the possibility of adequate articulation in word or image—a god to be experienced in awe and dread, but not thought, spoken or translated into practice. Miller on this point captures the Puritan disdain for Church of England procedures (but perhaps not the reformers' nausea, a vertiginous anxiety as intense as Hamlet's imaginations of Gertrude's nightly betrayals of the Father), captures the central insistence of early English Puritanism, which used the idea of the unknown god as an ideological device for delegitimating the Arminianism and adiaphorism of thinkers such as Hooker and Whitgift. When Puritanism moves to the New World, however, the reformers find themselves in the position of sociopolitical administrators rather than dissident radicals, a situation in which they desire to avail themselves of a utopian view of their own exercises of power as right service to a monological community organized around a clear and common spirituality. Biblical maxims have only limited utility for legitimating such a project, so Scripture comes to be supplemented by various schemes of typological and providential signification that represent current political activity as a continuation or, as Bercovitch argues, a perfection of what is prefigured in the Bible. But for Miller this ideological transformation is a matter less of triumph than of filial infidelity: "Calvinism could no longer remain the relatively simple dogmatism of its father. It needed amplification, it required concise explication, syllogistic proof, intellectual as well as spiritual focus. It needed, in short, the one thing which, at bottom, it could not admit—a rationale."[21] However much Miller may individually admire the practical compromises made by these theologues caught in the "coils" of present necessity, and however much he may insist that his heroes never forgot the "leap" to the inscrutable, he nevertheless regards the move to administration as the commencement of a decline into the dry rationalism of the bourgeois Enlightenment. The social articulation of the Protestant genius adulterates and betrays it, confining that genius to sporadic subsequent resurrections like those of Edwards and Emerson. Thus an administrator such as Winthrop would be for Miller a melancholy figure, a beautiful soul compelled by his concern for the world to betray his vision; and those critics who associate the marrow of Puritanism with the surrounding bone—the body of ecclesiosocial dogma—mistake a nobly tragic corruption of the thing for the thing itself.

Miller's work is therefore an appraisal of Puritanism from the point of view of negative theology, rather than a summary restatement of the Puritans' self-conception. He does not himself, however, often draw this distinction. Identifying his own imaginative experience of Puritanism's loss of its true force with the rhetoric of the second-generation jeremiads, for instance, Miller obscures an important difference: whereas for Increase Mather and his contemporaries declension was a falling-away from what they considered the first generation's splendid institutionalization of spirit, for Miller that institutionalization is itself a symptom of declension. Conceptually separate kinds of lamentation are allowed to blend together, and the tone of the jeremiad is made to seem to arise from a loss that the preachers of the jeremiad would in fact have seen as a victory, the building of the city rather than the forgetting of the crater. I stress this distinction between appraisal and exegesis first because Miller's intimation that American Puritanism *was a* negative theology represents the most serious challenge to my proposed analogy between the Puritan and Hegelian views of social history; and second because we must see the desire for positivity in American Puritan thought if we are to understand the Puritans' vigorous hostility to dissonances such as those they failed to discover in Rowlandson's narrative.

The crucial difference between Miller's dialectic and the Puritan dialectic lies in their different understandings of the disruptive power of the negative. From the perspective of Miller's theologized existentialism, the negation of political life is always and everywhere the summit of spiritual achievement. Barth: "As an apostle—and only as an apostle—[Paul] stands in no organic relationship with human society as it exists in history: seen from the point of view of human society, he can be regarded only an an exception, nay, rather as an impossibility."[22] Hence for Miller the eventual exiling of the two Puritans about whom he chose to write books, Williams and Edwards, proves that their opposition to the encroachments of pharaseeism was an unalloyed devotion to the knowledge of divinity as a crater in social being, rather than as a stage or foundation for government.[23] Proceeding from the sparse ethos of *Fear and Trembling,* Miller's commitment is decidedly post-Hegelian, taking the top off Hegel's system by removing the idea of social perfection through progressive syntheses and keeping only the restlessness and relentlessness of the antithesis, the negation of the type, rather than the type as negation.

But the Puritans were not inclined to represent their institutions as a series of more or less embarrassing capitulations to necessity. Though Miller's elevation of the antithesis may have the aura of the demystified or of a tough realism born from the barbarism of history after Hegel, it leads us away from the Puritans' own dominant conception of negation as the refinement of holy society through the work of history rather than the incessant demolition of all attempts to socialize the good. From Jewish tribalism through the underground enclaves of the early Christians to the nonconforming congregations, history was the progress of an idea of positive community, and negations were the means rather than the end, the expurgation of repellently alluring simulacra that mixed themselves into truth:

> My heart hath naturally detested foure things: The standing of the Apocrypha in the Bible; Forrainers dwelling in my Countrey, to crowd out native Subjects into the corners of the Earth; Alchymized coines; Tolerations of divers Religions, or of one Religion in segregant shapes; he that willingly assents to the last, he that examines his heart by day-light, his conscience will tell him, he is either an Atheist, or an Heretique, or an Hypocrite, or at best a captive to some Lust: Poly-piety is

the greatest impiety in the world. True Religion is *ignis probationis,* which doth *congregare homogenea & segregare heterogeneia.* [True religion combines likenesses and separates differences in the same way as the fire used by goldsmiths to separate impurities from gold.][24]

Thus, though Puritan theory may have continued to respect the sort of negation from above that Miller associates with the unknown god, for example in the dictum that belief in the completion of one's own conversion was an instance of pride rather than knowledge, such memories of the radical heritage subsided as the American Puritans' sense of political need emboldened their theological positivism. At that point negation was thought of less as a force that intervened into the coherences of the faithful than as a correction that the faithful visited upon what they considered to be the imperfect social and personal forms of others. I am not challenging Miller's argument that the theology of the unknown god was a durable factor in the ideology of the American Puritans, but rather contending that they chose to see positive institutionalization as a triumphal passage out of the interlude of the negative rather than as a regrettable accommodation to the practical demands of worldliness: they did not see themselves as he sees them, and their self-estimation was a crucial determinant of their discursive and political practice. Given their desire to see themselves as having passed out of the need for self-negation, the sort of theology Miller describes would in fact have functioned as a nagging and unspoken goad to supremacist demonstrations that appeared to obviate the need for self-criticism rather than as a revered creed or as an object of perfunctory acts of contrition. Miller's exclusive attention to the trace of negative theology prevented him from attending to Puritan exertions of power: a repeated and explicit experience of the vacuity of one's convictions about social propriety and a belief that such an experience was the essence of devotion are not likely to culminate in the sort of suppressiveness that punctuates and defines the history of seventeenth-century New England Calvinism; but a belief that negation has refined convictions by stripping away all the inmixed dross leads to confidence about the rightness of visiting such refinement on others not fortunate enough to have reached the summit yet. And if the memory of the radical legacy itches at the desire to see the city installed on a summit, then exposing and assaulting the inadequacy of another—becoming the minion of a god clear to oneself but unknown to others—will confer a reassuring feeling of successful achievement. Insofar as institutionalized American Puritanism was determined to view itself as having surpassed rather than merely suppressed the radical legacy that Miller calls its essence, it was bound to resort to violence for the sake of self-definition. If, then, as a generation of American Studies scholars suggested, Miller largely ignored the question of Puritan attitudes toward the frontier, and if, as a subsequent generation is beginning to argue, Miller failed to discuss the violence of Puritan racism and misogyny, these lapses result not from simple blindness, indifference, or approval, but rather from his sole focus on the issue that burned at the heart of his thinking, the introverted agony of the New England mind discarding obsolete commitments rather than the agony caused others by the torturous construction *of* the New England mind. (Insofar as the latter was often a palliative escape by means of projection from the former, Miller's thought can be said to probe critically the origin of violence he was not concerned to address directly.)

Of Puritanism's numerous opponents, the unassimilated and implacable grief that struggles to expression in Rowlandson's narrative is perhaps not the loudest or most conspicuous, or most confident, but it would have been among the most vexing because by its nature it challenges the fundamental premises of Puritan exemplaristic typology, and with them the social project they were intended to justify and sustain. And it is on the significance of the contest between grief and exemplarism that Hegel's tormented reading of *Antigone* is especially illuminating. The brevity of this chapter of *The Phenomenology of Spirit*[25] belies its importance as an exploration of the elemental problems confronting Hegel's social and religious commitment. Protestantism's founding text, the *Ninety-Five Theses,* arose from a controversy over the proper attitude toward the dead, and a close look at the later theses suggests that Luther's quarrel with the doctrines of purgatory and indulgences was not limited to his objections to profiteering: he also objects to the specious easing of the indulgence purchaser's discomfort at the thought of his own or others' deaths, to the Roman Church's reassuring implication that the negative can be placated by anything less than a total and meticulous reform of the self—self is the only adequate propitiation, money is like Cain's vegetables. The *Theses* instigate Protestantism's attempt to appropriate for its own purposes the terror of death in order to gain the authority and prestige required to assemble a total and single-handed administration of subjectivity. In this project, one of the major opponents may have been the quasi-autonomy of ancient mourning rituals that, according to John Bossy, were not during the late medieval period completely assimilated to ecclesiastical control:

> In practice, there was a good deal more to [dying] than [legal arrangements and the priest's performance]; death may be an individual event for the dying, but it is a social event for those who remain behind. While the priest made his way to the bedside, the tolling of a bell alerted the neighbours in rather the same way that an ambulance siren does nowadays. There were rites of informing the neighbourhood, for laying out the body in the house, for watching (the wake), mourning and reading the will; rites for carrying the body to church; rites of the funeral properly speaking, the office of the dead performed over the body placed before the altar; rites of burial; funeral baked-meats; obligations to be fulfilled towards the soul, commemoration and anniversaries individual and collective. This most elaborate

structure, which was at the close of the Middle Ages in a state of rapid enlarge-
ment, represented some kind of a compromise between divergent pieties, and
between *pietas* itself in the proper sense (that is, family duty) and the bare skeleton
of the liturgy. The natural religion of kinship and friendship, which the Church on
the whole managed to keep at a distance from the bedside itself, entered into its
element once the soul had departed from the body.[26]

If, then, as Bossy suggests, Protestantism was a "migration of the holy," a
demolition of the diversity of pieties preparatory to a totalizing coordination of
social practice under the aegis of a single notion of spirituality, then grieving
practices, previously "things indifferent," may have proven to be major loci of
resistance. Hegel's preoccupation with *Antigone* would in that case be primarily not an act of leaping to imagine the Greek past but an allegorization of
present tension, and acts of insistence on mourning, such as that of Antigone in
Hegel's imagination or of Rowlandson in seventeenth-century Massachusetts,
however solitary or isolated, would not be at bottom private or personal, but
rather individual remembrances of a social ethic under massive attack—an
attack that, if Ariès' thesis concerning the redesigning of death in the bourgeois
West is correct, was ultimately triumphant.[27]

But, for Hegel at least, the threat of mourning was not confined to its social
force, the durability and extent of its hold on a general consciousness. In
addition, the content of mourning, its intrinsic thought, presented Protestantism with a theoretical challenge to which a responsible apologist such as Hegel
aspired to be would have to answer with more than an overwhelming tonnage
of suppressive power. His sense of the importance of such a reply dictates the
placement of the reading of *Antigone* at the midpoint of *The Phenomenology of
Spirit,* where it facilitates a crucial transition in the book's argumentative development. In the course of the first half, Hegel develops a hypothetical biography
or bildungsroman of individual consciousness, starting with sense certainty,
moving to the discovery of deixis and abstraction, through the origin of unhappy self-consciousness in the battle for recognition, ending with the discovery
of the objective identity of virtue and reason. Though this final position represents the apex of individual consciousness, the fact that individual consciousness rather than the collective social "I" of spirit occupies the center of the
argument means that there will have to be a dialectical overturning, because the
individual's specious occupancy of that position is deeply implicated in the
fragmentation that Hegel saw reaching its gruesome nadir in the Reign of
Terror, a fragmentation he is writing the book to help remedy. His decision to
begin the book with the account of individual consciousness is therefore a
pedagogical rather than a philosophical choice, an address to the reader's
present condition, a condition from which he is to be pried free by successive
displacements and reformative identifications.

Therefore, having exhausted the potency of individual consciousness, Hegel now moves to the dialectically teleological chronicle of collective consciousness: a conversion narrative is replaced by a history of sacred community, though, as with Puritanism, there are structural rhymes between the two narratives. Unlike Puritanism, however, Hegel begins not with Hebraism but with what he considers the Greek ethical harmony, a zero degree of philosophical culture, in order to describe the cataclysm that split the simple whole, instigated open contradiction, and thereby began the deracinated community that will culminate in the Reign of Terror. The African and Asian communities on which he will present stridently Eurocentric lectures in the 1820s are not analyzed in the *Phenomenology,* not because they are inconsequential, perhaps, but because their tranquility does not seem to Hegel to break apart in a crisis of modernity. They are, however, present by surrogate in the person of Antigone, who obeys an "underground" law, the ancient obligation of ritual grief that the city-state violates in creating its splendid future. Suppressing this prehistoric "nature" that is the secret source of its energy, the city in the person of Creon creates the ancient law *as* nature or unconscious: that is, legitimating his assault on Antigone by labeling her a feminine unreason, Creon devises a self-fulfilling prophecy, because exiling Antigone and what she stands for from social discursivity produces a muted area of opacity within the polis. But though he thus *realizes his excuse,* he does not *win,* because the mute is not without efficacy; rather it is a demonized noncompliance that will shadow the city's future course, first as a curse, then as the Christianity of the catacombs mourning for Christ and opposing Roman legalism, finally returning to the sunlight to fuse with the bourgeois state in a moral political community that is the denouement of history as it is understood in the *Phenomenology.*

Insofar as he stands for an explicitly codified state rather than a purely private spirituality, therefore, Hegel is an heir to Creon (and notably more sympathetic to Creon than most romantic and postromantic readers). Hegel's commitment, however, at least at this point in his career, is to an ideal and as yet unrealized political order, which means that some conditions have not yet been met. Insofar as he contends that from Creon through Rome to the Enlightenment Western political life has nervously libeled and excluded ancient fidelities, he is an heir to Antigone as well as to Creon; Hegel stipulates the circumstances under which she will permit her exhumation. Here as elsewhere, as Henry Sussman argues,[28] Hegel's ethical commitment to imagining the cogency of alternate formations ends up diminishing (at least for some readers) the credibility of what he seeks to view as progression, rather than repression or suppression. Such a dramatic staging of the ascent of politics offers insights absent from the stark binarism of Puritan rhetoric—internal appreciations of the antagonist as (at least initially, before suppression) a form of reason rather than as an inchoate hostility to be assailed without hesitation, recognition, or self-critique. Hegel's staging of historical conflict offers, or at least permits, an understanding of the lines of tension and relation between the Protestant whole and the distinct socialities it bears in its midst, rather than confining such distinct bodies to the inferior category of chaotic declension as a means of interdicting communication and its transformative power, a power Puritanism could only see as loss of focus. *As a result of* this look into the antagonist, and despite the fact that Hegel the state ideologist will argue that the destruction of Antigone was necessary so that history could reconstitute her on a higher plane, fully integrated into a public whole, the archaeological Hegel's exegesis of *Antigone* at the book's midpoint retains a divisive tone and an unassimilated cogency that the teleological entropy of the book as a whole cannot dissolve, precisely because the conditions for the happy resurrection are only imminent or projected rather than present and accounted for when Hegel writes in 1806, as Napoleon advances toward Jena. As Creon cannot eliminate Antigone without remainder, stagnation, or malaise, so the dominant logic of the book cannot subsume this chapter. Dead bodies left unburied emit pestilence.

The desire to subsume, whether Creon's or Hegel's, is for Hegel a desire to establish a clear and socially accepted order of exemplification, to demonstrate that a person or event is best seen as a specimen or example of a transcendent category drawn from a coherent general repertoire of such categories. *Antigone* is consequently of special interest to Hegel because it depicts political life as an exploration of the relation between force and representation, specifically, as a struggle over the power to control the proper manner of remembering the dead, an issue that, again, was of great importance for Protestantism in its project of totalization. If the stresses Hegel puts on the text of *Antigone* (and the meanings he projects into it) carry his reading of the play away from Greek society, they do so in order to allegorize a confrontation endemic to Protestantism; if Hegel's Creon is in several aspects not Sophocles' Creon, this transmutation of Sophocles' intention is performed in order to present a Creon convulsed by the problems and ambiguities of Protestant sovereignty. To this end, Hegel imagines a Creon desperate to control representation, to legitimate the postwar Theban regime he heads by engaging in legend manufacture, vaunting the civic heroism of Eteocles and denouncing the noxious infamy of Polyneices in order to promote a consensual and nonfamilial genealogy of virtue to which he is the remaining heir. As Hegel remarks, this ideological labor is extremely problem-fraught, given the rival brothers' tenuous claims to sole possession of the throne and the consequent difficulty of seeing either one as a hero. Creon's prestige is recent and raw, deeply in need of consolidation and legitimation, and he is therefore aware of the tremendous power of *exemplification*, one of the central topics of the *Phenomenology*, as Derrida contends.[29] Creon risks raising the question of the brothers' relative political merits, even insists on the question, because, if he can persuade the citizens to venerate Eteocles (and vilify Poly-neices), he will have devised a putatively dialectical ideology that can move between an abstract notion of right (defense of the city rather than clear genea-logical claim to the throne as a source of virtue) and the memory of concrete experience. The example declares that the personal singularities of the brothers are only vehicles or vessels bearing their standings with respect to virtue; exemplification negates or annuls this extrinsic singularity in order to preserve in unobstructed form what is declared to have been the essence of their personal being. The example in this way implies that the negation of at least a portion of experience is an expression *of* experience, rather than a simple external oppo-site such as Kant's categorical imperative. The example lays claim to being an *immanent* representation, an articulation of what is posited as the gist of a social whole rather than as an aggressive individual participant within a diverse community. If the battle between the brothers allegorizes the damage that ensues from attempting to unify a heterogeneous society under a single head (an issue of great concern in Hegel's Germany, as in seventeenth-century En-gland), Creon's labor proves not to be a reconsideration of the project of forcible unification, but instead a search for a more sophisticated tool, *Aufhe-bung* rather than war—a dark version of William James's moral equivalent of war. But public knowledge of the continuity between war and exemplification, the revelation that Creon's legend is a forcible deduction driven by political interest rather than an adequate induction from fact, depends upon Antigone's obstinacy, which is for Hegel a resistance to exemplification, more precisely, a tacit contention that exemplification, rather than a sufficient resumé of its material, is on the contrary a violent social epistemology that seeks a forgetting of the existential-historical actuality of what it claims to represent. The strug-gle between Creon and Antigone is for Hegel a struggle over exemplification per se, over the question of its function and its violence, rather than over the establishment of a proper content for exemplification.

   The political situation of postwar Thebes is not nearly so clear as Creon's legends would have it (their excessive simplicity being precisely their appeal), given the absence of a rule of primogeniture, the consequent ambiguity about Oedipus' successor, and Eteocles' violation of the misguided agreement to share the throne in annual rotation. The political problem that instigates the play's movement arises from the question of the personal uniqueness of the person in whom power is embodied: the occupant of the throne is to be singular, not exchangeable or replaceable before his death without the destruction of the state. The war was therefore perhaps structurally inevitable once Eteocles and Polyneices had struck their ill-considered bargain. This devastating error re-veals them to be the true sons of Oedipus, because it repeats the disaster that ensued after their father's politicosexual replacement of Laius: seeking to control the chaos Oedipus caused, the sons ended up institutionalizing what the father had done in ignorance. History repeats tragedy as farce. One solution to the problem, as Hegel knew, is the bourgeois state, which enables the replaceability of the central human figure by emphasizing the singular sanctity of the constitution and by denying the impossibility of identity between the state and specific actual persons, a disjunction whose critical force mandates rotation in order to distinguish the state from simulacra. Unless, of course, a leader can successfully represent himself as one purged of personal singularity in order to emerge as a pure embodiment of the values of the polis, in which case the state is not debased to a specious pretense of identity with the birth, views, or talents of the leader, but rather the leader acquires the prestige of a mandate by having managed to seem to be not singly himself, but rather a selfless instance of the transcendental. Creon's recourse to the exemplary legend, and his claim to have dedicated his life to service—not to Eteocles but to what Eteocles *stood for* (*stood in for,* as the vehicle in a metaphor loses its essential specificity in order to *stand in for* the tenor)—is therefore at the heart of his endeavor to recompose society in a way that will not reproduce the causes of the initial catastrophe. Like Hegel trying to envision an other-than-Napoleonic end to the Reign of Terror or to German incoherence, or like the Puritans seeking an other-than-Stuart resolution to the seventeenth-century English *sparagmos,* Creon reacts to social heterogeneity by designing and promoting the legend of a spiritual genealogy of the group at last rising from the wreckage, reaching its majority not in his *person,* but in his *pure service.*

In the process, Creon condemns himself to having to oppose ideological enemies as well as self-interested conspirators, those who would contend that he is not the purest embodiment of the values he proposes as the society's essence, those who would contend that other values are more fundamental, or enemies such as Antigone whose insistence on her right and duty to remember the reality of her experience of the dead person challenges the founding premise of exemplification, that persons are adequately remembered as positively or negatively admonitory specimens. The strife that Creon creates between himself and Antigone, then, is for Hegel based on a theoretical disagreement over the proper manner to construe the singularity of the dead.

For Creon, the perfect political virtue of Eteocles and the perfect villainy of Polyneices do make them unique, but this uniqueness rests in their spectacular achievement, in their having made themselves into specimens so pure as to have transcended singularity completely—just as gold is uniquely suitable to be money by virtue of its ready conformity to the task of general representation rather than by virtue of its use value. For Antigone, though, this conception of uniqueness represents the annulment of what mourning aims to establish. She enters or is forced onto the political scene not to defend Polyneices as hero, not even to promote a cynical relativism, but to defend a wholly different way of thinking about singularity. Her task is to *stand for* the memory of Polyneices as person, rather than as exemplum—this is what one is commanded to do for the members of one's family (whether the cursed house of Oedipus or not). Family is, in Hegel's reading, not aristocratic lineage, nor is it the woman's domestic service and subordination, of which he may approve but which he considers subjunct to the state's need for citizens, and therefore not the crux of the family's vexing autonomy. Rather, family is at its heart the depth, intricacy, and proximity to completeness of its members' knowledge of each other—the closest thing to knowledge of another subject, not to be confused with the simplicity of sentimental love. Creon's inability to perceive Antigone's sense of obligation to preserve this knowledge is perhaps for Sophocles the essence of his tragic blindness, a blindness that eventually compels what might otherwise be an adjacent order of memory to become an adversary (thought it may also be that in Sophocles' universe there is no "otherwise"). But Hegel contends that Creon is jealous rather than blind, shrewdly mindful that establishing his legitimacy will require him to subordinate and appropriate all available social energy and that he therefore cannot allow adjacent or nonaligned energies to follow separate courses. In which case Hegel's Creon is less obtuse than Sophocles', but still blind in assuming that such autonomies can be broken and absorbed rather than demonized to the point where even greater disaster is inevitable ("fated").

Hegel's Creon, then, is concerned with the specific character of Antigone's defiance, rather than with its simple fact. Constituting the complexity of Polyneices in her work of memory, a work that falls to her alone because the city is cowed by Creon and because everyone else in the family is dead save Ismene, whose temporary fear has compromised her in Antigone's eyes, Antigone insists that exemplification is a repressive force not unrelated to the shameful rot in public view to which Creon has condemned Polyneices' body. Creon's refusal to oppose rot with ritual—to retire the overwhelming and noxious evidence of Polyneices' now-complete thingness, the ungoverned corrupting meat that irresistibly testifies that there is no subject here—is itself a kind of rot that dissolves Polyneices into an impersonal typological ground that has only an extrinsic or hyperpartial relation to what the sister will someday say the brother *was*. Antigone inhibits what Creon's symbolic typology would see as the movement of memory toward the clear sunlight of political signification, the sunlight that beats down on Polyneices' vacant residue, and she thereby stands apart from Creon's drive to close the wound of war, ignoring desperate political therapy in order to insist on the all too easily forgotten anomaly of the person. She refuses the logic of ideological memory (remember the hero, remember the traitor as one who should be forgotten) in order to reveal that logic critically, as a repressive amnesia seeking to override another memory (remember Polyneices)—in order to recover the obligation from the threat of expedient sublimation. The contest between Creon and Antigone is for Hegel over the nature of memory's reparations, over the difference between adventitious patriotism and mourning.

Hegel frequently invokes the play's symbolic verticality to refer to Antigone's mournfulness as a feminine underground or nature opposed to the solar law of the explicit state. Though this mythological emblematization undoubtedly persists in Sophocles' writing as a survival formation, the central dramatic place he gives to Creon's inhumation of Antigone resists the innuendoes of myth: she is not autochthonous from the start, but rather is *made so*.[30] Hegel correctly discerns the distinction Sophocles draws between the discovery of an underground and the construction of an underground, a distinction ignored by Creon's desire to use myth to portray Antigone as an ignorant force rather than as a coherent ethical alternative. I believe that is why Hegel's commitment to calling Antigone an underground *in herself* rather than *by Creon's fiat* is uneven and imperfect, wavering from paragraph to paragraph between a critical dramatic impersonation of Creon (one of the *Phenomenology's* prime rhetorical devices) and a simple identification with Creon. These vicissitudes of tone result from the fact that, though Hegel may identify with Creon's feeling that Antigone is a threat to social totality, his recourse to a naturalizing vilification is blocked by three of his own commitments. First, he believes that women are associated more closely with mourning than men not by virtue of women's natural proclivity to sorrow, but because of the more socially normal passage of men into state logic as a result of the need to conduct war. Position within the social structure, rather than the intrinsic characters of the sexes, accounts for gender differentiation in the question of mourning. Mourning is *left* to women, as it is left to Antigone alone after what she perceives as Ismene's defection from the obligation: it is theirs by default rather than special aptitude, and testifies to a willingness to shoulder an ethical burden otherwise in danger of extinction, rather than an inclination to emotional extremism. Exclusion from political life results in women's more comprehensive observance of manners of thought superseded or repressed in the political sphere. A domestic ideology that assigns a ritually circumscribed mourning to women in a gendered division of social labor and that prohibits participation in the kinds of representation that attend political action misfires in cases such as Antigone's, opening the critical potential of a mournfulness not subdued to exemplarity's measure. Being confined to work a sparse terrain, as Hegel had argued in his investigation of the consciousness of the Slave earlier in the book, one is more apt to come across hidden or derided resources than is the Master who only gazes at the map of his domain.[31] But this does not mean that those who make such discoveries are intrinsically more suitable to do so. If, therefore, Hegel's partial and troubled allegiance to Antigone's resolve amounts to a kind of feminism (however anachronistic that term might be with respect to either Sophocles or Hegel), this

would be a feminism that is historicist rather than essentialist, and that consequently neither celebrates nor calls for the elimination of the distinction between genders, but rather explains the need to attend to the voice of the excluded in terms other than those of liberal Christian magnanimity: rather than
a vaunting of the intrinsic value of the difference or a denunciation of its
exclusionary intent, Hegel's defense of Antigone entails a measured dialectical
judgment that exclusion enhances the likelihood of the survival of overridden or
superseded kinds of memory. Hegel's vexed suspicion that we should listen to
Antigone's critical truth celebrates not the fact that the task of mourning falls to
her alone, but rather the fact that there *is* someone for it to fall to, despite the
price for her, because her misery ensures that something other-than-Creon
survives. Second, as I will argue below, mourning is for Hegel not an inchoate or
animal drive but instead a rigorous teleological labor that opposes nature's
proclivity to indiscriminate rot, and thus it cannot *be* nature. And third, if for
Hegel women are not nature and mourning is not nature, neither is nature itself
really nature, in the sense of an extrahuman alien. As Derrida contends, the
Phenomenology is devoted to challenging the absolute otherness of a nature
with the proposition that the word *nature* is a repressive term devised to stifle
areas of human commitment that are found intolerable by thought that is
inadequate to the whole: "nature is spirit outside itself."[32] When Hegel sounds
as if he is joining his voice to Creon's without dispute or irony, therefore, the
fusion is *shocking,* precisely because the trend of his own argument works
against Creon's representation of Antigone (if not against the painful rectitude
of Creon's cause). The Hegelian challenge to nature per se, as well as to seeing
women or mourning as specimens of nature, would suggest that if that part of
spirit outside Creon's political reasoning appears to him in the form of a murky
alterity, this appearance is the result of a suppression (which is not to say that
his view will not *become true* as a result of the suppression, if the voice he fears
can be quelled). Neither Antigone's gender nor her cause can be called nature
because her devotion is a kind of *work,* intentional activity pointed at an end
(the memorial construction of a representation of Polyneices) and set against a
resistance (the decay into pure forgetfulness). If as Derrida suggests the corpse's
gravitation toward undifferentiated matter is an X that Hegel's system cannot
spiritualize, and therefore a durably inassimilable *nature,* then Antigone is
working against this dissolution just as Creon is, and she is therefore no more
natural than he is: even, perhaps, less so, if exemplification is analogous to
decay in its commitment to the effacement or obliviation of traits. Be that as it
may, Antigone and Creon differ here at the beginning of Hegel's social dialectic
not as nature and civilization, but as labor directed toward establishing singularity and labor directed toward exemplification—the law of the family
versus the law of the state.[33]

The kind of remembrance Creon seeks to promote is categorial—Polyneices as traitor, his "ethical self" liberated from "every existential form," in Hegel's words—a liberation that will seem abrasive from Antigone's position, because for her the "existential forms" Creon considers so much obscurity to be dissolved constitute the intricacies of Polyneices' "personality," a term that echoes with but is for Hegel much more complex and even painful than our common usage. Creon's abrasions, consequently, are for Hegel the result not solely or even primarily of his personal character but rather of the character of the social epistemology he enforces, which has little use for fine measurements and discriminations. (We might just as well ask whether the administration of exemplarism produces brusque functionaries: the difference between Sophocles and Hegel may well be that Hegel is more "structuralist," more inclined to derive character and behavior from functional participation in one of the moments of *Geist*.) Subtle representations of Polyneices' personality would only blur or diffuse the effect sought by civic reason: what Antigone sees as a reductive stripping of essence Creon sees as a necessary dismissal of inconsequential but potentially obfuscatory and therefore dangerous detail. This difference belongs to the assymmetry between their tasks—though both seem to bring a ready aptitude, by contrast with the initial hesitations of Ismene and Haemon. The epistemological violence of Creon's technique, then, comes into view for us because we can see or hear from what is violated: Antigone exposes Creon as a despot in the administration of memory. Only the expression of another view, even that of the little boy who says that the emperor has no clothes on, can reveal (if not triumph over) coercion as such, and for that reason small voices are dangerous despite their lack of magnitude. In this contention, Hegel moves past a sentimentalization of the play that would cast it as an opposition between spontaneous or unreflective fondness and the cruelty of expedient realpolitik by distinguishing between Antigone and Creon in terms of a difference between orientations within a field of possibility bounded on one end by the density of experience and on the other by the thinning of experience for the sake of a social agenda. Neither is more emotive; and neither is less theoretical, though Creon's inability or unwillingness to countenance the simultaneous operation of both his and Antigone's orientations toward the dead will eventually render him the vastly more ethically impoverished (and, for the teleological Hegel, historically necessary) of the two, howevermuch he considers himself to be laboring in service to the ethical good of the devastated city.[34]

The difference between their positions is a matter of the pace of the work as well as of the kind of representation sought. Creon's order of remembrance is ready-made before the brothers' death, and it would exist even had they never lived. The categories *traitor* and *hero* did not come into being through a process of thinking about Eteocles and Polyneices; they predated their contents, awaiting the brothers or some convenient others as receptacles. And, again, Creon is not concerned with making delicate adjustments between the vessel and what it

contains, since that would smear the sharp outline he desires. Creon's representation is thus ready to go, and he need only defend it against competitors, rather
than spend time compiling it in the first place. Antigone, however, does not have
a satisfying representation of Polyneices ready to hand. Rather, she has only the
destruction of her subject world due to the abrupt exit of one of that world's
crucial constitutive elements, an element rendered astonishing—rendered *real*—
by the sudden vacancy in the midst of the familiar. The remediation of such a
loss requires painstaking incremental work, the summoning of innumerable
minute memories, each of which must be dissevered from the habitual contexts
and fugitive sentiments that attached themselves to the event during initial
experience, then appraised for what it tells of Polyneices, then added to the
accumulating structure of what will, at some unpredictable and ungovernable
future point, be accepted by the mourner as a satisfactory representation of
him-who-was. No less than Creon, Antigone is using exemplificatory refinement to transcend the data of ordinary life: but rather than establishing the
manner in which Polyneices was an example of a type, she is striving to establish the manner in which the items of memory were examples of Polyneices.
The question of her mourning: who was he? If at the end she produces who he
was *for Antigone,* rather than objectively, a cynical judgment that this result is
no different from the representation Creon constructs for himself is invalid,
because the infinitesimal laborious fidelity of the mourner's work is *qualita-
tively* different from what it shows to be the deft facility of an opportunism.
The fact that neither is identical with the real, and that neither is therefore an
empirical realism, does not prove their equally arbitrary status, because one is
composed around the touch of the real; and, since there is no *more* proximate
mimesis than that, cynicism cannot claim a ground from which to assess relative adequacies. Mourning is the *most* mimetic area of thought and feeling
because its ineluctable premise is representation's total dispossession of its
object and consequent inability to control the unknown with the taken-for-
granted.

For Hegel as for Freud, mourning is an *intrinsically* progressive work because it produces its end in the course of its action rather than beginning with a
predetermined end to which it fits fact. Freud:

[The final representation of the lost object] is made up of innumerable single
impressions (or unconscious traces of them) and this withdrawal of libido is not a
process that can be accomplished in a moment, but must certainly, as in mourning,
be one in which progress is long-drawn-out and gradual. Whether it begins
simultaneously at several points or follows some sort of fixed sequence is not easy
to decide; in analyses it often becomes evident that first one and then another
memory is activated, and that the laments which always sound the same and are
wearisome in their monotony nevertheless take their rise each time in some different unconscious source.[35]

Hegel:

> The deed [of familial obligation] no longer concerns the living but the dead, the
> individual who, after a long succession of separate disconnected experiences,
> concentrates himself into a single completed shape, and has raised himself out of
> the unrest of the accidents of life into the calm of simple universality . . . The duty
> of the member of the Family is on that account to add to this aspect, in order that
> the individual's ultimate being, too, shall not belong solely to nature and remain
> something irrational, but shall be something *done,* and the right of consciousness
> be asserted in it.[36]

"Simple universality" here means decomposition, a blending-into-the-whole
that must be supplemented by the *doing* of mourning, which concerns itself,
according to Jean Hyppolite, with "what individuality becomes as a shadow,
when it is freed from all the accidents of life."[37] The death of the family
member is a forcible initial negation of ordinary life, which is not otherwise
characterized by self-interrogation for meaning. Mourning takes up and continues this negation, not in service to oblivion, and not at bottom in service to
mastery or aggression, but to defamiliarize memory's former reliance on the
context of the ordinary, to commence constructing a representation that will
exist as a thought and felt being—one that is contemplated rather than one that
haunts. As mourner, Antigone initially apprehends only the surviving ego's
ruination, the self as crater, and must construct in slow memory a portrait of
Polyneices that is adequate to her extensive experience of her brother. Such a
portrait would honor Polynieces by preserving him, translating him from the
shame of being unable to control the exhibition and corruption of his body, a
labor begun in the attempted burial, which does not remove him from thought
but on the contrary covers his unbounded shame with what Hegel calls the
assertion of the "right of consciousness" and thereby begins to bring him into
thought. And, in so honoring Polyneices, she begins to restore herself, not by
recovering wholeness, but by transforming the place-that-was-Polyneices from
being a ruination of representation to being an object of representation. The
area of zero or space left by Polyneices' departure is not closed in postmourning
subjectivity, but neither is it an impassible obstacle to the capacity to form
representations and engage in purposive living.

   The transfer of the dead zone from destruction-of-representation to object-
of-representation is not a linear or tranquil process. At the moment of death,
the survivor's ego supposes itself to know what has been lost. But this tender
image, hastily organized by the survivor's experience of his or her own ruined
self, is in reality a preliminary draft to be filled out and transformed by the
subsequent surging of numerous memories, each of which will contribute to a

vastly more complex and ornate notion of the dead. As Stuart Schneiderman contends, the "image of the beloved is not the same as the trace of that person's passage [through the mourner's life]. Someone who has been buried leaves a mark behind, a trace of his passage through our world. And that trace is inscribed indelibly in the unconscious—assuming that the object-choice and object-investment was made during early childhood."[38] The initial image is faithful to a coherence the survivor is desperate to preserve, but it is unfaithful to the dead, in the sense that a bad work of fiction is said not to be faithful to what it depicts. It must therefore be rejected. But the overthrow of the first image seems to the ego to be what Lacan calls "second death,"[39] a repetition of the first blow. Losing the dead again (and again and again) with each uprising bit of memory, the ego seeks to cling to the initial memory and to resist each reformulation, calling this a fidelity to the dead rather than to its own desire. In the process it comes to fantasize an omnipotence: if clinging to the image repels what feels like death again, then such clinging seems to have the power to immunize the lover and the loved and to refute the ego's putative impotence against the loss of its objects. But such "triumph," as Melanie Klein argues, however provisionally useful during the time of bleak discouragement and depressed helplessness, ultimately "impedes the work of early mourning."[40] The fortification of the draft image becomes, according to Nicolas Abraham and Maria Torok, a "crypt" or inert area within the self with which memory cannot communicate, against which it crashes without effect in the commence-ment of melancholia. Only by refusing such fantasias and by experiencing the incursions of the traces does the mourner prove herself faithful to the dead, does she render the proper homage and secure the right to pass on, out of the museum. Even if neither omnipotent nor whole, she is alive again, herself, rather than a broken ruin or residue performing adamant obsessive repetitions after the crucial life has been torn from her. In coming to know the track the dead made through them, the living honor what Lacan calls "the unique value / valor of the dead's being"[41] *and* distinguish themselves from what they have constructed as an object of representation: at the completion of mourning, the dead are honorably dead, that is, adequately assigned to being something symbolized, a carefully measured and internally described area of zero *in the real / that is the real*, rather than a crippling defect in a survivor who would otherwise be whole. At this point grief will have modulated into sorrow, com-pulsion into revery. But the procedure is prolonged and exclusive with respect to other commitments, certainly not completed with the alacrity of Creon's civic exempla. Antigone therefore cannot oppose Creon's representation with a more adequate representation at the early point of mourning depicted in the play, only with her enduring attention to the sudden astonishment of Poly-neices, which is enough to reveal Creon's reductiveness, but not enough to say what would not be reductive. Like Hamlet, she can only insist on her time and feel that public time is awry. Unlike certain dissidents who might be ready to proclaim Polyneices the hero, she cannot combat representation with representation, only stay separate from an irrelevant expediency. But if among the undue clarities of the public sphere her position thus seems weak, in the context of Hegel's conception of responsible philosophy it should seem strong: her apparent torpor is the external manifestation of the long process of memory challenging image, compelling it to respond to the real with self-revisions, a procedure that is much closer to what Hegel defines as dialectic than is Creon's untroubled tailoring of evidence to fit the image with which he commences. Mourning may be dialectic's purest case.[42]

But for Antigone, keeping expediency at a distance suffices only so long as that expediency does not become invasive, does not insist that there be no competitors or alternatives in its domain, in which case ignoring would have to become resisting. There is a third ground for the opposition between Creon and Antigone in addition to the kind of representation sought and the pace of the seeking, and that is the kind of renewal sought—and it is on this ground that the theoretical difference between the two orders of memory becomes political conflict. Antigone is attempting to return to some competence in her own life, to her marriage to Haemon among other things, but Creon is attempting to wrest personal power and political legitimacy from the postwar instability, an end he believes will require the full participation of the citizens. Mourning, however, is not simply one of any number of alternate pursuits that would distract from allegiance, such as reestablishing trade and so on; rather, mourning is in particular for Creon the major energy or resource necessary to fuel his machine, and Antigone's noncompliance is *especially* threatening to him. In suggesting this, Hegel is bringing forward his major addition to Sophocles, his contention that the exemplary state depends on a *sublimation of mourning,* rather than on the sublimation of *eros* that Freud will describe in *Civilization and Its Discontents* and *The Future of an Illusion.* In a sublimation of mourning, the negation of desire is performed by the death of the beloved rather than by self-discipline or primary repression, a situation to which exemplification can respond *solicitously,* as a generous provision of a ready and complete image of the dead. This ideological maneuver includes a promise that the repeated second deaths of mourning are unnecessary, that the work is done, the product delivered. The intense desire that this be so, a version of the compulsive clinging to the first image of the dead in order to avoid the work, renders the traumatized postwar population eager to emulate and thereby resurrect what is said to have been the essence of the dead—to make the dead live in memory rather than die in memory—rather than weary and inclined to subside into private work. The Hegelian and Freudian theories of sublimation are of course not mutually exclusive, but a putatively sympathetic response to negation represented as having happened in the course of things is intrinsically different from a justification of negation as necessary to the cause of civilization. Sublimation of the sort Hegel analyzes is more alert to desire's malleability and less vulnerable to skepticism, and therefore often the preeminently useful item in the ideological toolbox, because it seems to preserve rather than impose value. The sentimental state advertises a friendliness that its self-righteous counterpart lacks.[43]

Hegel argues that Creon learned the utility of sublimation during the recent war, when the urgency of preserving the city preempted and absorbed other uses of social energy:

> The Spirit of universal assembly and association is the simple and negative essence of those systems [such as the family] which tend to isolate themselves. In order not to let them become rooted and set in this isolation, thereby breaking up the whole and letting the [communal] spirit evaporate, government has from time to time to shake them to their core by war. By this means the government upsets their established order, and violates their right to independence, while the individuals who, absorbed in their own way of life, break loose from the whole and strive after the inviolable independence and security of the person, are made to feel in the task laid on them their lord and master, death. Spirit, by thus throwing into the melting-pot the stable existence of those systems, checks their tendency to fall away from the ethical order, and to be submerged in natural existence; and it preserves and raises conscious self into freedom and its own power.[44]

This is Hegel at his most Creonic, returning family to the category nature, outside "the" ethical order, and vaunting the destruction of autonomies, even suggesting that the nullification of internal disparity is a proper purpose for rather than simply a happy by-product of war. For my purpose here, the most important point in this passage is the discovery of sublimation, of the way in which the war machine negates the separatenesses of the energies it then absorbs, the figuration of death not as termination but as preparation for the transformation of nonaligned affection into love for the cause. At the time of the drama, Creon lacks the intensity of war to sustain sublimation, but he has not forgotten death's force and he realizes that grief can be exploited too, by a certain way of defining the nature of peace. Creon apprehends that private grief, if it is encouraged to misapprehend that to which it is obligated, can be converted into a supply source, a longing to reconstitute the dead, to close quickly the mortal wounds of destroyed survivor selves rather than to have to go through the ungovernably prolonged time of remembering. To tap this longing, Creon insists that Eteocles did not die in the pursuit of his own interest, but instead that he put civic virtue above his own life. This supposed gesture would

suggest two things: that Eteocles held his own singularity—that way of knowing him that the family had—to be inconsequential, not a crucial loss, and not
in need of mourning; and that what Eteocles considered his essence—political
loyalty—has not disappeared but remains *in potentia,* to be revived or resur-
rected in the Theban survivor's deeds of emulation. Conversely, in Creon's
logic, Polyneices' traitorous selfishness left nothing to be emulated, but again
nothing to mourn, because Eteocles' heroism has expelled singularity from
significance. Honoring Eteocles' death means honoring it as statement, which
means remembering Polyneices as meat lying on the ground, the visible and
olfactory figuration of what is left over after honor sanctified by death has
defined the canon of memorability. The genius of this rhetoric lies not primarily
in its declaration that mourning is impertinent or blasphemous, but rather in its
assurance that mourning is unnecessary, that solidarity with the postwar regime
based on emulation of the virtues Creon stipulates can obviate the night of
incoherence. A brief interlude of sorrow, then group renewal: would that it
were so.[45] Mourning is thus not simply discouraged, but instead discouraged
from following an intrinsic unfolding so that it might be diverted into the state's
bank account. Hegel's historico-teleological inclination sees this sublimation of
grieving as an instance of *aufheben,* the cancellation of a crude formulation of
spirit necessary to lift it into higher form, and at those points where Hegel's
ventriloquiation of Creon tends toward plain identification, as in the passage
celebrating the social therapy conferred by war, political rectitude emerges as a
refinement of grieving. But, insofar as there is an element of Hegel that is also
Antigone, Creon's appropriation seems at other moments less a refinement
than a repressive sublimation.

A repressive sublimation that fails. Rather than controlling Antigone, Hegel
contends, Creon drives her to articulate explicitly the implicit tenets of her
devotion, to become directly political: her grief for Eteocles does not emerge
into the domain of dramatic representation because it is not challenged by
Creon (although it would not be the same as Creon's heroization of Eteocles),
and her grief for Polyneices goes public only because its most elementary right
to be has been insulted. Exemplification per se does not incite her resistance,
but rather a demand that exemplification be the sole order of memory: had the
burial of Polyneices been permitted, had private emotion met with the tolerant
nonintervention of public respect rather than the predatory intrusion of public
preemption, Antigone might have contented herself with a milder disdain or
indifference for the legend and its "violence of human caprice."[46] However, her
hand forced by Creon's exploitive jealousy (thou shalt have no other memory
before mine), Antigone's disdain or indifference becomes explicit rebellion and
critique based on an open defense of the law that binds her; and the fact that she
does not oppose exemplification per se (an opposition that is in any case

theoretically impossible) becomes clear in her willingness to become an exam-ple of one who heeds the obligation, to become the small voice that reveals the despot. It is this willingness to become an example for which we remember her, though Ismene would in turn have to go past the contemplation of her sister *as an example of fidelity to mourning* if she were to heed Antigone's lesson in mourning for her, to remember a complexity in which her sister's noble com-mitment was embedded as a vibrant participant. But whatever Ismene will have to do, not only after the dramatic action of this play but also outside of the public space that is the Greek drama's site, this familial obligation is not our obligation because we are witnesses not to Antigone's excruciating reveries but to her forced exit from the practice of mourning into the defense of mourning, from private reflection into public statement, a transition that implies an inter-ruption of her mourning but not a violation of its principles: she is not our sister but an example of sisterliness, a role she chooses, and can choose without contradicting herself because mourning opposes not political exemplarity in itself, but rather the attempt to extend it into a monomnemonic supremacy.

Left to itself, mourning may therefore seem apolitical or even passive, con-tent to pursue its course and let Creon have his way. But that which is not directly political is not necessarily without political consequence: if mourning does not of itself challenge Creon but does its private business, it nonetheless maintains a reservoir of preserved human fact upon which counter exemplifica-tions such as folk legends can draw where there might otherwise be only the newspeak of the ruling party's legend. Though not subordinate to antithetical ideologies (vilifications of Eteocles/heroizations of Polyneices), and perhaps even discordant with them in turn should they aspire to Creonic supremacism, the material that Antigone is striving to remember would be an element in the hetereogeneous and nonsychronized collective archive that is an ineluctable precondition for antithetical formations competent to break through the smooth surface of what has been constructed as the true.

Such an *eventual* politicization of the legacy of mourning is not, however, at issue in *Antigone*, because Creon's encroachment on the obligation provokes immediate and direct politicization, Antigone's defense of mourning rather than her own or someone else's subsequent use of mourning's result in service to a new definition of political virtue. Needing mourning's energy and fearing its perhaps distant consequences, Creon assaults it directly, but, according to Hegel, thereby precipitates what otherwise only might have been, an enemy whose cogency opposes him on the public stage: "The community, however, can only maintain itself by suppressing this spirit of individualism, and because [mournfulness] is an essential moment, all the same creates it, and moreover, creates it by its repressive attitude toward it as a hostile principle"; "[Creon's] action is itself this splitting into two, [his] explicit self-affirmation and the establishing over against itself of an alien external reality; that there is such a reality, this stems from the action itself and results from it."[47] Hegel does not mean that without the repression there would be no repressed, as a certain contemporary cultural solipsism operating in the wake of Foucault would have it, but that without the repression mourning would not emerge directly as an antithetical player on the stage, as a reality *alien and external* to government.

As a vehement antithesis brought into being by Creon's jealousy, therefore, Antigone's defense of mourning poses crucial problems for the Hegelian system. The prewar harmony, according to Hegel, was ethically heterogeneous: it depended on inner disparities remaining latent or demotic, in the form of both/and rather than either/or. Reconstruction after the war, however, brings disparity into view by contrast with the unity forged during wartime and thereby instigates the work of history's mediatory unifications, which will replace harmony on a higher level. But the events of the play—which constrain Hegel precisely because he knows that he feels himself responding to them so strongly—lead to questions about the inevitability of seeing disparity as contradiction rather than as what Paul Zweig calls "a broad miscellaneous esthetic":[48] Creon forces disparity into contradiction in pursuit of his desire to preside over a unity with nothing outside itself. Thus the contradiction that seems to call for the arrival of social unification turns out to have been precipitated by the desire for social unification, a monomania-induced circularity that seriously compromises Hegel's assertion of the necessity and inevitability of the progression. Creon produces conditions he calls crisis and then uses them as a mandate, the violence of desirous power making a wreckage then said to be acute enough to demand submission to its initial plan, a ploy that suggests that it might have been otherwise. The harmony of ethical heterogeneity is not intrinsically or dialectically flawed, not in itself in need of remedial supplementation from above, only vulnerable to the insurgent and intransigent exclusivism of one of its members, the semiosis of the legend. The social heterogeneity of prewar Thebes, therefore, does not fail due to some inadequate theorization that calls for transcendental reformulation, but rather is only destroyed.

But not, for Hegel, destroyed without a trace. Creon creates his articulate political adversary and, burying her in the silence of earth, creates then a mute insistence, melancholia, an interminable, demonized, and vengeful grieving. When the avenues of exit from grief and reentry to life seem all to have been so clogged or polluted by political interest that there is no therapeutic path not complicit in the cause, grief remains immobile and poisonous, an infinite subverting rumination, and an infinite contagion. Seeking to stifle Antigone's grieving, Creon creates Haemon's grief by preventing the marriage, then doubles Haemon's grief when Antigone kills herself, then creates not only his own but also his wife's grief when Haemon kills himself, then doubles his own grief when Eurydice kills herself—though "doubling" can only be a figure here, given the incommensurabilities that loom over grief. The steps of nemesis come in his direction without fail; he is left with his hands full of exempla—*refinements of life,* according to his own logic—but little else. Now in the tragic anagnorisis Creon recognizes the power of the ancient law of which Antigone attempted to inform him, too late for him *as a person, as a member of a family,* concepts with little meaning in the system he has successfully promoted to dominance. Whatever recognition Creon may reach at this moment has little meaning for Hegel beside a slight tone of pathos, because this recognition cannot presage a *restoration* of the order that was. History must press forward to discovery, so nemesis is not the avatar of revival but instead a haunting, a miasmal medium in which designs result in their opposites and all is confused. By burying Antigone, Creon exiles the inevitable obligation she stands for from the city, even from the surface of the earth, commits it (he hopes) to oblivion, to a deep and unbreachable privatization and exclusion from public discourse that will leave exemplification as the sole standing order of remembrance. But Antigone is buried alive, which for Hegel means that Creon cannot eliminate an *Antigone effect* from the polis, only transform that effect from a dialogical ethical contestant into a mute virulent contagion that haunts public logic without respite or relief. *Now* he understands what mourning was, but too late, because it is that no longer, because he has transformed it into an area of sullen darkness impenetrable by and unresponsive to any ethical lucidity.[49] Rather than dialogue between his project and another, there is now only his project and a purely destructive and relentless force of adulterating resistance, irony:

> Since the community only gets an existence through its interference with the happiness of the Family and by dissolving [individual] self-consciousness into the universal, it creates for itself in what it suppresses and what is at the same time essential to it an internal enemy—womankind in general. Womankind, the everlasting irony [in the life of the community]—changes by intrigue the universal end of government into a private end, transforms its universal activity into the work of some particular individual, and perverts the universal property of the state into a possession and ornament of the family.[50]

Hegel's essentializing equation [mourning = ironic perversion = nature = woman) is not at this point in his argument necessarily a retraction of his earlier view of mourning as a human and ethical act because the equation of woman with mourning with irrationality is Creon's *creation,* the *result* of his violence, a demonization of women and mourning rather than their phenomenologically original condition. Once it is posited that the community can exist *only* by interfering with the family, that a community that is not universal and totalized is not a community at all, then any perception of individuals as anything other than the state's universal property will necessarily seem selfish, cloyed, frivolous, and perverted; as with the American Puritans, anything even simply alongside the errand is a force of declension. With the ascendancy of such reasoning to full power at the end of Hegel's *Antigone,* all who spoke for mourning are gone, so the undone work manifests itself only as the sociosemiological terrorism of vindictive deformation, odd slants of black light that introduce unaccountable fractures into meaning but no longer issue from a discernible ethical source.

But, though the passage is not a contradiction of earlier statements when it calls mourning and women nature, its tone does turn toward Creon, in its decision not to mention the etiology of deformation, and in its misogynist horrification. Whatever one Hegel thought about the ethics of mourning and its demonization is here usurped by what another Hegel considers necessary in order to move on with the historical mission of the universal community that Creon has initiated, an eagerness that mandates a repression of the knowledge of repression, a hiding of evidence to make even the dead seem to have been satisfied and to have grown irritated with the petty intransigence of women. To be sure, this second Hegel promises that there *will be* a moral state that *accounts for* or *makes reparation to* the ironic underground, that sublimates without ironic residue: but insofar as the reader is asked to wait patiently, insofar as a reunion between Antigone's vehement ghost and a Creon enhanced and edified by his progression through history is *not yet,* the resentment of melancholia is presently unappeased, and all the second Hegel can do is perform uncomfortable closures that fail to satisfy precisely because they transcend by a force of anxious denial rather than by the sovereign competence of *Aufhebung,* failing to appease a remainder that Hegel has himself brought forward. Hegel's suppression of his own insight into the ethics of mourning therefore jars with the putatively dispassionate contemplation of history's tribulations that he claims for himself in the preface to the *Phenomenology:* "The individual whose substance is the more advanced Spirit runs through this past just as one who takes up a higher science goes through the preparatory studies he has long since absorbed, in order to bring their content to mind: he recalls them to the inward mind, but has no lasting interest in them."[51] When Hegel returns to Antigone in *The Philosophy of Right,* his conflict will have been almost entirely remedied by a scrupulous avoidance of the topic of mourning.[52]

Hegel's reading of *Antigone* is not an exegesis for its own sake, but rather an employment of the play as an allegorical premonition of his own historical situation as he understood it, so the issue of fidelity to the text is not for him of primary concern. Consequently, though he does make some rather striking exegetical discoveries, he also interpolates meanings that are not Sophocles', most importantly, the view of Creon as functionary heeding the logic of a representational system rather than as an anxious despot seeking self-aggrandizement (though the two are not completely incompatible), and the emphasis on Creon's drive to sublimate rather than simply oppose Antigone and her mournfulness. These two innovations tend to divinize the state and thus to downplay Sophocles' contrast between the sacredness of mourning and political expediency in favor of an opposition between two orders of sacralization. These departures from Sophocles are precisely what makes Hegel's *Antigone* useful here, as a Protestant political view closer to the relation between American Puritanism and Rowlandson's narrative than the original would be. Hegel's *Antigone* provides a framework for viewing the tension between, on the one hand, a precarious and anxious political culture seeking legitimation through the promotion of a canon of exemplary human types evolving through history, a political culture that in the wake of King Philip's War takes the residual sorrow and fright to be an occasion for a still fuller consolidation of its prestige, and on the other hand Rowlandson's emergent insistence on the propriety of the work of mourning, an insistence that is prodded toward becoming an at least partial or implicit refusal of that culture. The connection I propose is neither between Sophocles and Rowlandson nor between Antigone and Rowlandson, but between *Hegel* and Rowlandson, not Hegel in toto, but the Hegel of the *Antigone* reading, a Hegel who is *an experience of both the allure of exemplarism and the violence with which it confronts mourning*—the Hegel who in his writing lives out the knot of divided loyalty, suppression, seductive sublimation, resistance, and coercive closure. This Hegel throws into visibility both the satisfaction and the *price* of American Puritanism, of a regime that attempts to purge itself of all appearance of self-interest, an austere Protestant Creon whose public persona is servant to a collective cause, a cause—the convergence of the City of God and the City of Man rather than the maintenance of order in one city among others, an *ontopatriotism*—that would drastically intensify the pressure to see noncompliant nonexemplarism as an outbreak of a purely inchoate underground rather than as an alternate formulation of the nature of the good.

Energized by the desire to believe themselves to be on the verge of such a culmination of history, exhilarated by the patently binaristic difference they saw between their towns and the terrain, the American Puritans produced a discourse that is remarkable first for its volume and second for its coherent general commitment to establishing and elaborating a system of exemplaristic representation. The amount of writing produced is astonishing, given the size of the population and the urgencies and dangers of establishing the New England colonies' physical and social infrastructures. Not all of the colonial writers' *oeuvres complètes* have the girth of Cotton Mather's four-hundred-item bibliography, and not all of their publications have the length of his unpublished

"Biblia Americana" or Willard's *Compleat Body of Divinity,* but there are many writers whose concentration and commitment amount to a kind of textual exploit. And the consumption of discourse matched production: Harry S. Stout contends that "[no] seventeenth-century culture was more uniformly literate than New England," and estimates that "the average weekly churchgoer in New England (and there were far more churchgoers than church members) listened to something like seven thousand sermons in a lifetime, totalling somewhere around fifteen thousand hours of concentrated listening."[53]

The contradiction between the demands of daily life and of discursive activity is in fact so severe as to suggest itself as the *motive* for discourse, rather than as an enemy to it: writing and preaching were manners of exerting control over the dispersive and centrifugal energies of unsettled life, powerful *because* they challenged those energies, rather than simply being things done in rare moments between more urgent commitments. This hypothesis is supported by the thematic coherence of American Puritan writing, which ranges over the spectrum of experience but always to lead experience toward its justification and completion in the imagined order. This subordination of experience to idea is performed by constructing the minutiae of life as instances of archetypes (though those who practiced the hermeneutic would say *discovering* rather than *constructing,* like a midwife encouraging the truth to its intrinsic emergence), thereby conferring clear significance on the novelty of New World life and fortifying the authority of the ruling discourse.[54] Though there are ephemera such as business communications and more or less secular appraisals such as William Wood's *New England's Prospect,* the virtual whole of New England writing is committed to the task of subduing experience's distracting patina of particularity, unfamiliarity, and anomaly in order to reveal what is specified as experience's truth. According to Sacvan Bercovitch, "even as [John Cotton and his contemporaries] urged each man to search into the minutest details of his life, they insisted upon the overarching plan which explained the social pattern of their lives, and so allowed them to fuse the particular, the social, and the cosmic . . . Their biographies [therefore] repeatedly assert the identity of the exemplary life and the colonial venture." "History is invoked to displace historicism": in a Puritan biography, "the actual [person] expands into an abstraction," and "the anomaly did not matter, only the common truths which the anomaly signified in context: the process of calling, temptation and salvation shared by all believers." "Saints' lives are not valuable for themselves, but because they make the true norms of identity accessible to all good men." What we might call a conversion of the real into the imaginary was, for the Puritans, a discovery and description of what was real in what would otherwise not be worthy of note, of that by virtue of which the person in fact *subsists.* "To transume history does not mean to reject or submerge historical details. It does mean that the 'real facts' become means to a higher end, a vehicle for laying bare the soul—or more accurately, the essential landmarks in the soul's journey to God."[55] Exemplification, then, was Puritanism's focal *project* (rather than simply an ingrained way of seeing), pervading not only the consortium of the intelligentsia but even the lower social levels,[56] and concerning itself with the moral significance of activities from the most vast, such as war, to the most trivial.[57] Exemplification is a collective scrutiny of the whole of collective experience, a group work that staves off and regulates the anomalies of the real, strenuously lifting the bewilderments and dissonances of actual historicity toward the certitude of readily recognizable abstractions that clarified at the same time that they coerced and legitimated—that were able to legitimate precisely because they could deliver the boon of clarity. Though legislators and magistrates often complied with ministerial wishes, especially during the first half century, Puritanism in the main pursued social power not through the development of explicit and direct legal means for enforcing piety (a technique that had not worked on them in England, and that they therefore viewed as a measure of last resort), but through the deployment of a capacious *way of thinking*. They devised an ideological rather than a primarily bureaucratic theocracy, in which power could seem impersonal and immanent, rather than external, coercive, or brutal.

In order to describe Rowlandson's textual confrontation with the Puritan hermeneutic of exemplification, I will be assuming that *for her* Puritanism was essentially a single and coherent entity, a collective subjectivity speaking *through* different voices, but not really *with* different voices, an assumption (on her part or on mine) that runs contrary to the challenge to the idea of a collective American Puritanism that has come out of the history departments of American universities in recent years. According to T. H. Breen, historians of early America have for some time now disagreed with Perry Miller's notion that there even was a New England Mind, pointing to significant disparities between diverse groups included under the rubric American Puritanism.[58] Their point is that a close look reveals seventeenth-century New England to be a plurality of minds, rather than a Mind. A close look, for example at the ordinary life of late-century Salem Village,[59] will always tend to uncover specificities and differences, the trees one has not been able to see for having looked too long at the forest. But the close look does not refute the existence of general coherences at a more abstract level, because a general idea necessarily takes on particular and hybrid forms in its local realization—especially in the case of a society such as New England where abstract unity is pursued through a deliberate and explicit social hermeneutic, rather than simply being present by virtue of a pervasive general *mentalité*. There is a certain intellectual gain in taking on Miller's holism with its heroization of uniformitarianism, but to dispel the idea of a meaningful abstract coherence, his critics would have to demonstrate two things: first, that the disparities that they discover are not differences *within* a field of possibility that for Miller *was* the New England Mind; and second, that the disparities were not arguments over *how to apply* certain consensually assumed programs—for instance, whether American Indian culture was to be erased by war or by Christian education—however much the participants may have so taken consensual assumptions for granted as not to mention them, or however much they may have lost sight of unchallenged consensual assumptions during the heat of controversy and in the peculiar confederations that actual politics produce. The movement away from Miller, which Bercovitch calls "a patricidal totem feast," where "a swarm of social and literary historians rushed to pick apart the corpus of his work," enables a fuller historical knowledge, but, insofar as a heuristic concentration on the specific becomes a theoretical statement that the abstract is only an imaginative or retrojective imposition on historical reality, it forecloses other knowledge—the astonishing labor expended creating and maintaining coherence around certain axioms, and the success of that labor, across social strata, spanning distances with tenuous communication networks bearing quite intricate and sophisticated ideological messages, reaching forward historically to the point where it is revealing to use, say, John Cotton's writing to contextualize Emily Dickinson's explorations of the quandaries with which her society surrounded her. Those who challenge the idea of an American Puritanism should consider Bercovitch's distinction: "By organic I do not mean monolithic. Recent demographic work has demonstrated both the diversity of American social patterns and the overlays, even in colonial New England, of various Old World forms. I see no conflict whatever between their conclusions and my own. My argument concerns an *ideological* consensus— not a quantitatively measured "social reality" but a series of (equally 'real') rituals of socialization, and a comprehensive, officially endorsed cultural myth that became entrenched in New England and subsequently spread across the western territories and the South." Only by treating the abstract entity American Puritanism *alongside* the inflections performed by particular persons, groups, and circumstances and the hybridizations included by other cultural infusions (such as those of Tituba in Salem Village) can the historically real be grasped in its complexity: if *American Puritanism* does not emerge in its pure form in its specific manifestations, neither are those manifestations fully intelligible without some description of the "webs of significance" that interlink them, producing an "astonishing cultural hegemony," the "tremendous vitality of the colonial church-state, from Winthrop's political achievements to Cotton Mather's gargantuan literary productiveness."[60]

With Bercovitch I agree that American Puritanism was not a mystically uniform sensibility but a collective project and a largely accomplished feat—at least, this is the form in which it appears to writers from Rowlandson and Bradstreet through Dickinson and even to Gaddis and Pynchon, where it presents itself directly, as voice or subject abstracted from the intrinsic singularity of the persons who bear its message, like its god immanent without ever being deeply local, a pervasive, elusive, impersonal, sustaining, intrusive, and crushing intelligence. Its real political achievement lent credibility to the cosmological axiom, a credibility that could then be reinvested for the dividend of further social legitimation. For each such writer, personal experience is represented as a *concrete experience of abstraction*. Rowlandson's violent and unchosen experience of radical cultural dislocation and transposition, for instance, would have enhanced her vision of Puritanism as a whole, and diminished her sense of the significance of, say, the difference between the two parties in the argument over the Halfway Covenant; and it may often be that the alienated experience of those who are marginalized—those who are least integrated into the whole—is proportionately more likely to lead to a view of the whole *as such*. Those who were least symptomatic of the New England Mind as Miller saw it may therefore be most inclined toward understanding the New England Mind as Bercovitch sees it; and those who see only the richness of variations and modulations rather than the enclosing consensual entity may fail to apprehend that entity's distinct political impact on lives. If, as Dickinson remarked in several poems, the historian of the ordinary must gaze through specificity to overarching cultural intentions in order to apprehend the concrete effect of those intentions on the lives of persons, then a historicism that derides theoretical attempts to describe the large formations that contribute to the determination of social phenomena will have the not really paradoxical effect of swerving away from an extensive description of the multiformity of actual experience.

Much of the success of the American Puritan synthesis derives from the versatile rhetorical structure of its major ideological tool, exemplification: by negating the specific significances of its objects in order to absorb them in transumptive representation, exemplification deracinated consciousness from immediate daily involvements—from the pressure to be of the world rather than simply in it—and readied consciousness for allegiance to transcendental commitments without requiring consciousness to *forego* attention to the daily in favor of a mysticism or monasticism; by challenging the "forgetfulness" of nonaligned involvement in what was at hand, exemplification provoked a centripetal "remembrance" of the cause that extended itself into the farthest-flung crannies of actual social life. Exemplification was not only, however, Puritanism's implicit *means of representation:* it was also a constant *object of representation,* symbolized by/as *death,* which was discursively constructed in such a way as to signify the cancellation of potentially confusing or diversionary aspects of the dead person's individuality in order to reveal his standing with respect to the absolute, his status as example, whether pious or abominable, his *instantiation of type.* Death clarified: for Puritanism as for Hegel, the "absolute lord and master" was not an enemy to humanity but rather an ally to the state's ideology, being both an analogy for and an aid to properly oriented meditative remembrance, which nullifies appearance in order to distill truth. Such an appropriative symbolization is of course endemic to all religious exercises operating under the signs of the cross and the broken seal of the tomb, but American Puritanism's peculiar inflection lies in two factors. First, the magnitude of the American Puritans' experience of deprivation—the loss of agrarian stabilities due to mercantile urbanization, then the loss of financial stability due to market fluctuation during the early decades of the seventeenth century, the general loss of what was perceived to be British social coherence, the loss of congregational peace due to the Laudian persecutions, then the loss of England itself, then epidemics, the grinding adversity of wilderness life, a minimally developed infrastructure, repeated relocation, war, dispersion, and the pervasive eeriness of the New World—constituted a ubiquitous and incessant cross. Second, American Puritanism developed a coherent ideological machine that, recognizing the sheer volume of grieving affect, discouraged mournful representation outside or alongside officially sanctioned exemplarism, and that insisted that demise not only be accepted gracefully but also introjected as a constant anti-affectional bearing toward life—a ubiquitous breaking of the seal on the tomb. The essence of "practical piety," according to Cotton Mather, was to "die daily."

Self-disciplinary meditation, the Puritan's constant obligation, would be a form of *self*-killing, not a suicidal termination of consciousness, but a surveillance and detection aimed at identifying and eradicating episodes of the *self,* the Puritan word for the amalgam of inclinations that went contrary to, or even merely did not participate in, the practice of virtue, nonparticipation being, if not vice, a standing invitation to it. Mather's defense of self-mortifying meditation would not let one rest with the hope of having turned out to have been exemplary at the end, in the eyes of God or of those saddened mourners who remain after. Rather, one must produce and maintain his own exemplarity, extirpating not only sin but the apostasy of any singularity that was more than superficial or ornamental, of anything that would jar with or blur the project of becoming a living emblem. Were this accomplished, one would be *in essence* a perfect duplicate of others renowned for achievement: like Puritan biography, Puritan identity is rigorously generic. One would of course differ in the extrinsic traits collected under the term *particular calling,* the talents one used as the vehicle or body for practical and expressive devotion—some were made to govern, some to preach, and so on in a divinely articulated social body; and, as Bercovitch contends in *The Puritan Origins of the American Self,* one could aspire to differ from predecessors by being a still-purer specimen of virtue, less encumbered by involvements with the distractions of particular identity, closer to a consummate disclosure of his tenor. But, again, one's central luminosity would not, strictly speaking, be his own, but instead a generic trait, and his particular noteworthiness would lie in eliminating any traits that rendered him *significantly disparate* from others who broadcast the same light. At the end, of course, one would turn out to have been exemplary no matter what, because those who fail to exemplify luminosity will be revealed as having been specimens of darkness, examples of nonexemplarity, worthy of being remembered as worthy of being forgotten, like Polyneices in Creon's eyes. Properly speaking, therefore, singularity did not exist save as an illusion to be dispelled by death's firm hand, whether throughout life by means of meditation or by default at the final clarification.

But illusion was for the Puritans potent, and its extinction was not to be awaited passively but instead vigorously pursued: the fact of a person's death prompted a search for his or her *meaning,* but it did not necessarily ensure a correct discovery of that meaning. Actual physical death encouraged but did not guarantee the passage to exemplary lucidity, so genericity had to be combative, intensively so in the affective zone surrounding the gravesite, in order that the profoundest opportunity in the career of the type would not be blown, the afflicted participants wandering off into pointless ruminations that only diverted funds from the collective account. The zone of the grave was Puritanism's area both of greatest bonanza and of greatest risk, a circle of human ground needing to be mapped and developed with the most sophisticated care to ensure that actual deaths became aids to *composition,* first by a waiver of close attention to the dead person's illusory singularities in favor of a measuring appraisal of where he or she stood with respect to the types of virtue and vice, and then by a call for those who survived to duplicate his or her achievement (or shun it, if the result of the moral calculus was bad). Death, that is, was not to be perceived as loss, as the human world's hemorrhage, but rather as transpositional or liminal event, the moment of the tenor's molting, when the type was suddenly no longer shadowy and the soul returned to its light or dark. Brief and constrained sorrow in response, a sensation of increased obligation, return to practice.

Hence perhaps the meagerness or even nonexistence of burial rituals during the first half century of American Puritan civilization.[61] Doctrinally, this seeming indifference can be explained as a Puritan opposition to nonscriptural ceremony, like the relegation of marriage to civil procedure or like the antipathy to Christmas. However, the specific hostility to mournfulness is sufficiently intense to suggest that there is more than doctrinal fastidiousness at work here, that the group experience of the dead body—the bolt of trauma that commences what grieving has to do—was discouraged because it was an obstacle to the carefully directed transference of affection from the person to the mandated representation of person. The omission of burial ceremony relegates grief to the status of *insufficient* reaction, but also, insofar as grief might entrench itself as an adamant attitude, represents grief as a blasphemous competitor to piety, a selfish insistence on affection that retards death's proper effect, the proliferation of clear truth; or, expressed from a non-Puritan perspective, that reserves or incarcerates energy that might otherwise be led to flow into the coffers of ideological fortification. This tension between improper and proper flow can be illustrated by the difference between Thomas Shepard's diary reflection on his wife's death, where only the most resolute and stalwart denial puts a halter on the sharpness of broken love become fury and weeping, and Edward Johnson's account of the death of Isaac Johnson, where the flow of tears becomes the flow of people to the south side of the river, to build Charlestown, a deed that preserves Isaac Johnson, that realizes what Edward Johnson's elegy promises: "Johnsons *turned dust, and yet hee's crownd and strengthend.*"[62] The differences between love for a wife and love for a leader and between diary and historical narrative of course account for the difference of tone between Shepard and Johnson in these selections, but my point is that this difference of tone illustrates the range between grief itself and the sublimation of grief. Johnson is an intensely feeling writer, but the feeling he expresses in the publicity of his writing flows in a sanctioned channel, something Shepard is laboring to find precisely because he apprehends the danger in what grips him, laboring to compel the vortex to be a stream. Restricting the survivor's encounter with the implacable sight of the corpse would help with such a labor, and the more elaborate burial ceremonies that arise in late century, at which the survivor distributed rather expensive gifts to the participants, might be less the abrupt reversal they appear to be than a different strategy for securing the same end, because the survivor's self-signification as geyser would also tend to repress the contemplation of the crater called the coffin. The practice of munificence exorcises the suspicion of poverty.

    Allan I. Ludwig and David H. Watters observe that Puritan culture, commonly thought to be relentlessly opposed to the image, permitted itself a great exception in the rich visuality expressed on its gravestones. Watters contends that the Puritan hostility to sensory mediation between the earthly and the divine was not so thoroughgoing as has been believed, a point echoed in Ann Kibbey's contention that Puritan iconoclasm was directed not against images per se but against the possibility of the sensory becoming interesting in itself, rather than beyond itself in its meaning: the regulation of contemplation rather than the destruction of art became the essential task. If, as Watters contends, the hostility of the British Protestants toward the power of images to mislead was expressed figuratively as a diatribe against erotic promiscuity, the opposite term for the American Puritans came to be marriage, not the celibacy that would be suggested by Perry Miller's insistence on the Puritans' thorough negativism. And, if the major difficulty in permitting images lay in the ease with which they could subside into the false, funerary art would promote a relatively more secure kind of looking, because the decay of the human body beneath the aesthetic figure would render an infatuation with the sensible less likely. By physical necessity a kind of literally self-consuming artifact, the significative unit of grave-and-stone had the highest chance of escaping the entropy that threatened all images, the tendency of mediation between the low and the high to become a reduction of the high to the low. But for the mourner the low is not yet nothing, it is still present though in the mode of the uncanny. As a result, mourning could instigate a collapse of meaning, so stone *figures* of abundance—fruit, cherubs, pendulous breasts, their stoniness emphasizing the figurality of their sensuousness—were accompanied by neomedieval images of the charnel zero below and by explicitly stylized (deindividualized) representations of him or her who is dead. (Only with the commencement of sentimentalism in the eighteenth century would the stone portraits of the dead begin to heed a mimesis of the specific person.) Recognizing that there are two orders of remembering, mourning and exemplarism, the art of the gravestone is enlisted to demonstrate the vacuity and shamefulness of the former, and then to carry its vigor to the latter.

This manipulation of mourning is more clear in the funeral sermon because the sermon is a verbal medium. According to Watters, stone markers became common only during the 1670s, a phenomenon he attributes to the deaths of the members of the first generation, to the deaths in King Philip's War, to the political incursions of the refurbished monarchy, and to what was perceived to be a general subsiding of piety—the second two of which were taken to be symptoms of a loss of control that might be reversed by an artful appropriation of the first two. Ronald Bosco and Harry S. Stout see the funeral sermon proliferating during the same period, along with more opulent burial practices, and, though Bosco sees this as a "liberalization"[63] because it pays more attention to death than had the earlier terseness, I am inclined to agree with Stout's judgment that the growing discursive figuration of death during this period— the period of Rowlandson's captivity—had more to do with using the emotional valence of death to aid in fortifying the imperiled charisma of the old way:

> To commemorate the faith of New England's first native-born generation, ministers began giving funeral sermons, which had as their overriding theme the enduring piety of the deceased. In the 1690s, examples of this genre constituted the most numerous printed sermons in New England. Like the printed final sermons of the

founders, funeral sermons used death to underscore the passage of generations and the covenant's continuity. Above all, they urged the rising generation to remember their predecessors and imitate their piety.[64]

The new loquacity in the dead zone, then, was not primarily a solicitous address to the condition of the mourner, but rather a closer development of a neglected resource: if piety was growing scarce, death was abundant at the end of the war; in time of crisis, a frugality arises, an unwillingness to leave veins unmined, especially if those veins are so rich as to invite competitive development. A culture that speaks at length about grief is not necessarily less oppressive than one that keeps silent, though what it promises, a sufficient culmination for grieving, can make it an alluring oppression.

The technique of the Protestant funeral sermon is plainly and decisively outlined in *The Practice of Preaching* by Andreas Hyperius, "Englished" and printed in London in 1577.[65] Hyperius divides the sermon into its major genres and lists the "places" and rhetorical attitudes appropriate to each: the minister will never be at a loss in responding to his congregation's recurring experiences "according to the capacitie of the vulgar people," and the sermon will be a member of a genre by virtue of a deliberate replication of a model. As one reads through Hyperius' manual, it becomes clear that the imitation of generic models is not simply a convenience for overworked or uninspired preachers because the task of the sermon is to reduce the angularity of experience down to the contour of timeless proprieties: the formal regularity of the genre reflects and promotes the emotional resolutions the genre exists to create, reflects and promotes *genres of experience*. The task is perhaps most vigorously advanced in chapter 13, "Of the kind Consolatory, or Comfortative," which delineates the manner for addressing those vulgars who have suffered disaster. This sort of sermon, according to Hyperius, is "peculiarly ordeyned to the easing and asswaging of sorrowe and griefe." To this end, he tells the preacher, you must show that you are not cold, that you know the feel or bite of loss:

> Hee that is determined to comfort others, must of necessitie so frame himselfe in all thinges, that he make them beleeve that he is earenestly touched with the griefe of the common calamitie, & that he is in the meane time ready bent to confirme and establish the mindes of others. I know not how it commeth to passe, he talketh a great deale better to our contentation, whom we perceyve to be endued with the lyke affection, that we are endued withall.

A pragmatist rather than a theorist, Hyperius does not look into why things work, but instead tells you what does work; your task is not primarily to feel, but to make them believe that you feel, because the echo they hear will bring emotion out of privacy, into the public circle of a congregational community at worship. Privacy, then, is this rhetoric's enemy (but a privacy Hyperius construes as feeling and reflection that lie outside the congregational circle, rather than outside sociality and discourse as such).

Once such access to grieving is gained, the emotions made available should be discouraged, rather than allowed to follow their native course. To this end, try shame: "It becommeth men chiefly to imbrace all manhood and prowesse, but especially constancye." Constancy, therefore, is not mourning, fidelity to the memory of love, but adamant adherence to norms of conduct even in arduous times: "All [that] be of a sound judgement, doe think it very uncomly and womannishe to lament without measure, & to take so impaciently the chaunce that happeneth." A manly constancy or Christian stoicism *measures* grief, that is, confines or delimits grief to a defined interval and a well-bounded area in the terrain of resolve, and the act of delimiting implies the capacity to do so, which in turn implies a transcendent consciousness that looks down on grief as object, rather than allows it to be the tone of subjectivity, by relegating destruction to its abstract category, vicissitude, "the chaunce that happeneth." If mourning aims eventually at competence to measure the loss, constancy aims immediately to measure mourning, and this ability to measure mourning, rather than the simple absence of mourning, constitutes manliness. In fact, the emotions assigned to the demarcated zone must *be* in the first place if grieving is *to be* in public, and so to be of use. But Pandora's Protestant teacher (or her Maxwell's demon) must supervise the opening of the area strictly if he is to prevent the flood that covers the land and renders the map pointless. The most famous practitioner of such surveillance is perhaps Claudius:

> 'Tis sweet and commendable in your nature, Hamlet,
> To give these mourning duties to your father,
> But you must know that your father lost a father,
> That father lost, lost his, and the survivor bound
> In filial obligation for some term
> To do obsequious sorrow. But to persever
> In obstinate condolement is a course
> Of impious stubbornness. 'Tis unmanly grief.
> It shows a will most incorrect to heaven,
> A heart unfortified, a mind impatient,
> An understanding simple and unschooled.
>
> (1.2. 87–97)

Claudius' fear at this point may be less that Hamlet will uncover the crime than that he will sequester affections that might otherwise be invested in the fledgling regime: "think of us as of a father . . ."

Such a fear would be well placed, because grief may reply to the attempt to shame it by contending that the mandated term is a "wicked speed," an infidelity rather than a constancy: "a beast that wants discourse of reason would have mourned longer . . ." (1.2. 150–52).[66] Accordingly, Hyperius' strategy is not limited to shaming. He also recommends an appeal to self-interest, to the easing of misery that comes with relinquishing grief: "What profiteth it thee to lye tumbling in deformitye, to wast and consume thy selfe with sorrowe? Thou art grievous both to thee and thine, thou disquieteth both thy body and minde in vaine." Remind them that grief is not a single sorrow but a self-renewing string of fresh mortalities: "Of the easiness. Thou so oft procurest to thy selfe a freshe newe heaviness, as oft as thou proceedest to bewayle thy case." Hyperius is an acute analyst of grief—knowledge of the enemy must be precise if practical edification is to succeed.

Having *publicized* the emotion, then discouraged its freedom by appeals to decency and comfort, you must then provide specific instructions on meditational techniques for lifting it into sanctity. First, encourage them to view their grief typologically—as a modern example of a historically repeating pattern: the application of biblical commonplaces "shall most conveniently bee done, by comparinge the things that have happened unto us, with those that in times past befell unto the Jewes." The immediate advantage of this is that it will introduce abatement into grief by making it into something looked at rather than a way of looking, an object of rather than a manner of contemplation. Not all biblical lamentations are as restrained as Hyperius might like, however, so he specifies the pertinent predecessors, the example of Christ, "a Captaine to be followed in humbleness, mortification, &c.," and the examples of "holy men, whose wonderfull pacience hath appeered, but yet more marvaylous seemed their deliverance accomplished by the power and goodness of God." The preliminary emancipation afforded by contemplation, which reduces loss to the status of *that which happens to the saintly,* is properly followed by a disciplinary suppression of grief: tell them to do what was done by those who had experiences like theirs. Typological meditation, therefore, repeats the pattern of opening-for-appropriation you have established with your sympathy: as your profession of fellow feeling brings grief into the public light, where it is rendered available to the norms of restraint you promote, so identification with the afflictions of predecessors can be converted to emulation of those predecessors' responses to affliction—the discovery of similarity can become the construction of similarity. In both cases, preliminary relief provides the incentive for subsequent acquiescence if the acquiescence can be made to seem a continuation of rather than a disparate successor to the relief.

In the process, you associate your own normative pronouncements with the prestige of the scriptural tradition. This enhancement of your own power will also follow from a second meditative technique, rumination on what sins caused the affliction. You must be cautious in such blame laying:

> If we take upon us at any time to render and declare, any causes, procoeding eyther of the providence, or of the justice of G O D or of any other occasion, for the which God scourgeth and punisheth us, we must not be over bolde in judgeing and determining of them, neither must we alledge any, except such as the holy Scripture without any ambiguitie hath set foorth, as generall and correspondent to the state of our times.

You may fortify your own authority by claiming to know God's motives in visiting them with affliction, but walk carefully here, make sure that the convergence between specific case and general type is easily credible, because otherwise you may seem to have strayed into pride, into inventing additions to Scripture, in which case your words will lose the charisma of impersonal transmission, and invite refusal or contest *on ethical or moral grounds*. As with the attempt to instill shame for excessive grief, the attempt to instill a sense of guilt for having brought on the cause of the grief confronts an *Antigone,* an alternate formulation of goodness always on the verge of discovering itself, risks losing the rhetorical advantage of representing the other as a chaos to the emergence of a *dialogue*. Despite such risk, though, the technique of blame is worth promoting because it promises the mourner a measure of control and thus relieves the sensation of helplessness in the face of devastation: however much he may not wish to take the blame for his own misery, he will nonetheless welcome the assertion that, had he had the knowledge you have, he might have avoided the present catastrophe; and that, acquiring the knowledge you have to confer, he can prevent the sequel. Though the bite of loss is not reduced by such contemplation, remorse reduces the sensation of utter victimage—unless you overdo it, convincing him that his sin is so intrinsic to his being as to render future catastrophes endless and inevitable: "It is lawful sometimes to acknowledge the sorrow or griefe to be justlye inflicted, yet must wee in any wise take heede, least in acknowledginge it occasion been given, that it take increasement, and become unmeasurable." Having brought him out of "womanish" intemperance, you may lose him to that demon again if you induce despair, an anticipation of infinite affliction, and a conviction that all means of remedy are futile. Grief is a wily adversary: even if you overcome its gravitation toward speaking a contrary ethic, it can exploit *your* ethic by convincing the mourner that he *is* his sin, rather than that his sin is a flesh that consciousness can shed in the act of emulation. This is a great danger for a theology insistent on original sin, as Jonathan Edwards revealed in his accounts of the suicides (including his uncle's) that exploded in the first stages of awakening to a perception of personal apostasy, a danger that requires careful distinctions such as Willard made in the funeral sermon from which I quoted in the epigraph to this chapter: "It is true that there is none so holy as to live without sin; but there are some that are so pure, as to be undefiled in God's eye and esteem, *Numb. 23. 21. God hath seen no iniquity in Jacob. Psal. 119. 1. Blessed are the undefiled . . .*"[67] Rowlandson's husband Joseph displayed a similar concern for warding off the sin of despair, for warding off melancholia that uses moral nomenclature, in what turned out to have been his final sermon, "The Possibility of Gods Forsaking a people." Having told the congregation that they deserve no more than to be cast into permanent misery, and having intimated that this outcome is likely, Rowlandson pivots at the last moment:

> Let Gods dear ones take heed of concluding against themselves, that they are under this judgement. They are readiest to conclude against themselves, and yet really in the least danger . . . God will not forsake them as he forsakes others not utterly forsake them: His forsaking of his is but temporary, and partial . . . They retain good thoughts of him in his withdrawment or abience [abeyance?]. As the Spouse in the Canticles, she calls him her beloved still.[68]

One spouse come out from the jaws of *temporary* judgment, from an abeyance of decent ordinariness that opened an abyss of pain, may have heard this blending of a promise of safety with a claim on wifely loyalty and responded with her own mixture of sentiments. She might also have suspected that, had her husband presented this reassurance in response to durable anxieties not of his making, his rhetoric would have been kindly, but that, insofar as the preceding part of his sermon had strenuously conjured the monsters, summoned them in the first place and ordered them to walk about the room, his goal was not to soothe but to maintain a measured fear that fueled allegiance to the values he promoted, a middle way between peace and the despair of those who know they will never be safe again.

Having reduced the specificity of loss with the category of saints' afflictions, having made grief an object of imaginative representation, and having adumbrated a means of control, you should now promise that future compliance will bring not only safety but also more than adequate surrogates for what has been lost. You should assure them that the evils they suffer are "recompensed with other commodities": "The Prophets doe in their consolations enterlace promises of divers things to come, of the coming of Christ, of deliveraunce by the same from spirituall tiranny and thraldome, and then of restoring the commonwealth of the Jewes, &c." The promise of recompense is, however, a dangerous technique, as is the imputation of guilt, because if you promise specific or concrete remunerations that do not arrive, you will be rendered ludicrous:

In like maner, when we promise that certayne and assured remedy of deliveraunce will follow, we must never prescribe any one singular meane, whereby the same may be accomplished. And that truely for this cause, least it falleth out otherwise, then we saye, we become laughing stockes: as wee know some, which covetinge to be taken for Prophetes and Soothsayers, when they promised all things prosperous, and all things happened cleane contrary, were openly laughed to scorne for their labours, and truely in my judgement not unworthyly.

Specification of recompense is here discouraged not primarily out of respect for the mystery of God's ways, but rather because whatever short-term enhancement of prestige you may get from the euphoria that follows a promise is liable to be proportionately dissipated by eventual disappointments; the prudent preacher looks to an accumulation of prestige that is modest in the short term but more dependable over the extended course of time.

However, even if new happiness or pleasure did arrive, it would not necessarily be taken as recompense. In its meticulous and intense commitment to the singularity of the lost object of love, mourning is apt to refuse the entire notion of commensurability or equivalent replacement, of payment *in kind,* because there is nothing else of the lost object's kind: the more exactly the contour and dimension of the crater are surveyed, the more likely it is that any new thing will seem at best a very crude fit—not that it will not be pleasurable or satisfying, but that it will not be a compensation, only a new thing, a point I take from Emily Dickinson:

> To fill a Gap
> Insert the Thing that caused it—
> Block it up
> With Other—and 'twill yawn the more—
> You cannot solder an Abyss
> With Air.
>
> (#546)

Aware of this mode of refusal, Hyperius does not propose that we remedy the problem of specific promises that fail to come true with vague promises of concrete happiness: eventually, some pleasant novelty is likely to (or at least may) arrive, an event you might be tempted to point at and say, see, this is it, but which the mourner may consider to be at best an attenuated echo of what is lost; at which point, you are once again in a position of dialogic contest rather than rhetorical dominance.

The solution is to make transcendental promises rather than vague concrete promises. Tell them that both the lost object and all subsequent objects are revealed as *of a kind* when they are viewed as emblems or adumbrations of spiritual value. Like the emotion that explodes from its loss, the object should be made to subside into category: "As well those that teach as those that learne or heare, shall regard more the internall consolation and quiet, which is setled in the minde and conscience, then the externalle and that which consisteth in corporal and earthly things." A Christian stoic decathexis that views corporal things as bodies or figures for transcendental meaning will view the specific differences among such things as inconsequential, as extrinsic and ornamental disparities apposite to an underlying sameness. From such a perspective, replacement becomes credible, as one commodity seen as a bearer of exchange value is a credible replacement for another seen in the same way so long as there is quantitative equivalence. Therefore, persuade them that both what is gone and what arrives in any future are best treated as occasions for edification through meditative contemplation, which rehabilitates *is:*

> Albeit [internal consolation] may out of the prophets more perspicuously be perceived, which if at any time they enterlace (by way of comforting) promises touching corporall benefits, especially in the kingdome of the true Messiah our saviour Christ to be received, yet neverthelesse will have the selfe same to be understood only of things spyrytuall and internall. For certes it is a familyar and as ye would saye a peculiar matter with them, to bring in and florishe over spirytuall thinges, under a certayne coollour or shadowe of thinges corporall, & that verily to the intent they might even by this meanes the more easily lifte up the rude minds of men from grose and earthly commodyties, to the contemplation of heavenly and celestiall graces.

Death, then, is to be a lesson in the protocols of perception: it teaches that the gross is really a shadow, that the lost object is not in itself of note, an embodiment of value, but rather an accommodation (commodity) of a transcendental value, a luminescence, certainly, to the rude mind, but, from the highest perspective, a color laid over truth. In this association of figurality with funereality you will certainly have assaulted the prerogative of the grieving heart, but you will have installed a credible theory of compensation (credible once the axioms are accepted), and so provided an incentive to relinquish misery.

Hyperius' brilliance lies in his recognition that religion can successfully *simulate* what mourning would eventually have arrived at: an ability to survey the chaos of grieving emotion, rather than simply being governed by it (typological emulation); a sensation of a measure of potential control (inquiry into cause); and a disengagement from fixation on the past and a receptivity to hope (compensation). Theology is a *bargain* because these things can be had without having "to lye tumbling in deformitye, to wast and consume thy selfe with sorrow." But the semblance of bargain depends upon hiding a cost: the stark freedom that would be eventually achieved by the minute memorial solicitudes of mourning is here sought through a cultivated derision—for the singularity of what was loved, for the love itself, and for the emotions that broke out when the love was broken; and the derisive self that is constructed above the corpse of mourning is not a freed self, but one carefully bound to imposed specifications of proper self-image, proper means of seeking, and proper things to seek. If such phantasmal gratification leaves the work of mourning undone, even unbegun, this is perhaps the desired end, because the deranged and subterraneanized misery of grief is now constituted as a *perpetual reservoir* continually provoking the phantasmal typic self to renewed derision and renewed acceptance of the introjected value system. To accomplish this, the sermon must walk a fine line, preventing the mourner from subsiding into his grief, but also discouraging an overzealous detachment from the energy of grief: "In comfortinge, eyther to increase sorrowe, as that a womannish kinde of wayling and shricking should follow, or so to induce gladness that a childishe rejoycement and exultation should thereupon ensue, both these poyntes doe indifferently incurre reprehension." The billiance of the type requires a somber background against which to show itself, a somberness that might at this point be called melancholia rather than mourning.

If Hyperius does not invent the Protestant funeral sermon, his meticulous attention to laying out a duplicable technique to aid preachers lacking strong rhetorical intuitions defines the genre's skeleton with the pragmatic candor verging on cynicism that is appropriate for an effective manual, though I probably push him too far toward Chaucer's Pardoner. When the funeral sermon emerges in New England in the 1670s, there are few essential modifications, save perhaps in the final attitude sought. Rather than a generally pious disposition, the Puritan sermon seeks a more concrete allegiance to the moral-civic code of the holy nation, an end that could hardly have been advanced by Hyperius, himself wavering between Luther and Calvin amid the religious and political heterogeneity of sixteenth-century Germany. Hyperius does present a brief vision of social service as desireable outcome: "afflictions doe minister cause unto us of humbling ourselves, of calling upon God, of exercising the duties of love towards our neighboure . . ." The Puritan sermon amplifies the "duties of love" in two ways: first, the transcendental consolations proffered by the sermon lie less in inward peace and postmortem reward than in the contemplation of the future greatness (or the future reclamation of the past greatness) of the New England errand; and second, typological emulation and transcendent compensation are combined in service to such spiritual nationalism by asserting that the dead person's life is properly seen as a vehicle for displaying exemplary virtue. His memorability lies in his having made himself a vehicle for value that can still be enjoyed by the living if they in turn make themselves vehicles, imitating what he imitated, in which case what was alive in him is still so. His sociospiritual representativity was his essence; emulating that representativity refutes the finality of death; and widespread emulation tends toward social consensus. "There never was death," as Whitman would argue in "Song of Myself," albeit with a different notion of representativity, "but it led forward life." (Such affectional fusion over the grave would prove more difficult when, as in Rowlandson's case, the dead person was an infant or young child, or—most intensely—when a child dies before being born, in which case imaginative conceptions of emulation and recompense would have to be generated without reference to concrete experience, and the raw fact of death would be proportionately more resistant to the typological reduction. This gap demands the sentimentalization of infant perfection to complete the system of sublimation, a project already commenced in Puritanism's "instances of early piety" literature, for instance Jonathan Edwards' portrait of Phebe Bartlett.)

Otherwise, Hyperius' perception of the genre was duplicated in New England. According to Gordon E. Geddes, "the goal was not repression but control." Geddes quotes Willard's pronouncement that mourning must be converted to "Godly Sorrow," an event that occurs "when our Mourning for any outward Loss or bereavement is accompanied with or diverted into the current of Contrition or Mourning for Sin." Seeking "to confine and direct the grief and mourning of the bereaved," Geddes contends, Willard allowed that the deaths of loved ones were "a proper occasion for the excitation of grief in us," but insisted that this feeling was apt to lapse into a refusal of comfort, such as that of Rachel in the Bible. Even Jesus wept when Lazarus died, so Christians should not be "'over-rigorous' in censoring displays of sorrow and mourning in others." But to allow permissible grief to take its own channel would be too permissive. Geddes suggests that the early Puritan hostility toward funeral sermons may have been based upon a feeling that such performances, "commonly fill'd with Immoderate and Untrue Praises of the Dead,'" invited a loss of control and so were thought best banned altogether. In his preface to James Fitch's sermon after the death of Anne Mason, for example, Joshua Scottow denounced the "Abusive, and justly to be condemned practice of too many, who in preaching Funeral sermons, by misrepresenting the Dead, have dangerously misled the living, and by flatteries corrupted many . . ." But this denunciation prefaces a funeral sermon Scottow considers permissible: the issue is not (or is no longer) the propriety of publicly representing the dead per se, but rather the strict discrimination between correct memory and misrepresentation, in order to *sift out inmixtures of the Puritan social unconscious, often present despite best intentions.* To this end, Geddes suggests, remembrances of the dead person's singularity were kept brief: "in the sermon itself, the deceased was usually mentioned only as the occasion for the sermon, or in the concluding paragraph." Such containment was reinforced by the practice of preaching the sermon at regular service rather than at the time of the burial. When the sermon was later published, "a brief biographical sketch would be appended, at least to the published sermon. By the second half of the century, these sketches tended to grow into lengthy biographies." Such extended attention to the life of the dead was not, however, a recognition of the utterly lost personality, a token of what Bosco calls liberalization. On the contrary, punctilious commentary on the minutiae of exemplary conduct (as in most of the biographies in Mather's *Magnalia*) bespeaks a heightened opposition to mourning, a sensation that everyday life is diverging from pattern and therefore requires detailed modeling rather than just abstract precept, a dedication to leaving no recollected event open to contrary or nonaligned interpretation. The life in all its moments becomes a single sign. Extended treatment, then, more completely emblematized "the lesson that death should have for the living," and functioned as a supplement of vividness in the cultural ambience that also supported the involuted fidelities of Rowlandson's narrative. Only by forgetting the singularity of the dead and heeding what was posited as his or her example can one escape the immoderate flow. As Willard put it, "If you can swim ashoar upon this plank you will not need to fear drowning in the torrent of sorrow."[69]

Fitch's sermon, which appears to have been the first to have been published in New England,[70] is typical, though Scottow's brief preface betrays a lingering nervousness about the revival of the genre, about what door is being opened. Only pages 10, 11, and 12 out of the total thirteen mention Anne Mason, and then only as a type, for instance, as a reminder of Dorcas who as "full of good works and acts of charity" and who was raised from the dead by Peter (Acts 9.36-42)—as Anne Mason will be raised from the dead by those who remember her in imitation. Fitch's inclination to stereotype is not simply a different order of mimetic convention from our own, because, as will those preachers who follow him, he is attempting to stave off the pressure of forms of memory that we might call realistic. (I am not contending that our notions of mimesis are not conventional, though the task of grief, if not the content of grief, seems to me to approach the status of the sort of universal convention that Levi-Strauss describes in his analyses of the incest prohibition, but that they are present-by-exclusionary-absence from Puritan discourse, rather than just absent.) Among this modern Dorcas' many virtues, in fact, was her transcendence of grief, a virtue to be emulated by those attending the present service: "I have personally seen her weep in her speaking of, and lamenting after Communion with Christ, but it was a rare thing for her to weep because of any outward loss or cross whatsoever."

In accord with Anne Mason's example, therefore, Fitch discusses Anne Mason herself only briefly, devoting the rest of the sermon (pp. 1-9, 13) to a treatise on correct memory. Quoting Psalms 37.37, "Mark the blameless man, and behold the upright," Fitch takes *to mark* to mean *to remember,* to lift a thing out of vicissitude, as in *mark my words.* The way to mark is to apprehend the marks of piety the dead woman displayed: the mourner should be exclusively concerned with the question "What are the Observable things in the Life and Death of the Godly?" *Observable* here means worthy of being observed, rather than capable of being observed. Such *marking,* after it has prevented less befitting markings, is still not adequate if it remains thought and feeling without becoming conduct:

> We should mark the Upright by way of imitation; if we do not in this sense mark them we mark them in vain, and behold them to no good purpose; the Lord requireth us to mark the life of the Upright as a living example, that may live with us, and that when they are dead; and to consider the end of their conversation, that we may live and die as they.

Such imitation will ensure that nothing worthy of mark has died:

> If you would have comfort against your loss, lament after the Lord Christ his Spiritual presence; this Upright one makes the Upright such and keeps them such to their end: are they so precious, Oh how precious is Jesus, the savour of whose Ointment is such that the Virgins love him, *and his love is better than wine, therefore the Upright love him, Cant. 1. 3, 4.* Oh pour out thy heart to Christ, and say, I lament my loss of an Upright servant of thine: Oh thou canst make up my loss by thy presence.
> Preserve the memory of the Upright by imitating of them; It's a pleasing thing to love when it can no longer enjoy the presence of the Beloved, yet to preserve the memory of the Upright by imitating them . . . would you show love indeed to her. Oh preserve her memory, and that must be by imitating her, think and speak of, Oh weep and pray over the observable things in her Life and Death, that you prize Communion with God as she did, that you may love Prayer and Self-Examination as she did, and abound in good work: *Thus shall her memory be blessed to you, Prov. 10. 7 and you shall be blessed at your latter end.*

Christ is the first adequate vehicle for or mimesis of the undying divine, revealing clearly the marks of the meaning he bears, revealing them most clearly in the clarificatory act of dying; others such as Anne Mason are mimeses of his mimesis, as we may be in turn, and so on. Vehicles drop away, but the Upright is always so; compensation is not really compensation—since nothing is lost or falls away—but rather a revelation of the fact of this sempiternal erection. *Nothing is missing.* A Christian homily, certainly, but one that Fitch is putting to nearly unprecedented use in the Massachusetts of 1672.

I have represented the Puritan symbolization of death as coercive in order to open a critical area apart from the rather considerable body of commentary that would see such an address to grief to be an abundant consolation. Contemplating the imposition of typological significance in Puritan self-conception, for example, John Owen King believes such imposition *relieved* melancholy because it resolved or conferred form: "It is not a question of choosing between words and experience, or between a language of conversion and conversion itself; prescription is a language with which to order and craft experience."[71] If it were a matter of a single order of representation set over against an otherwise inarticulate experience of suffering, then the exemplary scheme would be a relief. But my contention is that such an ennobling of exemplification depends upon maintaining the binarism disseminated by Puritan ideology—us versus chaos—and thereby perpetuates the repression of other orders of representation that were extruded from permissible discourse so that their intrinsic energy could be appropriated. The category *nature,* that which is *beyond the pale,* is ideologically repressive because it is constructed to include "womanish" or "immeasurable" or "irresponsible" grief (among other things) as a kind of beast's howling, rather than as a competitor ethic.

But to the extent that I have represented Puritan funerary discourse as repressive, I have perhaps not directly enough presented its desirability, its aura of solicitude, an aura so cogent that many of the practitioners of this discourse (like their heirs and exegetes in the centuries to come) may have gone to the work with a sincere desire to annul disaster. Failing to see the desirability of this structuration of feeling would leave us unable to comprehend its success: no ideological system of such social generality maintains itself in such an extent of space and time without being able to seem to gratify the emotional needs of its proponents and adherents. At the most basic level, the exemplary representation of the dead person's virtues is not necessarily opposed to what conclusion the mourner might eventually reach: Anne Mason probably was the paragon Fitch said she was, and those who stayed on after her might have been proud to have been like her; even Antigone might have felt that ambition and lack of concern for peace were dark sides of Polyneices' boldness. Add to this the fact that the funeral sermon offers a simulation of the end of grief, a coherent image of the dead person where there is otherwise only pain; that the funeral sermon proposes that that which the dead essentially *was* endures, that only the extrinsic lies in the ground; and that it delineates a course of engagement with the world through emulation rather than a prolonged and seemingly aimless wandering among memory traces. To all of this add the frequency of death in seventeenth-century New England, a world where, to borrow from David Stannard, "the nights were blacker, the days more silent, the winters more horrifying and cold than most men [and women] of the twentieth century can imagine,"[72] a world that, focused by his wife's suffering, produced Joseph Rowlandson's horrified vision of abandonment and victimage:

> God's forsaking a people is a sore judgement, in that it exposes them to all judgements. Sin is a great evil in that it exposes to all evil, this is a great evil of punishment, in that it exposes to all punishments. If God be gone, our guard is gone, and we are as a City, in the midst of Enemies, whose walls are broken down. Our strength to make resistance, that's Gone, for God is our strength, as a carcase without life, to beasts of prey, so are a people forsaken of their God . . .[73]

There is God and there is rotting meat and there is nothing in between.

Imagine the dread of commencing mourning again, the last task not complete, the two or more losses mingling and compounding the labor exponentially: such incentive would have rendered the sublimation of mourning irresistible. But gratifications are not always adequate, and the sermons' vigilant, alert, and anxious attention to griefs that threaten to refuse the consolation the sermons propose suggests that grief endured as a continual furtive presence—in need of vilification, as a wildness, a desecration of civility. Hence the importance of Mary White Rowlandson's innocent narrative, where countermemory emerges from the silence of being an eternal irony in the heart of the community and teaches those who come after what was really down below.

3

Lot's Wife: Looking Back

She is a mother ensnared in God's Plan. She has witnessed the destruction of Lancaster/Sion. She and her children are commodities between two hostile armies. What is their legality? What are they worth.?

Other to other we are all functions in a system of war . . .

A Sovereign thinks the sun. Form and force begin with Him. If there is evil in the Universe it is good and therefore marvelous. Law scans the grammar of liberty and surrender. Catastrophe is a matter of fact. Who can open the door of God's face?

Love is a trajectory across the hollow of history . . .

—Susan Howe

In the work of mourning, it is not grief that works: grief keeps watch . . . Grief, incising, dissecting, exposing a hurt which can no longer be endured, or even remembered.

—Maurice Blanchot

And in his earnest address concerning the Last day, [Christ] says (Luke 17:32): "Remember Lot's Wife." From this we readily understand what it means to look back, namely, to depart from God's command and to be occupied with other matters—matters outside one's calling—like the man who has been commanded to follow Christ and wants to bury his dead first (Matt. 8: 21). . . . Therefore one must hold fast to this teaching—that the saintly woman is compelled to suffer this punishment—in order that it may reach all succeeding generations.

—Martin Luther

Now, if we weigh all the circumstances, it is clear that her fault was not light. First, the desire of looking back proceeded from incredulity; and no greater injury can be done to God, than when credit is denied his word. Secondly, we infer from the words of Christ, that she was moved by some evil desire: (Luke xvii. 32:) and that she did not cheerfully leave Sodom, to hasten to the place whither God called her; for we know that he commands us to remember Lot's wife, lest, indeed, the allurements of the world should draw us aside from the meditation of the holy life. It is therefore probable, that she, being discontented with the favor God had granted her, glided into unholy desires, of which thing also her tardiness was a sign: for Moses intimates, that she was following after her husband, when he says, that she looked from behind him: for she did not look towards him; but because, by the slowness of her pace, she was less advanced, she, therefore, was behind him.

—John Calvin

In his description of Lot's wife in the epigraph above,[1] Calvin exposes grief's peculiar phenomenological movement: drawing aside, gliding away, too much in motion; sticking fast, lagging behind, standing still. This doubleness is not, however, an intrinsic or immutable trait of grief, but rather the way grief looks from a specifically Protestant perspective, the way it appears to a consciousness that considers itself to be at once both preserving and canceling a tradition: upholding ancient norms from which grief strays; moving toward a historically unprecedented splendor, with grief lagging behind. The judgement that grief is too fast *and* too still, then, requires two consciousnesses, that of intransigent mourning, and that of an appraising eye that constitutes grief as intransigence, and that bestows on its opponent a symmetrically reversed image of its own double time. The opponent might for its part tend toward viewing itself as proper but as on the one hand caught up in the pure malice of an indifferent velocity and as on the other trapped in marmoreal and unresponding monoliths without discernible movement of inner life.[2]

Having experienced sorrows arriving at such a pace as to seem simultaneous rather than serial, a victim of the defeat of fixity by the atrocity of vicissitude, of total and instantaneous reversal, Mary White Rowlandson has, as she writes, drunk "the wine of astonishment" (365), and cannot help but long for a serviceable theology that would restore at least regularity if not the credibility of love. As Susan Howe writes, at "sun-rising, on a day of calamity, at the inverted point of antitypical history, Mary Rowlandson looks out at the absence of Authority and sees we are all alone. Spite is the direction of creation. In a minute death can and will come. All collectivities will be scattered to corners . . . This terse book tells of prefigured force and the dooms of life. For a time its author was elided, tribeless, lost."[3] Subject to what Elaine Scarry describes as "the intense pain that destroys a person's self and world, a destruction experienced spatially as either the contraction of the universe down to the immediate vicinity of the body or as the body swelling to fill the entire universe,"[4] Rowlandson suffers the assault of fright as Freud defines it,[5] not a concrete anticipation of an approaching danger (fear), but rather the response to something that expeditiously bursts on the scene, *unmaking* the scene: "I have seen the extreme vanity of this world: one hour I have been in health, and wealth, wanting nothing: but the next hour in sickness and wounds, and death, having nothing but sorrow and affliction" (365). Recalling having been helpless before the primal insult, demotion to utter dependence without possibility of appeal to contractual obligations or even modest conventions of decent restraint, she assumes the tone of Ecclesiastes here, and that view is apt, but not the tone, because as teller she still feels not weary cynicism but anxiety, fear of fright, the apprehension that reversal may renew itself without courtesy of notice. From the beginning of the narrative: "Now is the dreadful hour come, that I have often heard of (in time of war, as it was the case of others), but now mine eyes see it" (323); "When we are in prosperity, oh the little that we think of such dreadful sights, and to see our dear friends, and relations lie bleeding out their heart's blood upon the ground. There was one who was chopped into the head with a hatchet, and stripped naked, and yet crawling up and down" (325). The havoc does not conclude with things being laid to rest, instead they are prompted into grotesque and unprecedented motions, motions akin to the unrest that still uncoils itself within Rowlandson as she writes. At the end of the narrative, "redeemed" in cash negotiation and living in prosperity again, she cannot reconcile with the various avatars of tranquility, even with the tranquility of cynicism or skepticism, because the heart cannot be so scrupulously sparse in its engagements as to be neighborly with the mania of being that she has witnessed:

> I can remember the time, when I used to sleep quietly without workings in my thoughts, whole nights together, but now it is other ways with me. When all are fast about me, and no eye open, but His who ever waketh, my thoughts are upon things past, upon the awful dispensation of the Lord toward us; upon His wonderful power and might, in carrying of us through so many difficulties, in returning us to safety, and suffering no one to hurt us. I remember in the night season, how the other day I was in the midst of thousands of enemies, and nothing but death before me: it is then hard work to persuade myself, that ever I should be satisfied with bread again. But now we are fed with the finest of the wheat, and, as I may say, with honey out of the rock: instead of the husk, we have the fatted calf: the thoughts of these things in the particulars of them, and of the love and goodness of God towards us, make it true of me, what David said of himself. Psalms 6. 6. *I have watered my couch with tears*. Oh! the wonderful power of God that mine eyes have seen, affording matter enough for my thoughts to run, that when others are sleeping mine are weeping. (365)

Her claim that the sleeplessness and the tears come from gratitude is perhaps not false, but perhaps also not completely true: the passage on the world's extreme vanity follows immediately after, and David's weeping in Psalm 6 is provoked by boneweariness, terror, sorrow, and a plea for relief—not by thankfulness for relief that has arrived. To use one of her epigraphs, the god who makes alive also kills, and the unpersuasive intensity with which she attempts to call the workings and the running thoughts solely the effect of relief and gratitude indicates that the paragraph is propitiatory rather than fully candid, indicates, therefore, that the anxiety that is the paragraph's manifest topic also dominates her *in the moment that she writes.*

It may be that the captivity was not Rowlandson's introduction to the infringements of force. According to Melanie Klein, "the [child's] mourning is revived whenever grief is experienced in later life,"[6] and Rowlandson's earliest experience—the disappearance and return of the father, the disappearance of the Somerset home, the extraordinary new habitations of ship and home, "for a long space of time . . . in ye woods from ye meanes [of grace]," at a time in her young life when such transformations could not have been reasonably explained to her—could have only been for her enigmas or testimony to the intrinsically evanescent ontology of homes. It may have deeded her a burden of unreconciled suspicion and sorrow that echoed powerfully with and was rehabilitated by the weeks of wandering during the captivity, by being dragged across the blank face of an earth. Whether caused or recalled by the captivity, however, hers is now a focal perception of bleak velocity, the conversion of the world into pure anomaly, bare ground: "we travelled about a half a day or little more, and came to a desolate place in the wilderness, where there were no wigwams or inhabitants before; we came about the middle of the afternoon to this place, cold and wet, and snowy, and hungry, and weary, and no refreshing, for man, but the cold ground to sit on, and our poor Indian cheer" (332). The site is cold, wet, and snowy, and people are cold, wet, hungry, and weary, but the syntax of the sentence does not respect such a distinction between the scene and its occupants, mingling the poverties of the two into an undistinguished aggregate: not even a place, really, without settlement, and not a person, without coherence—if a home, not "for man," but only for an entity that could not be imagined.

This is the state of grief, which is not a state but the termination of states dissolved in a cold flow. When organizing foci—home, custom, possessions, family—perish, there is no support or material to draw upon in generating a new coherence, not even a provisional coherence. But she tries nonetheless, receding from the scene of fright into a self-incarcerating incommunicativeness or sullen shelter that mimics the economy of a home but lacks expression and tenderness. And even this recusant simulation of an interior is not durable:

And here I cannot but remember how many times sitting in their wigwams, and musing on things past, I should suddenly leap and run out, as if I had been at home, forgetting where I was, and what my condition was: but when I was without, and saw nothing but wilderness, and woods, and a company of barbarous heathens, my mind quickly returned to me, which made me think of that, spoken concerning Samson, who said, *I will go out and shake myself as at other times, but he wist not that the Lord was departed from him.* (342–43)

Hence the symbolic power of her decision to segment experience into successive "removes" or marches, which is not merely an organizational or heuristic convenience but instead an emblem of grief's jolting and uneven meter—pauses for gathering or collecting a spare coherence, but never long enough, precipitations back into velocity. It is therefore with some envy that she imagines sufficient pauses during the Israelites' captivity, sufficiently long to permit feeling to search its repertoire for adequate expressive vehicles:

Then my heart began to fail: and I fell a-weeping which was the first time to my remembrance, that I wept before them. Although I had met with so much affliction, and my heart was many times ready to break, yet I could not shed one tear in their sight: but rather had been all this while in a maze, and like one astonished: but now I may say as, Psalm 137. 1. *By the rivers of Babylon, there we sat down: yea, we wept when we remembered Zion.* (336)

She is not allowed to sit long enough to compose herself, but is always again hurried on along the unknown vector of captivity:

Now away we must go with these barbarous creatures, with our bodies wounded and bleeding, and our hearts no less than our bodies. About a mile we went that [first] night, up upon a hill within sight of the town, where they intended to lodge. There was hard by a vacant house (deserted by the English before, for fear of the Indians). I asked them whether I might lodge in the house that night to which they answered, What will you love English men still? (325–26)

The dissolution of the world is not done once, but promises to repeat itself to infinity, a situation she figures with the recurrent image of a river's force and the desire to remain dry: "They quickly fell to cutting dry trees, to make rafts to carry them over the [Baquag] river; and soon my turn came to go over: by the advantage of some brush which they had laid upon the raft to sit upon, I did not wet my foot (which many of themselves at the other end were mid-leg deep) which cannot but be acknowledged as a favor of God to my weakened body, it being a very cold time. I was not before acquainted with such kinds of doings or dangers. *When thou passeth through the waters I will be with thee, and through the rivers they will not overflow thee,* Isaiah 43. 2" (333); "on the morrow morning we must go over the river, *i.e.* Connecticut, to meet with King Philip; two canoes full, they had carried over, the next turn I myself was to go; but as my foot was upon the canoe to step in, there was a sudden outcry among them, and I must step back; and instead of going over the river, I must go four or five miles up the river farther northward" (335); "We began this remove with wading over the Baquag river: the water was up to the knees, and the stream very swift, and so cold that I thought it would have cut me in sunder. I was so weak and feeble, that I reeled as I went along, and thought that I must end my days at last, after my bearing and getting through so many difficulties; the Indians stood laughing to see me staggering along: but in my distress the Lord gave me experience of the truth, and goodness of that promise, Isaiah 43. 2. *When thou passeth through the waters, I will be with thee, and through the rivers, they shall not overflow thee*" (348); "Then we came to a great swamp, through which we travelled, up to the knees in mud and water, which was heavy going to one tired before" (350). I quote at length here to illustrate the manner in which Rowlandson explores significance by means of fixational motif (fixation itself being an attempt at control and stabilization, an attempt to secure in the act of memory what was forbidden in the experience). Of the uncountable events that transpired during the captivity, none is recalled so repeatedly or so concretely, or with such a recurrent imagistic gestalt (river-weariness-legs) as *crossing waters.* Despite the concrete vividness of these memories, therefore, Rowlandson's aim is not primarily to present an objective account, but rather to return to a primal scene that bears but has not released its arcane significance. Her quotation from Isaiah represents a foray into exegesis—and if the verse was in mind as she crossed the rivers it may have catalyzed the gestalt in the first place. But, as so often happens in this text, the biblical gloss is inadequate to the meaning-laden scene because it does not take account of all of the scene's significant attributes: being pushed from solidity into sundering force; the frailty and inadequacy of mimic homes (the raft and her body); the fear of dissolving in a pure dispersal; the cruel recurrence of the event. Rather than being allowed like the Israelites to sit by the side of the river, to contemplate it as an exterior thing and thus to posit a self set off from it, she is forced in, not once to negate and then recombine in refined form, but incessantly and without product.

But if grief is on the one hand a doomed attempt to constitute an obstinate reserve that resists immersion in the river of fright and sorrow, it is also a nomadic restlessness, or refusal of stabilities that offer themselves as adequate replacements for the fair lost world. In the episode that culminates with the reference to the rivers of Babylon, the pause to feel results not in fortitude, but in a flow of expression, in the commencement of an exchange with the Indians, an exchange that postulates rudimentary common humanity and originates a transpersonal home to replace adamant self-enclosure: "There was one of them asked me, why I wept, I could hardly tell what to say: yet I answered, they would kill me: No, said he, none will hurt you. Then came one of them and gave me two spoonfuls of meal to comfort me, and another gave me half a pint of peas; which was more worth than many bushels at another time" (336). The food and the kindness are the grace of renewed sharing. But however strong her desire to reopen, she cannot forget that such generosity comes from those who degraded her in the first place and who are feeding her, like the witch in Hansel and Gretel, with an eye to their own eventual gain. This stirring of trust and rest is, therefore, though forgivable, a lapse, a *failure* of the heart, which keeps moving away from false comfort.

Grief is a cold stone that won't be swept along, but also a river that doesn't eddy. For all of the times that Rowlandson detests the constant motion that the Indian Master imposes upon her, as many times she represents herself as constant movement. There is on the one hand the despairing fatigue of one who has been forced onward: "I could hardly bear to think of the many weary steps I had taken, to come to this place" (338): "My head was always so light, that I usually reeled as I went; but I hope all these wearisome steps that I have taken, are but a forewarning to me of the heavenly rest" (340). *And* there is the restlessness of refusal: "Whereupon I earnestly entreated the Lord, that He would consider my low estate, and show me a token for good, and if it were his blessed will, some sign and hope of relief. And indeed quickly the Lord answered, in some measure, my poor prayers: for as I was going up and down mourning and lamenting my condition, my son came to me, and asked me how I did . . ." (329–30); "When I was returned [from a subsequent visit with her son Joseph], I found myself as unsatisfied as I was before. I went up and down mourning and lamenting: and my spirit was ready to sink, with the thoughts of my poor children: my son was ill, and I could not but think of his mournful looks, and no Christian was near him, to do any office of love for him, either for soul or body. And my poor girl, I knew not where she was, nor whether she was sick, or well, or alive, or dead" (339). To remain still is impossible with so much unknown and unresolved.

The phrase *going up and down mourning and lamenting* ("There was one who was chopped into the head with a hatchet, and stripped naked, and yet crawling up and down") does not appear as a whole in the Bible, but the first half does, in the first chapters of Job, which are echoed and cited so frequently in Rowlandson's narrative as to suggest a very heartfelt familiarity: "The Lord said to Satan, 'Whence have you come?' Satan answered the Lord, 'From going to and fro on the earth, and from walking up and down on it'" (1.7, also 2.2). If as writer Rowlandson is replying to her culture's request to know whence she has come, the weaving of Satan's words into her reply adumbrates her unholy restlessness; if at times in the narrative the Indians emblematize a devilish unsettlement, always tearing her away from the labor of reconstitution, her own Joblike refusals of false comfort have something blasphemous and nomad-ological to them as well. In the account of the visit of her son, for instance, she punctuates her expression of gratitude with that remark that the prayer was answered *in some measure,* which is to say, not enough, only enough to excite a deeper despair.[7] Rowlandson's persistent and jumpy sensation that she is being conned, offered trash she is supposed to accept in lieu of the vanished, provokes her refusal to stop or settle. Unmoving intransigence, unresting impatience: this is the existential crux or chiasm of grief, which detaches at its own rate rather than at imposed rates, which refuses to settle for or move toward spec-ious surrogates, which resists movement in other directions while it is compos-ing its gait: "I could not keep still in this condition, but keep walking from one place to another" (329); "On Monday . . . they set their wigwams on fire, and went away" (334); "What through faintness, and soreness of body, it was a grievous day of travel to me. As we went along, I saw a place where English cattle had been: that was comfort to me, such as it was: quickly after that we came to an English path, which so took with me, that I thought I could have freely lain down and died" (335). One familiar fiber come across in the snarl forbids all other futures. Fast and slow, she will converge only at that distant point stipulated by a private law that is occult to her as well as to those who would keep her moving and settling down. "Someone is here. Now away she must go. Invisible to her people. Out in a gap in the shadows."[8]

Both stunned and accelerated, Rowlandson has herself taken on the liability to unannounced reversal she has discovered to be the earth's driving principle. Each semblance mutates into an opposite:

> In that time came a company of Indians to us, near thirty, all on horseback. My heart skipped within me, thinking they had been Englishmen at the first sight of them, for they were dressed in English apparel, with hats, white neckclothes, and sashes about their waists, and ribbons upon their shoulders: but when they came near, there was a vast difference between the lovely faces of Christians, and the foul looks of these heathens, which much dampened my spirits again. (349)

On the other side, hostility sometimes inverts itself as kindness, as in the gift of the spoonfuls of meal, but the pleasant aspect of transformation does not mitigate the traumatic force of incessant astonishment, since pleasure can al-ways slide back again, and sliding doesn't stop. When the world turns inside out, what has been manifest becomes what is hidden, and will return itself to view again when what was first hidden becomes hidden again, etc. Rowlandson thus anticipates not Ahab's vision of the earth's pure diabolism, but rather Ishmael's vision of the circulation of pure anomaly and mutation, not dialectically but senselessly and infinitely, each item of experience being wholly singular and without the redemption of a stable and credible explanatory context. "The more so, I say, because truly to enjoy bodily warmth, some small part of you must be cold, for there is no quality in this world that is not what it is merely by contrast. Nothing exists in itself."[9]

In the midst of such dismay, the inclination to seek symbolic meaning to explain the demise of ordinary meaning, already encouraged by her religious upbringing, by her husband's ministry, by those such as Increase Mather who read the manuscript and encouraged her to accept publication, and by her imagined audience, becomes irresistible.

The recourse to explainability is an attempt to cure the malady of solitary things that are without precedent or intrinsic sequel. As Richard Slotkin and James K. Folsom contend in their commentary on Rowlandson and Job (309), she imagines a *god of paradox,* not a *paradoxical god* but a god whose hidden intentions guarantee the world, intentions that, if discovered, would reveal senselessness to be only appearance, not the truth of things. The interchange of aspects is itself the outside of a coherence: cruel Indians are sometimes kind because God restrains them, as he restrained the lions for Daniel (356), which did not make the lions less leonine, but only enforced a pause in their nature. God assists his people's enemies because the people are grown lax, not because they are not his people; God defeated the Indians at their moment of greatest victory because it was at that moment that the English had been sufficiently humbled and the Indians had therefore become more useful as reminders of the fate of proud power than as instruments for destroying English pride (354). Even when such meanings are not yet manifest, the intending god gives clarity a credible future, not by revealing that either malignity or solicitude is the essence and the other accident, but by adumbrating an exegetical frame in which their interchanges are regulated and rational. Only the child's base craving leads it to see the parent as unpredictably changing back and forth between cruelty and sustenance; maturity lies in seeing that *all* of his actions are part of a single edifying design. The disaster had to occur to teach ordinary reason that existence is not an automatic transmission of gratification, to teach ordinary reason that it must come not only to respect but even to desire supplementation by a superior perspective.

Once this first leap from astonishment to explicability is accepted by desire as an axiom (as well as vigorously reinforced by the society to which Rowlandson has returned), other clarifications follow, such as typology. She is not alone, her suffering is not singular or anomalous, but instead by design analogous to the sufferings and confusions of others such as David, Daniel, and Job. Not too long after being taken captive, during the Third Remove, she meets an Indian who gives her a Bible he took along with other plunder from the attack on Medfield, gives it to her probably out of lack of interest in the book rather than concern for her. But he is only the vehicle of a providence, a second cause, and the Lord's motive is certainly kindness, because the Bible, like the English path, is a trail leading to a clearing. Unlike the path, however, the Bible leads not back to the material comforts that have been lost, but forward to higher insight. Other gifts, by appeasing her wanting, would encourage her to subside into the complacency that provoked the disaster in the first place, and the suffering would have been for nothing—an intolerable possibility. But disaster + Bible, like grave + stone, stimulates an elevation of perspective to a plane of finer security. This may be why she so frequently calls biblical verses *places,* a colloquial term for *topoi* or commonplaces, but in this case perhaps also *sites,* clear ground for dwelling in the midst of obscurity and mutation. The ultimate text textualizes her, as Hyperius recommended, her identifications joining her to the great tradition, while at the same time providing the great tradition with a modern instance and so confirming its continuing vitality and concrete reality. If some of those with whom she identifies, for example David, were punished for good reason, they were nevertheless still great, still chosen, still remembered for the magnificence of their response to chastisement.

Hence the confirmation and gratification she secures from her repeated experience of scriptural expressions not as illustrative metaphors but as literal realities, such as the verse from Isaiah concerning passing through the waters. While hurting from the wound she received during the attack, she recalls Psalms 38.5–6. *"My wounds stink and are corrupt, I am bowed down greatly, I go mourning all day long"* (328); during the Seventeenth Remove, Rowlandson is forced to carry a pack and her strength fails her, which brings to mind Psalm 109.22–24, *"I am poor and needy, and my heart is wounded within me. I am gone like the shadow when it declineth: I am tossed up and down like the locust; my knees are weak through fasting, and my flesh faileth of fatness"* (349); during the next remove, having been driven by hunger to eat a boiled horse hoof, she remembers Job 6.7, *"The things my soul refuseth to touch, are as my sorrowful meat"* (350). Sorrowful meat is for her not a simile for affliction, as it was for Job, but rather, like rapids, wounds, and weak knees, affliction itself, not because figurality has dissolved but because what seemed to be the ornamental expressiveness of speakers such as Job and David is coming into view as the actual and divinely authored figurality that is punctuating and italicizing her life. Rather than a series of dissipations of the figure in the real, these rhymes between Scripture and experience are eerie realizations of the figure, the sacred happening here and now to her. Whereas the ordinary Christian's meditation might be aided by imagining that his sorrows are like Job's because they are like having to eat sorrowful meat, she is presented with the boiled hoof. Job's words thus do not express in a general way her melancholy: they specifically predict the events of her life, a prefiguration that stimulates the uncanny but self-enhancing feeling that she in particular *exists as fully as is possible,* more fully than the others who came through the war, that she is in the midst of being a legend, a state that subsequent folklore may ratify but will not create, that she has been chosen to occupy a zone where the divine intervention is so direct and unequivocal as to obviate the ease of contemplative pleasure and to permit no mistake. With the force of a bolt, the scriptural verse tells her that *that hoof was meant to be.* There is nothing loose, idle, or random in what happens to her because she has inhabited an area of *constant message,* where meaning is never subject to the buffering calm of conjecture or speculation.

The destruction of the ordinary during the attack comes to seem to her, therefore, not as the vanishing of order in chaos but as the clearing away of the spurious clarities of the daily in order to make way for sound significance: we interrupt this program for a bulletin, to echo Pynchon. If the American Puritans felt that the endings of their British lives had been an interruption of chronic historicity in preparation for the incursion of the sacred, for life readied to be the noise-free channel of message, Rowlandson's glowing experience amounts to a still intenser election; and if the war was a violent restoration of the group's mantic faculty, her physical journey through horror would seem to have been a focused synecdochic analogue and guide to the common experience. The literalized scriptural figures that punctuate her experience, in other words, are part of her process of *becoming-a-vehicle.* As such, her life exits from the perhaps banal state of spouse to second-order minister and becomes, for others but first for herself, an object of awe, a sacred object, a talisman, something fantastic and maybe a little repellant in the midst of the ordinariness being reconstructed after the war, a space of strange magnetism at the heart of the community bending its conventions and communications in unprecedented directions, something with an atmosphere of *suspense.* By considering the unity between her experience and the great tradition, therefore, she demotes the utter singularity of what she has undergone without losing sight of its exceptionality: anomaly and uncontrollable reversal are not the blindness at the heart of the creation, but rather the aspect the sacred wears for those unprepared to recognize it. As God's intentions glimmer through the fog, so too her self emerges as a well-defined being—New England grown lax, and corrected for its impious torpor—rather than an incoherent grieving rag. Typology supplies grief with a version of what it seeks, a completed representation of what was torn away, i.e., carnal appetites, and of the person left behind, i.e., the saint recalled to her vocation. Rowlandson *is* the type of what Increase Mather called "formality" in religious practice, of a decent and discreet manner that followed the motions of faith but preferred pleasure such as (in her case) tobacco, good food, good company and rest on the Sabbath, and—the utterly lost thing—Sarah, wounded in the attack, dead in the wilderness, brusquely buried by the Indians without Rowlandson's knowledge or participation. She *is* an emblem of worldly things loved inordinately, without thought of their creator, and therefore justly torn away. This is of course a harsh light in which to see herself, and the perception of its harshness is not an anachronistic addition by the contemporary reader: but it is a light, and therefore opposed to the miserable obscurity of what would be otherwise, so its appeal is strong despite its rigor.

The bolt of recognition she experiences when reading about biblical sufferers, however, remains an incomplete revelation because it does not illuminate *all* of what happened to her. Though there is hope for clarity to come, full clarity is still not yet, the gap between sense and experience abides. Therefore, she writes, stringing together those events that have the feel of significance, searching for a wondrous point-for-point covergence. She *speaks herself* as did Job and David when they dwelt in that gap, and thereby acknowledges and accepts a typological representation that might otherwise only be imposed upon her life story. By speaking herself she emerges from taciturn seclusion to establish a *commonplace* of open emotional exchange with the community that reads her reading herself, seeking to placate a longing that had already possessed her when her heart failed and she wept before the Indians. If she were only *spoken about,* for instance in a sermon by Increase Mather, an object rather than also a subject in the community's talking, this would dismay the community because it would mean that an important piece of itself was outside of itself, and it would dismay Rowlandson because it would mean that she was still in the land of shadows, not truly redeemed and returned to life. She is willing to testify and they are willing to have her do so, but the testimony is premature because the matching between pattern and experience is not yet completely worked through. And such prematurity manifests more than an uncompleted task, reveals instead an experiential material that resists transcendental formulation, a resistance that reveals in turn either that she is still defective, or that the formula is coercive rather than purely resolutive. In either case, the abiding discrepancy suggests that the convergence of their desire for her testimony with her desire to testify does not prove that the same kind of testimony is in both cases desired. Happy to experience the convergence, she does her best to make her performance suit their expectation, but there is still the restlessness, the walking up and down, because the pattern of explicit significance that she attempts to accept and embody has been designated as the only path back to life: the definition of living is externally controlled rather than susceptible to creative amendment on her part no matter how much invention she exerts in the task of application. The labor of extending those moments of uncanny identity between Scripture and experience is therefore likely to become a coercion of experience by ideological shape rather than remaining an inquiry into experience. Completing the mesh between pattern and experience will not be simply a process of continuing what is begun but will instead require the transformation of identification into emulation that Hyperius recommended as the desideratum of funerary rhetoric. Pattern discovered becomes pattern imposed: the blessed mercy in finding several tokens of sense serves as bait for wholesale complicity in a cultural project eager to make use of her, to control her reflection on the means of life.

Rowlandson's desire for her own relief, together with her readers' desire for relief from their own particular postwar traumas, takes the form of a longing for pattern, a longing that the society of the example correctly and shrewdly perceived as an unprecedented opportunity for consolidating the prestige and power of the New England Mind. Hence the unmistakably overheated excitation of the war's major theorist, Increase Mather, and his concomitant *jealousy*, his anxious scramble to ensure that every event of the war be properly understood. His anxiety, as Slotkin and Folsom contend (62–77), is most evident in his *Brief History of the WARR With the INDIANS in New England* (1676), composed almost day by day as the disaster unfolded and therefore frequently strained in its attempts to do on-the-scene exegesis:

> *June 15.* This day was seen at *Plimouth* the perfect form of an *Indian Bow* appearing in the aire, which the Inhabitants of that Place (at least some of them) look upon, as a *Prodigious Apparition.* The like was taken note of, a little before the Fort Fight in the *Narragansett* Countrey. Who knoweth but that it may be an *omen* of ruine to the enemy, and that the Lord will break the bow and spear asunder, and make warrs to cease unto the ends of the earth?[10]

Though Mather has scrupulously recalled a similar image that appeared in the sky before the fort fight, which was an English victory, the status of the celestial emblem is nevertheless vague: it is at lest possible to think that a giant bow in the sky would betoken Indian strength and further English defeat, a possibility of misinterpretation to which Mather is quite alert, as his sarcastic aside ("at least some of them") indicates. Despite the invocation of the fort fight precedent to control interpretation, the meaning of the apparition is still snarled in, still bears the traces of, the hermeneutical malaise that the war has brought forward:

> The Swamp was so Boggy and thick of Bushes, as that it was judged to proceed further therein would be but to throw away Mens lives. It could not there be descerned who were *English* and who the *Indians.* Our men when in that hideous place if they did but see a Bush stir would fire presently, whereby 'tis verily feared, that they did sometimes unhappily shoot *English men* instead of *Indians.* (90)

Mather is not the first Puritan writer to use the swamp as a sign for the confusion of signs: the trope is nearly irresistible in Indian war narratives, because the project of draining swamps was just begun in seventeenth-century Massachusetts, and because the Indians, knowing that the English were reluctant to pursue them there, often went to swamps to regroup. But Mather develops the image with a certain compulsiveness in order to use it as a figurative vilification of the countervailing interpretive possibilities he is attempting to stave off with his writing. The swamp is for Mather simply *the real,* the irony at the heart of the community, with its appalling power to pervert the typological order, but also with its astonishing potential should correct interpretation succeed. He is writing to drain the swamp, to ensure that everyone knows without trace of doubt who is behind the bush shaking it. The figuration of unclarity as the swamp, the clear view of unclarity, prefigures success, because it keeps typology integral and universally capable, but for the Increase Mather of the *Brief History,* as for Rowlandson, the perfect convergence is *not yet.* Experience is still defective.

His explications are less troubled in *An Earnest EXHORTATION of the Inhabitants of New England. To hearken to the voice of God in his late and present DISPENSATIONS,* a sermon preached a short while after the English victory and published in 1676.[11] His greater confidence is largely due to the facts that he is writing at a greater reflective distance and that the war is over: he has had more time and leisure to devise ingenious strategies for wrestling the real into shape, and reality has returned to ordinariness and regularity, and therefore impinges less pertinaciously on the type. But though he may have cured his discourse of all swampiness, he knows that his audience cannot already have so immersed themselves in the renewal of the ordinary as to have forgotten the recent trauma. The confidence he gets from greater expository coherence, therefore, leads not to rhetorical equanimity, to group self-congratulation, but rather to an edgy and pushy insistence that his audience acknowledge his view. Without acknowledgment internal coherence is worthless because the type cannot be only an agonistic member of the society's discursive repertoire, it must dominate, organize, and coordinate that repertoire.

Mather decides that he must undo the provisional sense of safety the audience has begun to compose, first by impressing them with the strong possibility of renewed fright, new Indian insurrection, by inculcating anxiety, fear of fright; and second by contending that such a return of disaster will be brought on precisely by the sense of safety, by a preoccupation with the concerns of rehabilitated quotidian existence that leads to neglect of typological meditation. This causality replaces anxiety with fear by providing a concrete and lucidly perceived danger and proposes a clear course of action to prevent disaster. Destroying calm, he leads them from the memory of fright to anxiety to fear to an anticipation of a higher and more secure version of the calm he has just destroyed, a safety that is contingent upon their fervent and wholehearted embrace of his discourse: you don't have what you think you have, it's not only a mirage but a direct cause of what you think you've escaped, only (what) I (stand for) can bring you peace. He unsettles trust and conjures misery, gorges himself on the opulent meal of desire and dread spread across the table of the postwar world.

One of the major signs that the population is returning to the laxity that brought on the war in the first place is their failure to *"Hearken to the voice of God in the ministry of his word"* (174), a flaw now conspicuous even among magistrates: "mind what the messengers of God speak in his name, *for surely the Lord will do nothing, but he revealeth his secrets to his Servants the Prophets"* (174), preeminently Mather himself—"I will (by the help of Christ) speak faithfully, as I shall answer it before him that hath set me a *Watch-man,* another day" (185). Whatever modesty the parenthetical remark concerning Christ's help may suggest is annulled by the thought that Christ has chosen Increase Mather to be the one he helps, an extraordinary election that is proven by Mather's ability to discern and describe the secret meanings of the late travail, to reveal who was shaking the bush and for what reason:

And none more guilty than the poorer sort of people, who will needs go in their Silks and Bravery as if they were the best in the land. Though it be also true that the rich and honourable have many of them greatly offended by strange Apparel, especially here in Boston . . . *Moreover the Lord saith* (if the Lord say it who dare slight what is said) *because the Daughters of Zion are haughty, therefore will he discover their nakedness.* Hath not the Lord fulfilled this threatening, when the *Indians* have taken so many and stripped them naked as in the day they were born. (177)

No question mark needed. The obvious literalization of the scriptural trope itself strips discourse of heterodox meaning and exerts its clarifying force against lower-class and female aberrations to which heterodoxy has opened the door. Mather here avails himself of a venerable patristic figuration of Christian waywardness as the sartorial hedonism of those who clothe the body of truth with an excess of ornament.[12] But the misogynist trope that emerges at this point in the sermon is less important in the sermon as a whole than is Mather's racist trope, his equation of New England's sinful life-style with Algonquian culture—a trope that will prompt Rowlandson's own descriptions of her captors' heteroglot fashion choices. The racist trope is more attractive to Mather in the present circumstance because the Indians are currently a greater horror than are women, and because this trope allows him to explain the war as a clear message, and thus to demonstrate his mantic capability: you were attacked *by* the Indians because you had become *like* the Indians, and so if you want to avoid being attacked by the Indians again you will have to become *unlike* them, according to the explications of *likeness* supplied by the watchman. The *character* of the disaster plainly reveals its etiology: but of course this plainness conceals Mather's dependence on maintaining the plausibility of certain assumptions about what Algonquians *are*.[13]

In this rhetorical climate, Mather could not have helped but be exultant to discover Rowlandson's narrative, because she is not a theologue supplying meaning but rather a member of the audience come forward to acknowledge what she has heard as a valid tool for making sense of what happened to her. This apparent conformity with the argument he was advancing about the war provokes the enthusiasm that pervades the preface, where he contends that Rowlandson's experience was exceptional only in its heightened representativity, in its presentation of New England's condition and correction in stark and excruciatingly bare outline. Hers is the skeleton of New England's experience. She is God's rhetorical device for laying bare the meaning of the war and ensuring that the meaning will not be forgotten. Her suffering "was a dispensation of public note and of universal concernment":

> This narrative was penned by the gentlewoman herself, to be to her a memorandum of God's dealing with her, that she might never forget, but remember the same, and the several circumstances thereof, all the days of her life. A pious scope which deserves both commendation and imitation. Some friends having obtained a sight of it, could not but be so much affected with the many passages of working providence discovered therein, as to judge it worthy of public view, and altogether unmeet that such works of God should be hid from present and future generations . . . (320)

Through the reading and remembering of her act of reading and remembering the "several circumstances" and "many passages of working providence," the postwar New England consciousness—itself grieving, jumpy, desperate to reconstruct a secure regularity—will become the medium through which eternal pattern enters contemporaneity, and restores and rejuvenates itself. "Marking" what is "upright" in her recollection, to recall Fitch's terms, the reader will perceive her as she is hereby certified to have perceived herself, not as a person, really, but as "an *instance* of the sovereignty of God," "an *instance* of the faith and patience of the saints, under the most heartsinking trials" (332; italics added), an occasion for public edification: "Reader, if thou gettest no good by such a declaration as this, the fault must be thine own" (322). The end here is not simply to remember, but to remember properly by comprehending the meaning rather than only imagining the vivid circumstances of the working providence:

The works of the Lord (not only of creation, but of providence also, especially those that do more peculiarly concern His dear ones, that are as the apple of His eye, as the signet upon His hand, the delight of His eyes, and the objects of His tenderest care) are great, sought out by all those that have pleasure therein. And of these verily this is none of the least. (320)

If "this" refers to the narrative as well as to Rowlandson's salvation, and if the narrative is "of these," i.e., one of the works of the Lord, then even as a writer she is a matter worked upon, rather than an author. An instance or item of providence, Rowlandson is not primarily subject but object, a thinking, speaking, and acknowledging object, to be sure, and an object glowing with aura, but an object nonetheless, and this objectification is exactly what she acknowledges, what makes her glow. It is her *best intention.*

Twentieth-century criticism has in the main taken it for granted that Rowlandson is so thoroughly one of "those that have pleasure therein" that this best intention has been assumed to be the only intention. The selections from the narrative in Milton R. Stern and Seymour L. Gross's *American Literature Survey: Colonial and Federal to 1800,* the most useful general-purpose text for early American survey classes, seem to have been chosen to highlight the maximally typological sections of the narrative. Stern and Gross's act of selection, therefore, recapitulates the marking of the upright, not in order to demonstrate the glory of the working of providence but in order to demonstrate that Rowlandson's purpose was without exception to demonstrate the glory of the working of providence:

The title is indicative of New England attitudes: the narrative maintains the old Puritan belief that God is on the side of the settlers and that all hardships are means by which Sion's Savior tests the faith of the chosen. It was only right that, as children of Satan, the Indians should be exterminated and their lands appropriated by their Christian conquerors. Readers applauded the sentiments and were thrilled by what they saw as a living example of Christian perseverance in the "plantation religious" of the New World.[14]

Their view issues from the critical paradigms dominant during the period of their anthology's composition and revision (1962–75), and represents a preliminary foray into supplying the narrative with critical intelligibility. More surprising is a recent seconding of their assumptions by Jane Tomkins. In an essay on English and American perceptions of Indians, Tomkins contends that whites have always seen Indians only through the filter of the paradigms they inhabit, and that this is all that is ever possible. The Indian *an sich,* for Tomkins' reassuring neo-Kantian complacency, can never be brought into view, so why worry ourselves with the question? The concept of realism is fatuous. As I will argue in Chapter 4, Rowlandson seems to me to be a counterexample to this argument, because the wreckage of her world prompted her to see the Indians, if not in themselves, in other lights than that of the type. For Tomkins, though, as for Stern and Gross, Rowlandson's narrative is no more than a typological automatism. Citing a passage where Rowlandson mentions having met Philip, Tomkins remarks that the passage "makes it hard to see her testimony as evidence of anything other than the Puritan point of view," a judgment that confirms her opinion that Rowlandson "sees everything that happens to her as a sign from God":

> What seem to us the peculiar emphases in Rowlandson's relation are not the result of her having *screened out* evidence she couldn't handle, but of her way of constructing the world. She saw what her seventeenth century English Separatist background made visible.[15]

Tomkins thus selects the evidence that confirms the thesis, screening out evidence that she does not desire to handle, thereby herself making it hard to see Rowlandson's testimony as evidence of anything other than a strictly doctrinaire Puritan point of view. Whether or not Rowlandson is constitutively deaf to something it would be impossible to hear anyway, Tomkins' Rowlandson is, like the Indians she was told about when she was a child, a creature "totally of the imagination,"[16] a desiring imagination that, albeit with a different desire, more than confirms Per Amicum's wishful assertion that Rowlandson wholeheartedly agreed to be an *instance,* more than confirms because for Tomkins Rowlandson didn't even have a choice. Mather need not have worried about the mournful woman writing, because she couldn't help but recapitulate his truths.[17]

In their preface to the narrative, Slotkin and Folsom agree with Tomkins: "it is certainly true that few Puritan texts hold so uncompromisingly as this *Narrative* to a demonstration of the ostensible moral they set themselves" (304). But phrases like "it is certainly true" bespeak nervousness, and Slotkin and Folsom in fact go on to find the narrative quite untypical. After positing contradictions within Calvinist theology and transformations within New England orthodoxy in order to keep Rowlandson within the circle of conformity, they finally declare that "it is in many ways a psychological text as well as a theological or historic document":

> For there is another dimension to her *Narrative* than the moral one, a dimension that explains as well as any other single factor both the power of this particular book and the popularity, among serious readers, of the whole genre of Indian captivities. This dimension is, for lack of a more precise term, an internal, psychological one. (307)

Slotkin and Folsom's first judgment that Rowlandson's writing is controlled by a typical moralism may have been shaped by the critical enterprise of Slotkin's *Regeneration through Violence,* which is a broad sketch of large ideological formations and the ways texts reflect those judgments, an enterprise that is not advanced by attending to the specificities of single writers. There is nonetheless a certain Creonism at work here, an inclination to typify, for instance when Rowlandson is released from doctrinal typicality only to be absorbed into the typicality of the captivity narrative genre. But the conclusion that typology is *among* the book's expressive patterns is an advance; and the invocation of a "psychological" dimension perceptible to "serious readers" is useful, though it must be added that Rowlandson's nonaligned "psychology" is not devoid of intellectual, social, and ethical determination, and that the theological dimension for Rowlandson as for Mather is governed by desire, and is therefore not "unpsychological."

More recently, some critics have begun to follow Slotkin and Folsom's second judgment in concluding that the exemplification cannot be taken as the whole of the authorial intention, though it may be the beginning intention, that there is a certain emergent dissonance or volatile dialogism. David Downing, for example, points to an important tonal discrepancy: "Rowlandson generally recounts the events of her captivity in a vigorous and homely style, combining close observation with simple, direct expression. However, when she pauses to consider the significance of a particular detail, her style becomes more elevated as she employs biblical quotations and metaphors to convey her meaning."[18] Rowlandson usually signifies the difference between the sacred word and her own word by italicizing quotations from the Bible, but, as Downing contends, this sanitary discrimination also extends into the tone of her own word, dividing her maximally typological ruminations from what Slotkin and Folsom collect under the term "psychological." The power of the scriptural, to echo Bakhtin, is inadequately assimilated into the text's milieu of style: "Authoritative discourse may organize around itself great masses of other types of discourses (which interpret it, praise it, apply it in various ways), but the authoritative discourse does not merge with these (by means of, say, gradual transitions); it remains sharply demarcated, compact, and inert: it demands, so to speak, not only quotation marks but a demarcation even more magisterial, a special script, for instance."[19] Demarcated, compact, inert—encrypted. Bakhtin's taxonomic description of the incomplete integration of the authoritative voice here perhaps obscures the phenomenology of mourning in Rowlandson's narrative. Grief is incompletely integrated into the consolations of theology, which is present not in the perfunctory or halfhearted way of extrinsic obeisance, nor as a simple opposite to grief, but is instead a promissory simulation of grief's eventual end. The essence of what is longed for, the authoritative word appears often to her as a hypothetical future for desire, and she is as a result *interested in it,* rather than either compliant or resistant. Rowlandson's theological tone therefore exists, but not as belief, rather as the atmosphere of something that she desires will turn out to have been adequate.

The tonal discrepancy that Downing describes is an index of the text's afflicted temporality, a dimension that would be obscured by Bakhtin's tendency to emphasize simultaneous arrays. If theology is longed for, it is *not yet,* it is subjunctive rather than present, and what is present stubbornly remains. Theology has not completely percolated into voice, or rather voice has not completely percolated into it. Despite the redemption from captivity, the writing self is still a grieving self, and wary about enticing hospitalities—as it was when the Indians offered her kindness. Pausing at front doors, but still a sojourner rather than an inhabitant, she is still an *Indian,* not in the enjoyment of inordinate pleasure but in the restlessness and nomadism, the unsettledness, if only *for the time (of) being,* which is the time of the writing: *not on schedule.* She watched the following ceremony during her captivity, but her exceptionally long account of it suggests that it still bears fascination and occult meaning for her as she writes during the time of white redemption:

> Before they went to that fight [at Sudbury], they got a company together to pow-wow; the manner was as followeth. There was one that kneeled upon a deerskin, with the company round him in a ring who kneeled, and striking upon the ground with their hands, and with sticks, and muttering or humming with their mouths; beside him who kneeled in the ring, there also stood one with a gun in his hand: then he on the deerskin made a speech, and all manifested assent to it: and so they did many times together. Then they bade him with the gun go out of the ring, which he did, but when he was out, they called him in again; but he seemed to make a stand, then they called the more earnestly, till he returned again: then they all sang. Then they gave him two guns, in either hand one: and so he on the deerskin began again; and at the end of every sentence in his speaking, they all assented, humming or muttering with their mouths, and striking upon the ground with their hands. Then they bade him with the two guns go out of the ring again; which he did, a little way. Then they called him in again, but he made a stand; so they called him in with greater earnestness; but he stood reeling and wavering as if he knew not whither he should stand or fall, or which way to go. Then they called him with exceeding great vehemency, all of them, one and another: after another while he turned in, staggered as he went, with his arms stretched out, in either hand a gun. As soon as he came in, they all sang and rejoiced exceedingly a while. And then he upon the deerskin, made another speech, unto which they all assented in a rejoicing manner: and so they ended their business, and forthwith went to Sudbury-fight. (353)

Earlier in the narrative, Rowlandson described Algonquian ritual briefly and conventionally—infernal dancing in the woods. Here, however, topos is breached by intrigue, by a feeling that the ceremony says something to be noted—an attentiveness usually reserved for divine providences such as the horse's hoof. The account is not reportorial: many details are left out, such as apparel (of which she makes note on other occasions), the tone and content of the chanting, etc. What we get is an allegorization of a certain social conflict:

1. A consensual group, arrayed around a charismatic leader who occupies a designated site (the deerskin), inciting itself to ritually sanctioned violence, the sanction depending on acknowledgment from a designated outsider.

2. The outsider, at first sent away but then hesitant about return; equipped by the group with tools of aggression, but uncertain about whether to add them to or withhold them from the group violence; indecisive, moving in then away, not vehement in refusal, but staggering, weak, apparently about to fall, still not completely willing to collapse into the circle, dangerous despite the weakness. Or:

1. New England, Increase Mather at the pulpit, the regenerated devotion to the Errand, the nation's eagerness for her book.

2. Rowlandson and the captivity; writing and interpretation; mournful writing and the present time of the narrative, its abiding threat to the consensual cause.

Here, perhaps more powerfully than anywhere in the narrative, Rowlandson's innocent *receptivity to message* carries her outside the circle rather than beckoning her in. The account of the powwow allegorizes the act of writing of the narrative that includes it, emblematizing the wariness and hesitation of this voice that moves sometimes toward and sometimes away from the legitimated canon of emblems, not in the circle, not standing at an unequivocally defiant distance. "He stood reeling and wavering as if he knew not whither he should stand or fall": "I was so weak and feeble, that I reeled as I went along, and thought that I must end my days at last, after my bearing and getting through so many difficulties; the Indians stood laughing to see me staggering along . . ."

The account of the powwow is emblematic and even typological, but neither the vehicles nor the tenors are drawn from Puritanism's archive (armory) of meanings. The rhetorical device of the type is bent from its proper direction. Like the irony at the heart of Hegel's community, Rowlandson's narrative is a zone of appropriative distortion. And even her flashes of identification with the Bible are not automatically congenial to Puritan sagacity. The Bible is a complex anthology drawn from an extensive social aggregate and written piecemeal over a long duration, not the univocal utterance of a master voice, and typological associations between experience and Scripture therefore do not automatically fortify what Puritanism chose to see as the Bible's message—the Canticles, for instance, as Ann Kibbey argues, required considerable exegesis

to be brought to a semblance of utility for the Puritans.[20] Such associations do
not of necessity entail ideological solidarity, but can instead sanction dissidence, especially when the associations are made with dramatized expressions
of complaint, such as those in Psalms and Job, which are, according to Downing, the two books of the Bible most frequently cited by Rowlandson.[21] Job
was, after all, *blameless,* and chosen for affliction because of his blamelessness,
and Rowlandson's identification with Job therefore runs directly contrary to
Per Amicum's contention that she is the type of New England punished for its
sins and taught to remember the Lord. Furthermore, as Slotkin and Folsom
note (309), much of the Book of Job is taken up by Job's angry rejoinders to the
"false comforters" who urge him to accept rationalized representations of himself, of the meaning of his affliction, and of his future, representations that he
feels are perhaps not entirely false but certainly simple, premature, and worthy
of being repudiated as encroachments on divine prerogative, as distorted vi-
sions of a divinity that offers grounds for neither hope nor comprehension.
Upon arriving to witness Job's misery, Eliphaz, Bildad, and Zophar measure
out seven days of respectful silence, and then commence with homilies and
maxims that make Job furious:

> Lo, my eye has seen all this,
> my ear has heard and understood it.
> What you know, I also know;
> I am not inferior to you.
> But I would speak with the Almighty,
> And I desire to argue my case with God.
> As for you, you whitewash with lies;
> worthless physicians are you all.
> Oh that you would keep silent,
> and it would be your wisdom!
> . . .
> Your maxims are proverbs of ashes,
> your defenses are defenses of clay.
> Let me have silence, and I will speak,
> and let come on me what may.
> I will take my flesh in my teeth, and put my life in my hand.
> (13.1–5, 12–14)

Because Job refuses the factitious lucidities of the comforters, who are eventually reproved by God as well, and because, though his prosperity is *restored*
(the text implies that new sons and daughters replace the dead as handily as new
oxen for old, which could be the case only if paternal desire were only a desire
for dynasty and therefore a specimen of the affectional fungibility Antigone

mocks), he never knows that the cause of his suffering is a little gentlemanly experimentation conceived to mitigate the ennui of heaven, as Melville might contend (why does an omniscient god have to *discover?* doesn't such a desire for probation foreshadow Thomas' need for evidence, or the husband who was too curious in Cervantes?), Job's god is to the end a paradoxical god rather than the god of paradox, as violent and unpredictable, he announces, as the behemoth that swims at the base of creation, the senselessness of whose force is essential rather than merely apparent.

Insofar as Rowlandson's identification with Job entails a similar view of absolute force not as a parental infliction of pain in the cause of love but as an unchartable oscillation between destruction and happiness, her distance from the synthetic lucidities of covenantal insight amounts to a revival of the frightening god that Miller called the marrow of Puritan divinity. In her case, though, the radical legacy is revived in order to protect the truth of her experience of disaster and confusion against the imperious allure of Puritanism, rather than to protect clear faith against the power of Church of England ritual. If so, then her knowledge is a crater in the midst of the society of the example and a resurrection of Puritanism's *dangerous memory.* Benjamin:

> To articulate the past historically does not mean to recognize it "the way it really was" (Ranke). It means to seize hold of a memory as it flashes up at moments of danger. Historical materialism wishes to retain that image of the past which unexpectedly appears to man singled out by history at a moment of danger. The danger affects both the content of history and its receivers. The same threat hangs over both: that of becoming a tool of the ruling classes. In every era the attempt must be made to wrest tradition away from a conformism that is about to overpower it. The Messiah comes not only as a redeemer, he comes as the subduer of Antichrist. Only the historian will have the gift of the fanning the spark of hope who is firmly convinced that *even the dead* will not be safe from the enemy if he wins.[22]

Convulsed by a memory of the dead despite her *redemption,* Rowlandson appeals to scriptural tradition in such a way as to make it swerve from the rhetoric of the funeral sermon and toward what Auerbach saw as the Bible's communication of the obscurity of depth, and thereby implicitly relegates Puritan typological exegesis to the manifestness of what Auerbach called legend and associated with the Hellenic:

> I said above that the Homeric style was "of the foreground" because, despite much going back and forth, it yet causes what is momentarily being narrated to give the impression that it is the only present, pure and without perspective. A consideration of the Elohistic text teaches us that our term is capable of a broader and deeper application. It shows us that even the separate personages can be repre-

sented as having "background"; God is always so represented in the Bible, for he is not comprehensible in his presence, as is Zeus; it is always only "something" of him that appears, he always extends into depths . . . [The legendary] runs far too smoothly. All cross-currents, all friction, all that is casual, secondary to the main events and themes, everything unresolved, truncated and uncertain, which confuses the clear progress of the action and the simple orientation of the actors, has disappeared. The historical event which we witness [in the Bible], or learn from the testimony of those who witnessed it, runs much more variously, contradictorily, and confusedly; not until it has produced results in a definite domain are we able, with their help, to classify it to a certain extent; and how often the order to which we think we have attained becomes doubtful again, how often we ask ourselves if the data before us have not led to a far too simple classification of the original events![23]

But my association of Puritanism with Hellenism as Auerbach describes it is not quite correct: like Hegel distinguishing himself from Kant, Puritanism considers itself post-Judaic rather than non-Judaic, orients itself around the wonder of manifestation rather than of simple manifestness, around a divinity generously come from behind the veil as a gesture of approval for his saints. If manifestation were to be erroneously taken for granted as automatic manifestness, then it would seem no longer to need maintenance according to the watchman's instructions.

Consequently, the obscure god described by Miller and Auerbach is preserved in Puritan ideology *as threat,* as *that into which favor will subside* if wholehearted compliance wanes: as partner in the Covenant, God performs in a visible foreground, but reserves the right to return to his mystery should the human partner lapse. Hence the rhetorico-political utility of the irregular horror of war and of Rowlandson's intense experience, which demonstrate the reality of the danger, and the utility of peacetime and the narrative, which can be called reconstitutions of manifestation, formidable specimens of Puritanism's central ritual, covenant renewal. But hence also the truly dangerous power of the woman's narrative if it represents the background as *more than an interlude or passage,* as being's *chronic circumstance* rather than as a morally deliberate and explicable interruption of being's usual lucidity, and thereby converts the realism of complex experience from an ideological device into a critique of the spurious and opportunistic patina laid over being by false comforters. In the latter case, the only recourse would be to represent the narrative and its author as chaos, rather than as a representation of the experience of chaos, as a dwindled but potent remainder of the monstrosity recently overcome—to bury Antigone's insistence on a manner of burial, a strategy that Puritanism erroneously concluded was unnecessary in the case of Rowlandson's narrative.

I disagree, therefore, with Howe's contention that Rowlandson's recourse to the Bible is in every case a restraint rather than an expression of nonconformity:

> Mary Rowlandson's thoroughly reactionary figuralism requires that she obsessively confirm her orthodoxy to readers at the same time she excavates and subverts her own rhetoric. Positivist systems of psychological protection have disintegrated. Identities and configurations rupture and shift. Her risky retrospective narrative will be safe, only if she asserts the permanence of corporate Sovereignty. Each time an errant perception skids loose, she controls her lapse by vehemently invoking biblical authority.[24]

Here as elsewhere, Howe is the deepest reader of Rowlandson's narrative, which she calls "a relentless origin," "composed in a bloody fragment of the world."[25] But I think that Rowlandson's appeals to Scripture in some cases express an anti-ideological typology, thereby challenging the safety of corporate sovereignty and the incipient positivism of the watchmen and expressing or providing a vehicle for the errant perception.

However, using the Bible in this way at one important point requires Rowlandson to read against its grain: when the normative frame is more fully developed than it is in the Book of Job, Rowlandson's identification with the suffering character must circumvent or deliberately overlook the moral stigma laid upon misery's complaint against the course of things, *excavating* or *exhuming* the character's discourse. This sort of textual revisionism is required when Rowlandson associates herself with Lot's wife, who is explicitly condemned in Genesis:

> On Monday (as I said) they set their wigwams on fire and went away. It was a cold morning, and before us there was a great brook with ice on it; some waded through it, up to the knees and higher, but others went till they came to a beaver dam, and I amongst them, where through the good providence of God, I did not wet my foot. I went along that day mourning and lamenting, leaving farther my own country, and travelling into the vast and howling wilderness, and I understood something of Lot's wife's temptation, when she looked back; we came that day to a great swamp, by the side of which we took up our lodging that night. (334)

This is an especially dense nest of symbols—the destruction of a place of pausing, forced movement, the foot and the river, the Deuteronomic description of the wilderness as "vast [waste] and howling," and the swamp—the last two of which were Puritanism's major figures for the New World earth. The reader alert to Rowlandson's expressive motifs will recognize this as the waking dream's core, where gratitude for the divine generosity reverses or mutates into anti-typology, a planet around which we orbit so quickly that there is only a flicker rather than a clear distinction between light and dark hemispheres.

The identification with Lot's wife is more complex than the identification with Job, not only because of the overlay of the narrating voice in Genesis, but also because the wife does not speak in the Bible. Nor are her thoughts and feelings recorded. There is only the act of turning:

> Then the Lord rained on Sodom and Gomorrah brimstone and fire from the Lord out of heaven; and he overthrew those cities, and all the valley, and all the inhabitants of the cities, and what grew on the ground. But Lot's wife behind him looked back, and she became a pillar of salt. And Abraham went early in the morning to the place where he had stood before the Lord; and he looked down toward Sodom and Gomorrah and toward all the land of the valley, and beheld, and lo, the smoke of the land went up like the smoke of a furnace.(19.24-28)

Lot's wife's subjectivity is as utterly eradicated as are the cities of the plain: all that remains is an unmistakable emblem, like the rising smoke. It is important that in neither case is the extirpation entire—rather than disappearance, which would prevent an aversive memory of sin, there is a conversion of living subjectivity into emblem. Destruction is exegesis. The double violence directed against the cities and against Lot's wife is therefore an act of figuration, after the completion of which Abraham not only can but must look back—must never stop looking back, as Christ's citation of Lot's wife in Luke suggests. The most striking stylistic trait of this passage from Genesis is its resolute externality, its cautious avoidance of the subjectivity of the destroyed: anything about the culture of Sodom and Gomorrah save what are called their moral excesses, the absence of what God and Abraham decide between them to call a good man; the home—friends, memories, possessions—that led Lot's wife to look back, in fondness, Rowlandson assures us, rather than out of simple curiosity about the providential detonation, to mourn, to begin to apprehend the shape of the loss, the crater; Lot's feeling after his wife's transfiguration or conversion; Abraham's feeling as he gazes on all the ruin. These hearts, centrally, her heart, are textually obliviated as entirely as were the cities: perhaps because if we were to know that, a good woman, she had been fond of her home, that she was sorrowful because it had enclosed a certain intricacy of life, then the use of Sodom and Gomorrah as pure examples of a repellant carnality, of places where not a single good person could be found, would be compromised by an emotional ambiguity, as would her conversion into a type of what Hyperius might call a womanish measurelessness. The *price* of Sodom's destruction would be conspicuous: it had been a place where life was organized around more than the pursuit of excess, where there was a history rather than just a string of heterodox orgasms. Thus if this resolute externality produces what Auerbach calls a background, our inclination to explore that background is strictly prohibited. The interior is a place that the reader must pass over. The rigor with which the text interdicts the irruption of grief in the midst of destiny reveals precisely the anti-exemplaristic power of grief, its power to reveal that the price of disobedience, about which the text is richly expressive, is set off against a price of compliance, about which the text is eager to be silent. But the narration is informed by the knowledge of grief's inevitability, and therefore of the necessity of speaking about it, *briefly,* in order to demonstrate its worth-lessness and blasphemy, to attempt to prevent it from persisting *alongside* the severe normativity the discourse is meant to instill in the reader. Consequently, the narration brings grief in to control it, but with an anxious and jealous terseness *so* severe as to invite conjecture, centuries later, one reader looking not for the moment *back* but for the moment *below,* and so overthrows its own good intentions: "I understood something of Lot's wife's temptation . . ."

Rowlandson's identification with Lot's wife may have been suggested by Protestant commentary on the episode as well as by the Bible itself, as my epigraphs to this chapter are intended to suggest. Luther begins by speculating that "since women are rather weak by nature—she either forgot the command of the angels, or she thought there was no longer any danger after she had come into the open country from the city," but he realizes, under the guidance of Luke 17.32, where Christ discourages love for this world's things with the exhortation "Remember Lot's wife," that her motive was grief: "From this we readily understand what it means to look back, namely, to depart from God's command and to be occupied with other matters—matters outside one's call-ing—like the man who has been commanded to follow Christ and wants to bury his dead first (Matt. 8: 21)." For all of his world-historical intervention into the governance of mourning, Luther nonetheless seems here a little unset-tled by the obduracy of the judgment, because he goes on to assert, three times, that her death was "instruction for us, rather than a condemnation of the woman, who, I fully believe, was saintly and saved," a possibility that, in Rowlandson's case at least, might tend to induce a certain asperity rather than reconciliation. Luther's insecurity is still not laid to rest, though, and he is compelled to speculate further: "Perhaps Lot's wife was terrified by the awful crash of the thunderbolts, and the collapsing cities and looked back for that reason." A degree of rubbernecking is to be expected in the presence of the sublime, but it seems to me that this commonsensicality has the additional function of momentarily easing Luther's feeling that the punishment is some-thing of an atrocity. Finally, he openly and sympathetically imagines grief, but only for Lot: "From our own sentiments we can readily gauge how hard it was for the saintly man Lot on such an occasion and because of such a sin to lose his very dear wife, with whom he lived for so many years and who had followed him so dutifully during so long an exile."[26]

Calvin also finds it necessary to speculate around the issue of this "memorable prodigy": "It may now be asked," he writes, allowing that some questions are nearly as irresistible as the desire to look back, "why the Lord so severely punished the imprudence of the unhappy woman; seeing that she did not look back, from a desire to return to Sodom? perhaps, being yet doubtful, she wished to have more certain evidence before her eyes; or, it might be, that, in pity to the perishing people, she turned her eyes in that direction." But, in the passage I quote as an epigraph, the verse from Luke controls Calvin's inquiry into the interdicted background as it controlled Luther's: "her fault was not light," "she did not cheerfully leave Sodom," she was "draw[n] aside from the meditation of the holy life," she "glided into unholy desires," all of which interior movement is revealed by the exterior slowness that God will simplify into immobility: "her tardiness was a sign." But despite this harshness, Calvin follows Luther in balking at the punishment, which may be why he forces himself to be so harsh: "And although it is not lawful to affirm anything respecting her eternal salvation; it is nevertheless probable, that God, having inflicted temporal punishment, spared her soul; inasmuch as he often chastises his own people in the flesh, that their soul may be saved from eternal destruction." Once he has rescued meditation by diverting attention from the wife to her pedagogical function, Calvin's equilibrium is restored: "If the severity of the punishment terrifies us; let us remember, that they sin, at this day, not less grievously, who, being delivered, not from Sodom, but from hell, fix their eyes upon some other object than the proposed prize of their high calling."

My point is not that Rowlandson must have read Luther or Calvin, but that the post-Reformation reader of Genesis, prodded by the unforgiving disproportion between crime and punishment, was apt to take the minute chronicle of Lot's wife as a too-eloquent silence rather than as an effective prohibition, as a strong temptation to the sort of speculation evident in Calvin's "perhaps," "it might be," "we infer," "Moses intimates," "it is probable"—speculation that might be brought to quickness by personal experience: "I understood some thing of Lot's wife's temptation." The inordinate attempt to silence, like Creon's burial of Antigone, produces an area of visible darkness, a heterodox typical potentiality. Repressive brevity misfires and creates its opposite, a textual phenomenon analyzed by Horkheimer and Adorno with respect to a passage concerning Telemachus' execution of "the faithless women who had reverted to prostitution" in the *Odyssey*:

Emotionless and with an inhuman composure rivaled only by the *impassibilité* of the major nineteenth century novelists, Homer describes the movement of the nooses and coldly compares the women's appearance as they hang to that of birds caught in a net; the reticence and composure of the narration are the true marks of eloquence. The passage closes with the information that the feet of the women "kicked out for a short while, but not for long." (22: 473) The precision of the descriptive artist, which already exhibits the frigidity of anatomy and vivisection, is employed to provide evidence of the dying convulsions of the subjected who, in the name of law and justice, were cast down into that realm from which Odysseus the judge escaped. As a citizen reflecting momentarily upon the nature of hanging, Homer assures himself and his audience (actually readers) that it did not last for long—a moment and then it was all over. But after the "not for long" the inner flow of the narrative is arrested. *Not for long?* The device poses the question, and belies the author's composure. By cutting short the account, Homer prevents us from forgetting the victims, and reveals the unutterable eternal agony in which the women struggle with death.[27]

In such a case the minute delineation of externality that Auerbach claims makes Homer's an art of the surface is strained, which creates the implication of an antithetical background, an event replicated at least for some readers by the notice posted over Lot's wife's death. But the background in the account of the wife is not the background Auerbach finds characteristic of the Bible. The chronicle of Lot's wife is the reverse of Job: rather than a manifest grief and a recessed or mysterious divinity, there is the quite manifest and personalized divinity who dickered with Abraham over Sodom's fate shortly before, and the recessed enigma of grieving. A staging of the contest, therefore, that is rhetorically closer to Rowlandson's contemplation of the mystery of her grieving in the midst of Puritanism's explicit positivity, to her labor to say something in the midst of the watchman's noise, than is the dramatic situation of the book of Job. Her shocking confession of her identification with the blasted zone of Lot's wife is as brief as is the story of the original, and as eloquent: the waking dream's core, a drain. At the moment of confessed identification with Lot's wife, Rowlandson sends a message to Mather and the system for which he stands that is as clear as it can be, or as she chooses to have it be: I allow you access to what I have to say, but this book does not belong to you.

Lot's wife seems to have been a rather regular figure in Puritan representation. As Bradford had used the Exodus as a prefiguration for the emigration to New England, for example, Samuel Whiting, in *Abraham's Humble Intercession for Sodom,* used the exit from the cities of the plain, because this allowed him to address the issue of inordinate fondness for what was left behind:

> Every mournful ditty is not good music with men; nor beast-like roaring melody in the ears of God . . . For consolation against our loss of near relations, Brethren, Sisters, Fathers, houses, earnest and dearest friends: we in this country have left

these: but if we can get nearer God here, he will be in stead of all, more than all to us; he hath the fullness of all the sweetest relation bound up in Him. We may take that out of God, that we forsook in Father, Mother, brother, sister and friend, that hath been as near and dear as our own soul.[28]

Though this is not a funeral sermon per se, Whiting nonetheless addresses grief in the manner recommended by Hyperius. Mournfulness is first identified and thereby invoked in the public circle, then discouraged as an incipient bestiality or nature, then represented as unnecessary because the superior substitute that annuls loss is readily available to those capable of taking it. The only major difference from Hyperius lies in Whiting's association of consolation with "this country," with the theocracy where we are nearer God: if not every mournful ditty is good music, some are, those that move graciously from the lost signifier to the immortal signified, father to Father. Though Whiting does not mention Lot's wife, this is a *signifying omission,* because if New England is like Abraham's house escaped from Sodom, then the bad mournful ditties are like those that might have been sung by her to whom Whiting does not even allude.

In New England, Lot's wife is not just a sinner, but also a traitor, and therefore an important cautionary figure, an importance that glimmers through Cotton Mather's attempt to provide rational credibility to the story:

Genesis 19:26
Q. One Touch more, if you please, upon the History of *Lot's Wife* being turned into a *Pillar of Salt?*
A. The Jewes give her name as Adith (in [--------------] c. 25) because of her continuing a *Testimony* of the Displeasure of God. She standing still too long, some of the dreadful shower before mentioned, overtook her, and falling upon her, it wrapt her Body in a *Sheet of Nitro-Sulphureous* Matter, which congealed into a crust as hard as *Stone,* and made her appear as a *Pillar of Salt,* her Body being as it were candied in it. Thus Dr. Patrick expresses it; and I have not seen this matter anywhere better expressed. It is probable that the fable of Niobe was derived from [?] who, as the poets feign, was turned into a *Stone,* upon her excessive passions, for the Death of her Children.[29]

Per Amicum, probably Cotton Mather's father, is also alert to the danger and utility of the example of Lot's wife. Seen properly, the pillar of salt is a useful admonition; but a dangerous tool because it can instigate a reversal of the intention that lays hold of it. As such, the example of Lot's wife participates in the general American Puritan anxiety over what Derrida calls *supplementarity* or *homeopathic pharmacology,* aids to the maintenance of the truth that can become dangers if not properly managed. The anxiety orbits most regularly around rhetoric as a supplement to discursive veracity and women as supplements to patriarchal dynasticism, both of which are potential vehicles of manifestation but also incipient sensual perversions of the truths they bear, media liable to forsake their vehicular function and adulterate the signified with the character of the vehicle.[30] Hence the close attention to women's writing in Per Amicum's preface to Rowlandson's narrative. He concedes the danger of a woman writing, but contends that such writing is not necessarily apostate—if it were, Puritanism's supervisory social hermeneutic would be incompetent, and the entire political project would be pointless. Strictly controlled and regulated, women's writing can lend a powerful assistance to male theorization precisely because of the amount of heartfelt capitulation it expresses. Per Amicum thus not only defends but vaunts *this* woman's writing as sound and orthodox, as vision's successfully navigated passage through social peril. But his defense is rather overinsistently emphatic and repetitious, therefore perhaps a kind of *denegation* that confesses the force of the worry it dismisses: is he *sure* that the text is sound and worthy of imprimatur? Though his ill-concealed stress may result from a general suspicion of women's writing, Rowlandson's narrative would be especially worrisome, first because it is the product of (1) a woman (2) writing (3) about mourning, combining three dangerous supplements in one text; and second because, in my judgment, the narrative *is* strikingly dissonant—Per Amicum's nervousness is a more perspicacious act of literary criticism than are the conclusions of those such as Tomkins who see the narrative as being at one with its best intentions.

Per Amicum's specific apprehensions about Rowlandson come to the fore when he evokes the scene of horror at Lancaster as it was viewed by Joseph Rowlandson a couple of days after the attack rather than as it is viewed by Mary White Rowlandson during the attack, then buries the horror under the hermeneutic load of a triple homily, and finally invokes the usefully maladept type of Lot's captivity in Genesis 14:

Notwithstanding utmost endeavor of the inhabitants, most of the buildings were turned into ashes; many people (men, women and children) slain, and others captivated. The most solemn and remarkable part of this tragedy, may that be justly reputed, which fell upon the family of that reverend servant of God, Mr. Joseph Rowlandson, the faithful pastor of Christ in that place, who being gone to the council of the Massachusetts to seek aid for the defense of the place, at his return found the town in flames, or smoke, his own house being set on fire by the enemy, through the disadvantage of a defective fortification, and all in it consumed: his precious yokefellow, and dear children, wounded and captivated (as the issue evidenced, and following narrative declares) by these cruel and barbarous savages. A sad catastrophe! Thus all things come alike to all: none knows either love or hatred by all that is before him. It is no new thing for God's precious ones to drink as deep as others, of the cup of common calamity: take just Lot (yet captivated) for instance besides others.

A dense passage, as packed with Per Amicum's core motifs as the passage where Rowlandson associates herself with Lot's wife is with hers. Per Amicum tries his hand at the knack of Rowlandson's writing, the vivid and concrete presentation of the primal scene of attack, to capture our attention by rousing our horror. His end, however, is not a lifelike tableau per se, because the aroused emotion must be directed toward the abstraction it is to illustrate. A didactic specimen, then, of the proper manner of reading. To this end, Per Amicum puts our eyes in Joseph Rowlandson's head, so that his imagined appraisal of the scene is to govern ours, so that Mary White Rowlandson's compository subjectivity will always also be an object in a critical view: deep regret, perhaps judgment ("a defective fortification": the inadequate piety or *flawed possession* that brought on the attack *during his absence,* during the time between his setting and rising), immunity to intemperate grief (like that of Abraham gazing at the smoking cities some time after), and rectifying interpretation that diminishes the singularity of the scene (which is exactly its *captivating* horror) so that the scene can merge into general type—"all things come alike to all," "as deep as others," "the cup of common calamity." Though its force is requisite as a beginning for meditation, Per Amicum is attempting to preempt the gaze that would linger at the scene, the captive('s) gaze, a still-defective fortification. But he discloses the nervousness of his attempt to forestall this other way of looking when, of all the possible biblical emblems of adversity, he chooses the rather minor episode of Lot's captivity, which does much more than signify "common calamity" because it parapractically points to the occluded point of view, *hers,* that is being suppressed to be sublimated: Mary White Rowlandson was taken captive, not Joseph Rowlandson, so Lot's captivity ("for instance besides others") is a more apt emblem for her experience than it is for his; and if the emblem thus invites us to gaze at the destruction with her eyes (despite Per Amicum's best intentions), such a gaze would be that of Lot's wife, not Lot's, a gaze that will not move forward or upward into the repressive reassurance of the triple homily. Per Amicum *knows what is in this book.*

The putatively innocuous choice of Lot's captivity as a figure for Joseph Rowlandson's affliction, supposedly only one from among interchangeable dozens that might have served Per Amicum's purpose equally well, says by not saying the name that the Bible never says, Lot's wife, a countertype that threatens what Per Amicum claims to be the orthomnemonics of the ensuing text:

> This narrative was penned by the gentlewoman herself, to be to her a memorandum of God's dealing with her, that she might never forget, but remember the same, and the several circumstances thereof, all the days of her life. A pious scope which deserves both commendation and imitation. (320)

The commonplace banality of this passage is the source of its ideological efficacy. In other words:

1. Rowlandson herself affirms the truth that is to be taken from experience, which is therefore not applied from above without her complicity. This demonstrates that the truth *is* the truth rather than an enforced demand. The preface *summarizes* the narrative without *coercing* it.

2. Her unforced affirmation unfolds through her commitment to writing, a labor of devotion that gradually raises her to a transcendent perspective that she will subsequently maintain for the rest of her life. She "pens" *so that* "she might never forget."

3. If the penning is a labor of overcoming *something*, then there is another way of reflecting on what happened to her that might have dominated her had she not scrupulously eradicated it. This *other-than-pious scope* would have been a forgetting not of the experience itself, but of the ways in which the experience was an episode of "God's dealing with her." The writing therefore opposes a way of remembering that would be a forgetting of the right way of remembering.

4. The work of penning not only establishes the pious scope for her, but also unveils it for the reader, who is to commend and imitate, thereby also affirming the truth as truth rather than as imposition and forswearing erroneous memory. Or at least the reader *should* commend and imitate, because her labor is a gift that *deserves* the reciprocality of admiring emulation. But the fact that this is a *potential* rather than an *inevitable* outcome of the publication means that the *other-than-pious-scope,* vanquished from Rowlandson, is nonetheless still *at large.*

A great deal follows from accepting the premise that Rowlandson's experiences are "curious pieces of divine work" (320). If work is the attempt to embody an intention in a resistant medium, then there is always counterforce and the possibility of miscarriage—the irony at the heart of the community—in memory. Derrida: "a letter does *not always* arrive at its destination, and from the moment that this possibility belongs to its structure one can say that it never truly arrives, that when it does arrive its capacity not to arrive torments it with an internal drifting."[31] If the letter from the Lord is to arrive through the experience of the woman, the "curiousness" of memory is so great that, despite *her* best intentions, it prevents the message from being a piece of anything but itself. Per Amicum's commotion around the symbol of Lot's wife and the spectral presence of memory reveals that his overfrequent assurances of danger avoided are directed against his own incompletely concealed disquiet over what he is risking in pursuit of the woman's intense affirmation, a disquiet, again, that bespeaks a more profound understanding of Rowlandson's narrative than that displayed by modern critics who announce the text's normality without hesitation. Horror, then, announces a presence: what Per Amicum would see as mislaid-in-passage might from another angle be seen as *found:* recovered (uncovered) from (beneath) appropriation. Culture happens in zones of risk.

Rowlandson's identification with models such as Job and Lot's wife discovers subdogmatic complexities in the Bible, a plurivocity that echoes with the tensions of grief and thereby establishes an intertextual rather than a didactic typology, one that is more rich than point-for-point analogies, a medium in which positive consolation participates but does not govern, at least not with the sort of full assent that is the object of Per Amicum's desire. There is so much witnessing of hurt and vanishing clarity—days spent watching Sarah oscillate between living and dying, little to do but observe—that memory's ineluctable loyalty to what has been witnessed prevents her from seeing the Bible solely as a treatise on the virtue of loss. Rowlandson's frequent recourse to biblical reassurance, for instance, tends to return tenaciously to utopian passages promising a total and meticulous restoration to desire of its *specific* objects rather than to passages demanding a grateful acceptance of tutelary deprivation because such passages invite her to comprehend the loss *in its full specificity.* "But the Lord helped me still to go on reading till I came to Chapter 30 [of Deuteronomy] the seven first verses, where I found, there was mercy promised again, if we would return to him by repentance; and though we were scattered from one end of the earth to the other, yet the Lord would gather us together, and turn all those curses upon our enemies. I do not desire to live to forget this scripture, and what comfort it was to me" (331). Trust remits its excellent sustenance to emptiness:

> Heart-aching thoughts here I had about my poor children, who were scattered up and down among the wild beasts of the forest: my head was light and dizzy (either through hunger or hard lodging, or trouble or all together) my knees feeble, my body raw by sitting double night and day, that I cannot express to man the affliction that lay upon my spirit, but the Lord helped me at that time to express it to himself. I opened my Bible to read, and the Lord brought that precious scripture to me, Jeremiah 31. 16. *Thus saith the Lord, refrain thy voice from weeping, and thine eyes from tears, for thy work shall be rewarded, and they shall come again from the land of the enemy.* This was a sweet cordial to me, when I was ready to faint, many and many a time have I sat down, and wept sweetly over this scripture. (332)

The comfort of the verse lies in its power to deliver expression from out of tension: the utopian imagination of an exact regeneration of the past, by allowing her to think for a moment that the horror is only temporary, also allows her to stop hiding from the thought of the horror; or, further, such fantasizing *requires* her to contemplate the scope of loss, because the fantasy of reunion feasts upon a meticulous imagination of what is presently gone. As Sartre argues in *Search for a Method,* longing *designates* the flaw or inadequacy of the present—it is a critique: and in the case of Rowlandson's fondness for verses promising total reunion (promises of the kind that Hyperius urges the careful preacher not to make), longing facilitates what grief cannot yet bring itself to do directly. When the horror of the future is annulled in fantasy, the horror of the present can be thought, a step in mourning, if not the completed journey. By savoring the promise that the lost will be restored, she relocates herself momentarily and provisionally from the actual present to an imagined future, and thereby becomes competent to acknowledge the horror, to represent it to herself rather than inhabiting it. The power of the verse therefore lies primarily not in the credibility of the promise, but in its pragmatic efficacy—its functionality in the procedure of mourning's gradual self-emancipation from fixation on victimage. Her belief in the fulfillment of the promise, rather than her gratitude for its utility, is, however, unlikely, because the scattering of the family includes one child extruded from the circle of life as well as from the circle of white civilization. We understand the promise of repair as a promise of heaven rather than of worldly recuperation, and the Puritan emphasis on the resurrection of the body in the afterlife did as much as can be done to concretize the consolation of heaven: but the verse nevertheless veers too close, at least for Rowlandson, to the sort of specifically promised compensation that Hyperius says is liable to blow up in the preacher's face. Remember that for Rowlandson the wonder of experience lies in the uncanny literalization of Scripture—Job's sorrowful meat means just that, the horse's hoof. Hence the assertion that *return from the land of the enemy* is to be understood anagogically, as referring to the soul's entry to paradise, would be apt to seem somewhat deficient—an imbalance between the literality of the afflictions and the allegoricity of the reimbursements. However, even if the thought of heaven were to suffice for her, this would mean that the repair is only projected, that it is *not yet* in the temporality of narration. The peacetime restitution of ordinariness, despite its relief for stomach, knees, and so on, is not the ordained consolation for the loss, and the credibility of the promise remains to be seen.

Rowlandson's repeated concentration on verses promising minutely mimetic repair, rather than on verses celebrating the wisdom and beneficence of deprivation, suggests what Emerson saw as the crudity of prayer that craves individual things rather than affirming the general benevolence of being. ("And while He was on earth He mended families. He gave Lazarus back to his mother, and to the centurion he gave his daughter again. He even restored the severed ear of the soldier who came to arrest Him—a fact that allows us to hope the resurrection will reflect a considerable attention to detail."[32]) But unsublimated craving is not in Rowlandson's case simply oblivious to wonder: the utopian hope that desire can be gratified without transfiguration to the point of unrecognizability preserves the thought of the dead, resists the obliteration of loss by abstract categorization—an obliteration that was for Emerson, as he confesses in "Experience," a temperamental inclination rather than a philosophical achievement. In resenting the requirement that desire must accept surrogates with only slight and symbolic likeness to lost originals, such hope holds Puritan spiritual economism to its promise, rejecting a sophisticated ideological shell game—it's not under that one, it's under this one. Sarah is dead: what is the recompense? The several returns to the promise of redemption become a demand and a refusal of the watchman's assertion that reconstruction is done here and now in the rehabilitation of the New England Mind. When Puritanism associates compensation with the vigor of theocracy, it enhances its opportunity for prestige through desperate allegiance, but it also heightens the chance of refusal by those who remember what is lost well enough to judge that what has arrived is at best a bad metaphor for what has gone.

Of course, the Puritan moralism that reappears in Emerson's critique of crude prayer would suggest that Rowlandson's abiding dissatisfaction was a result less of the inadequacy of the substitutes than of inability to apprehend their wonder, in which case the deficiency that brought on the judgment remains uncured. Rowlandson is certainly aware of this perspective, which hovers on the periphery of her thought, keeping her awake at night with the fear of renewed disaster: given the divine provenance of war, penetrating all human fortifications, even London is not in theory safe from Indians if hearts are unreformed. But, though she cannot lay aside this interpretation of her dissatisfaction because only the future can test its merit, she does not accept it as the sole possible explanation for the discrepancies between feeling and prescribed wisdom. If the moral explanation is not disproved, it is also not yet proved, and therefore not the only currently possible explanation for the discrepancy. At several points, therefore, she notes the inadequacy of doctrinal typological identification but she disputes the contention that she is the source of this inadequacy: the leap of significance plays only fitfully, and her attempts to represent significance as being consistently at hand are as a result rather forced. For instance, after an especially vehement argument with the captors that ends with her being chased around by several carrying hatchets, the best she can produce is an all-purpose homily, 2 Samuel 24.14, *"I am in a great strait."* She had shortly before conceded that her desire to identify with Scripture often failed, perhaps with the halfhearted and pallid effect of the quotation from 2 Samuel:

> Then also I took my Bible to read, but I found no comfort here neither, which many times I was wont to find: so easy a thing it is with God to dry up the streams

of scripture comfort from us. Yet I can say, that in all my sorrows and afflictions, God did not leave me to have my impatience work toward himself, as if his ways were unrighteous. (343)

She briefly entertains the view that wisdom has vanished because it is offended by her sin: "But I knew that he laid less upon me than I deserved" (343). This hypothesis, however, is momentary, soon replaced by another:

Afterward, before this doleful time ended for me, I was turning the leaves of my Bible, and the Lord brought me to some scriptures, which did a little to revive me, as that of Isaiah 55. 8., *For my thoughts are not your thoughts, neither are my ways your ways, saith the Lord.* And also that, Psalms 37.5., *Commit thy way unto the Lord, trust also in him, and he shall bring it to pass.* (343)

Scripture explains why Scripture feels insufficient: like the incompletely regenerated reader postulated in Augustine's *On Christian Doctrine*, Rowlandson receives a mixture of message and mystery from the text, mystery being a transmogrified way of representing irrelevance. This second hypothesis prevents anger and fear by lifting the logic of righteousness out of the range of human contemplation: her remark about impatience that was not allowed to work against God concedes that there was impatience and that it might have worked against God had this result not been forestalled, forestalled not because the righteousness of her suffering was clearly demonstrated but because she agreed to accept the premise that righteousness is not clearly demonstrable, to be patient, to wait for a lucidity. Anger depends upon what is believed to be a clear knowledge of its object; it cannot survive mystery (though it can repress the knowledge of mystery in order to preserve itself). But if the Bible saves its authority and dissolves her anger through the postulate of this built-in nonfalsifiability, this is not necessarily good news for the Puritan watchman because the rehabilitation of the Bible is accomplished at the cost of explicit canons of righteousness, which are the backbone of covenantal theology, the foundation of the theocracy's prestige, and the source of the judgment that her experience of discrepancy results from *her* continuing sin. Thinking of God after the manner of Job keeps her from atheism but does not therefore leave her convinced of the specific notion of God promulgated by Increase Mather. Rowlandson's experience of identification with and allegiance to what she accepted as the word of God, in sum, does not translate into accord with the ideology of Puritanism. On the contrary, it reconstitutes Miller's enigmatic god, resurrects Puritanism's dangerous memory, legitimates an extension of the discrepancy between feeling and dogma into the present of the text—not to annul feeling to make way for dogma, but rather to keep dogma in abeyance.

And thereby to leave open a space for the exploration of mournfulness: if the limits set on feeling by righteousness are ultimately obscure, then neither condemnations nor defenses of mourning can properly say when the stream of grief has exceeded its channel. Refusing to accede fully either to the economy of transcendental surrogation or to a dogmatic censure of her refusal of full assent, Rowlandson pushes Puritan theory away to the distance of a possible but not inevitable future for interpretation. At the same time she keeps the present as an anomalous zone in which she can adhere to the minimality that grief knows, that the incursion of utter reversal into the lighted world has wrecked that world—the lesson of what Nietzsche calls "time and its *it was*." The pushing away of consolation manifests itself most powerfully in stubborn and incantatory repetitions and other fixated attachments, thinking and feeling that do not advance but stay in place (or no-place) in-sisting on the facticity that the doctrine of compensation would repeal, staying close:

> It was nine days from the first wounding, in this miserable condition, without any refreshing of one nature or other, except a little cold water. I cannot, but take notice, how at another time I could not bear to be in the room where any dead person was, but now the case is changed; I must and could lie down by my dead babe, side by side all the night after. I have thought since of the wonderful goodness of God to me, in preserving me in the use of my reason and senses, in that distressed time, that I did not use wicked and violent means to end my own miserable life. (328)

The transformation she describes is one of several that experience has brought onto her: whereas I used to smoke, to observe the Sabbath in a perfunctory way, to sleep soundly at night . . . now I . . . The recounting of these maturations takes on the tone of Christian conversion, where trauma recalls the sufferer to profounder commitments. But, at least in addition, she is also and more simply taking the measure of what sort of being she now is, with a certain astonishment and incredulity surveying the terrain of her conduct in order to decide if she can believe herself to be the same person, or even still a person. Such an appraisal, however tentatively amenable to the model of conversion, is not necessarily reducible to the model, and the compelling vigil she describes does not fit neatly with the concept of Christian duty. *Both* natures (hers and Sarah's? the body's and the soul's?) being without refreshing, she does shed an inability to confront fact, but in order to *become a fact,* an extinguished subjectivity whose nowhereness and hypertrophied thereness simulate the corpse, rather than to become a meditation. She can hardly be said to be moving on toward wisdom, but rather to be seeking to stop the renewed onslaught of what Lacan calls second death, the procedure of revisionary memory. Stop it here: as if by staring at the physical remains of love and disaster she could recompose it, comprehend its magnitude and be done. The thought of a future of mourning is at this point unacceptable, and leads inevitably into thanatos; by dying she can spare herself mourning, remain loyal to the first fond image constructed during the vigil, be spared both the gross infidelity of enjoying when the loved one enjoys no longer and a future that will be horribly different no matter what its content. After the disappearance of value (rather than of a value), the erasure of the mourner's body should be a redundancy so far as fear is concerned, and a blessing with respect to the burden of an empty destiny. Theology intervenes here to prevent her reasoning from securing its end, but not in the promissory mode of remuneration, only in the stark and isolated commandment *live*, don't wait, just continue. The Kantian severity of the commandment, the absence of rationale, in fact saves her *because* it does not appeal to reason or incentive, and therefore does not clash with her disbelief in desirable futures; and it circumvents guilt, because it allows whatever will to live that still stirs in the ruin not to have to see itself as such, to call survival a kind of self-abnegating pure service without mixture of self-interest.

However, if in this way theology speaks into the chaos to prevent its multiplication, it does so by combating one effect of Puritan theology, the conflation of the mourner's sense that she is worthless because the source of emotional value is gone, with the dogmatic judgment that she has been brought to this state because she is morally worthless. Strictly speaking, these are separate kinds of self-derogation, but they can be blended by means of Puritan symbology: the feeling of worthlessness in mourning is represented to the mourner as a true sight of the worthlessness that provoked the disaster in the first place. Practical theologians from Hyperius at least through Edwards, as I argued in the preceding chapter, recognized the need to combat the culmination of this line of reasoning—suicide—but with an unstated understanding that it was reinforced if not set in motion by their own appropriative schematization of mourning. Rowlandson's open description of the desire to die thus foregrounds, perhaps intentionally, the fact that the command to live has to be an isolated mandate distinct from the rest of the dogmatic milieu precisely because it is an extrinsic element imported to arrest dogma's innate tendency. For her part, Rowlandson recognizes that the mourner's desire to die tends toward a bifurcated moral valence, either something God forbids or something that mutely conforms to His own judgment:

> One of my elder sister's children, named William, had then his leg broken, which the Indians perceiving, they knocked him on the head. Thus were we butchered by those merciless heathen, standing amazed, with the blood running down to our heels. My eldest sister being yet in the house and seeing those woeful sights, the

infidels haling mothers one way, and children another, and some wallowing in their blood: and her elder son telling her that her son William was dead, and myself was wounded, she said, And Lord, let me die with them, which was no sooner said, but she was struck with a bullet, and fell down over the threshold. I hope she is reaping the fruit of her good labors, being faithful to the service of God in her place. In her younger years she lay under much trouble upon spiritual accounts, till it pleased God to make that precious scripture take hold of her heart, 2 Corinthians 12. 9. *And he said unto me, my grace is sufficient for thee.* More than twenty years after I have heard her tell how sweet and comfortable that place was to her. (324)

A succinct emblem of being's character, the bullet grants the wish it condemns. Despite Rowlandson's earnest desire that her sister be remembered as a saint, a desire to bequeath an exemplaristic remembrance, the episode has a disturbing circularity. The verse from Corinthians is not a command to live but a sparse promise of consolation, a promise that, despite Rowlandson's assurance that it took hold, did not: the survival of the youthful doubt is suggested by the urgency with which the sister clung to the verse over the years, and proven by her desire to die when trauma enters Lancaster. The biblical place did not keep her in her place so she was laid to rest, and Rowlandson's *interest* seems to me to proceed from identification, by which I do not mean to exclude loving sympathy. The sister's death is a complex event—both the fulfillment of the wish and the judgment against it, an ambiguity that Puritan exegesis could unravel only by declaring that the mourner's feeling of the worthlessness of life is an inappropriate and perhaps evasive conclusion to draw from the contemplation of her moral worthlessness. Only by declaring that one's life is not one's property, and therefore that suicide is theft, additional guilt rather than contrition, can dogma dissever thanatos and guilt in order to preserve its needed resource, living and compliant mourners, to combat not only apostasy but also an exegetical intensity that goes too far by taking the bullet as a simple statement— You're right, your life isn't worth living, because you are not of worth, or, still more radically, approaching the sister's focal despair, because life *isn't worthy*.

Rowlandson's close interest in her sister's inner history, in her desire and the fate of her desire, suggests that she identified with her sister, at least to the point of suspecting or wondering whether she too was not less than at one with what her society defined as faith, long before the captivity, which brought to the front doubts that long preceded it. If so, then such a speculative identification, a kind of intracontemporary typological leap that must have threatened to succumb to the transhistorical type of the Wayward Woman, would testify to a perception on Rowlandson's part of a difference from rectitude within herself of which behaviors such as smoking and enjoying the Sabbath were manifestations. If such behaviors seem to us rather slight reasons for Rowlandson's suffering, even granting the premise of an economy of punishment, our mistake may be in seeing symptoms as substances, in failing to apprehend that Rowlandson worried that her very being was awry. Importantly, however, the account of her sister, though it *worries in the direction of* the Wayward Woman, does not wholly cross over into that zone of coercive clarification: the type hovers about the episode but is not allowed a full or sufficient exegetical domain. The account of the sister, like the sister herself, is awry, a condition we can perceive only because the type is present in a spectral rather than a transuming mode. But, if the type is therefore a rather ominous or threatening possibility for the teller as well as the tale, it also has a certain utility, because the woman-to-woman analogy it adumbrates brings to the surface and collects remembrances of Puritan women, thereby allowing an exploratory meditation on the condition of being at a varying distance from propriety, a meditation that retains a realism or social concreteness so long as the moral power of the type is kept confined to its virtual mode and prevented from assembling all such remembrances under the sign of its simplicity:

> Amongst them also was that poor woman before mentioned, who came to a sad end, as some of the company told me in my travel: she having much grief upon her spirit, about her miserable condition, being so near her time, she would often be asking the Indians to let her go home; they not being willing to that, and yet vexed with her importunity, gathered a great company together about her, and stripped her naked, and set her in the midst of them, and when they had sung and danced about her (in their hellish manner) as long as they pleased, they knocked her on head, and the child in her arms with her: when they had done that, they made a fire and put them both in it, and told the other children that were with them, that if they attempted to go home, they would serve them in like manner: the children said, she did not shed one tear, but prayed all the while. (331–32)

Though in part one of many expositions of the Indians' cruelty, Rowlandson's account of the death of Goodwife Joslin (no more than a week from childbirth, in Rowlandson's view) once again uses the topic of the Wayward Woman Punished to explore tentative identifications. Though Joslin's pregnancy commits her to a future and thereby plays the part that the injunction to live plays for Rowlandson, she despairs, that is, doubts and mistrusts the course of things. When the Indians decide to kill her to end their irritation with her and to make her an example to others who attempt to escape their condition, therefore, her death takes on the mark of a providence: their dislike for her attempts to intervene in their manner of conducting the business of selling back hostages signifies God's dislike for her despair over his elected scheduling of affliction and relief. However plangent and affecting despair may be, it arises from a certain petulant definition of a proper schedule of events, and an impatience with other schedules. But in the case of Goodwife Joslin, the question of the schedule is precipitated by the course of the pregnancy: rather than anything that could be derisively called mere whim, an inner necessity seems to imply that the time for delivery has come. Two unchosen and imposed itineraries, providence and gestation, clash with each other in her life, and she seems to have died for having sided with the weaker rather than the less moral force. In this episode, deserves-to-die is not intertwined with wants-to-die as it is in the death of Rowlandson's sister, but in both cases grief begins to emerge as a more or less credible response of desire to its victimage at the hand of an omnipotent whim, of a puppetmaster. The juxtapositions sanctioned by the typological act of constituting the Wayward Woman Punished therefore culminate, through the power of conviction that arises in the constitution of a series, in a challenge to the moral integrity of the instigating type.

In both episodes, Rowlandson is exploring versions of herself, specifically, of the entanglement of the mourner's feeling of the worthlessness of a life that goes this way with the moral judgment that such feelings are worthless, an entanglement that seems to culminate in a punishment for the wish that is also the fulfillment of the wish. Thus the desirable theology that Puritanism sought meets with its grotesque and nearly perfect realization, a realization so powerful that it can be combatted only by an external and unrationalized mandate to live appended to the system in order to prevent the system from *going all the way*. Though the Puritan ministry availed itself of this mandate in order to preserve live congregations, the mandate did not issue or emanate from the otherwise integral reasonings of the New England Mind. The recourse to the mandate, therefore, whether motivated by a humane if belated horror at what they had produced and/or by a more pragmatic concern over the dwindling of the congregation, is a moment of implicit insight and confession on the ministers' part, a sudden awareness that the attempt to appropriate mourning is liable to generate its intractable antithesis, melancholia.

By heeding the injunction to live during her vigil over Sarah's corpse, Rowlandson defers the inner compulsions of both typologization and self-destroying despair, accomplishing at least a postponing of melancholia, if not a decisive advance out of it. She decides to *live to look* at the body. Rather than emulating the body, she will contemplate it: she will represent it to herself rather than making herself into a representation of it. Thus she uses the ontological difference between the gaze and its object to instigate a difference between the living and the dead, proleptically simulating what will eventually be *for her* an adequate comprehension of the loss, and devising a tolerable reason for the continuation of her own life. The injunction to live, nonaligned with Puritanism's focal movement, emerges as the law of mourning, a prosthetic augmentation of the body of dogma that by its existence necessarily reveals a defect in the body of dogma and thus always implies the credibility and integrity of the counterethic from which Puritanism takes its prosthesis.

But, as with all her attempts to assemble a situation that is at least stabilized, a ground on which to begin, this spare equipoise does not endure:

> I went to take up my dead child in my arms to carry it with me, but they bid me let it alone: there was no resisting, but I must go and leave it. When I had been at my master's wigwam, I took the first opportunity I could get, to go look after my dead child: when I came I asked them what they had done with it? They told me it was upon the hill: then they went and showed me where it was, where I saw the ground was newly digged, and there they told me they had buried it: there I left that child in the wilderness, and must commit it, and myself also in this wilderness condition, to Him who is above all. (329)

Only the enemy's dubious report assures her that Sarah's corpse did not lie in the sun like Polyneices', or that, if it was buried, it was buried *here*. The Indians have, after all, shortly before demonstrated their inclination to an unbearable mordant humor:

> Then they set me upon a horse with my wounded child in my lap, and there being no furniture upon the horse's back, as we were going down a steep hill, we both fell over the horse's head, at which they like inhuman creatures laughed and rejoiced to see it, though I thought we should there have ended our days, as overcome with so many difficulties. (327)

Having thus revealed their willingness to enjoy the banana-peel kind of humor without restraint by considerations of decency, the Indians are not to be trusted as having given Sarah a decent burial. The proper sequel to the vigil would have been *Rowlandson's* act of burial, at a *given moment,* disaster localized in the sight of the corpse, then the corpse localized in / as its *place.* Even if the corpse *is* buried, and buried *here,* and even if it was buried with some form of ceremony, it was not buried by her or by her designated agent. The procedure of the obligation is interrupted, and the preliminary stabilization afforded by the gaze is destroyed. Disaster is not once done: there always seems to be something left outstanding, something seemingly undoable so long as the dead one is pervasive rather than *committed to place.* The is no *site of Sarah* but rather an afflicting *everywhereness,* a consciousness that is a haunted maze, which Rowlandson labels her "wilderness condition." Susan Howe: "They are things: abducted from the structure of experience, Rowlandson wraps herself in separateness for warmth. Tyranny precedes morality. Her little girl was broken in a rift of history."[33]

In the face of such incessant renewals of abduction, Rowlandson attempts to hasten the arrival of stability by wrapping "herself in separateness for warmth," killing affections that have lost the chance of fulfillment, a venture revealed most painfully, perhaps, as Slotkin suggests, in the decision to speak of Sarah's corpse as an *it*, or *meat:*

> I had not seen my son a pretty while, and here was an Indian of whom I made inquiry after him, and asked him when he saw him: he answered me that such a time his master roasted him, and that himself did eat a piece of him, as big as his two fingers, and that he was very good meat . . . (342)

This report turns out to be another piece of Wampanoag wit, wit that draws on what the Indian supposes will sting, the change of person to meat, which assumes terrifying proportions as an object of narration, for example in the cooking and "serving" of Goodwife Joslin or even at the end, in the way Rowlandson visualizes redemption during the sleepless nights:

> I remember in the night season, how the other day I was in the midst of thousands of enemies, and nothing but death before me: it is then hard work to persuade myself, that ever I should be satisfied with bread again. But now we are fed with the finest of the wheat, and, as I may say, with honey out of the rock: instead of the husk, we have the fatted calf . . .

The fat of the animal, according to Leviticus, because it is the richest part, properly belongs to the Lord: it is to be relinquished, or taken from us if not relinquished. If therefore she now herself eats the fatted calf, it cannot be without the thought of its *takenness:* the meat that one has like the meat Sarah that the Lord has always entails a mourning somewhere else, and Rowlandson's voraciousness thus always alludes to the disquiet of the improperly buried body and amounts to an identification with and an impersonation of the frightful power itself. *She* takes and eats. Carnivorousness, like the mortification of one's own affectional inclinations, represents an attempt to overcome victimage by becoming a specimen of the indifferent appetite that set upon her home, to forestall the renewal of fright by becoming both the indecent tutor and the assaulted victim in one and therefore adept at the apotropaic prevention of invasion from without. Early in the narrative, the project of self-tutelage in brutality takes the form of repetitive intonation:

> To add to the dolefulness of the former day, and the dismalness of the present night: my thoughts ran upon my losses and sad bereaved condition. All was gone, my husband gone (at least separated from me, he being in the Bay; and to add to my grief, the Indians told me they would kill him as he came homeward) my children gone, my relations and friends gone, our house and home and all our

comforts within doors, and without, all was gone (except my life) and I knew not but the next moment that might go too. (326)

Thought adds to misery by accomplishing homicides in the imagination to accompany the homicides in fact, an overdetermined deed with a double valence: if on the one hand such meditation tends toward acceptance of the fact that the vanishings are real, it also seeks to impersonate the force that instigates the vanishings, and thus to annul that fact of her vulnerability, to recompose a feeling of control that admits the reality of woe but not of helplessness. She recites the lesson in order to achieve the coldness of a killer, a coldness that will come closer to completeness in proportion to her ability to dissociate herself from also being the recipient of killing. To this end, she will find it highly useful to externalize the suffering Rowlandson in the person of another, to project the part of victim onto another so that her cultivation of coldness can reach purity not in a sympathetic identification with this other mother, as in the reminiscences of her sister and Goodwife Joslin, but, precisely, in an utter indifference to one whose situation is so much like her own:

> That night they bade me go out of the wigwam again: my mistress' papoose was sick, and it died that night, and there was one benefit in it, that there was more room. I went to a wigwam, and they bade me come in, and gave me a skin to lie upon, and a mess of venison and ground nuts, which was a choice dish among them. On the morrow they buried the papoose, and afterward, both morning and evening, there came a company to mourn and howl with her: though I confess I could not much condole with them. Many sorrowful days I had in this place: often getting alone; *like a crane or a swallow, so did I chatter: I did mourn as a dove, mine eyes ail with looking upward. Oh, Lord I am oppressed, undertake for me,* Isaiah, 38. 14. (346)

She invokes the memory of her own solitary suffering and the Indians' lack of feeling for her complaint to justify her indifference to her mistress' loss of a child: what goes around comes around. The tone she is seeking for herself, however, is not finally vindictive or spiteful satisfaction with the symmetry in the event, but inertness: the death of the child left more room in the wigwam, and being kicked out the night it died resulted in a pleasant variety in the arrangements for room and board. If this cultivated indifference is for us appalling, I think that it is for her too, that she would not fail to appreciate that tone because she is seeking to mimic the source of her own horror, because, again, this simulates the feel of having a preemptive power. Being horrified by her own indifference would be evidence of success, though whatever satisfaction she may derive here would depend on blocking any inquiry into what part of her it is that is still horrified, this time by herself.

On the next page: "As we went along, they killed a deer, with a young one in her, they gave me a piece of the fawn, and it was so young and tender, that one might eat the bones as well as the flesh, and yet I thought it very good" (347). Like the disaster that took everything from her, she cleans her plate (as it were, the world in which there are plates being gone). As the thought of the two English mothers allowed Rowlandson to consider her own victimage, so the thought of the Indian and animal mothers uses ethnic and species difference to dissever sympathy in order to enjoy victimization: but the fact that she is choosing specifically maternal victims reveals that transcendence is built upon occluded identification, that there is sympathy beneath sadism enabling sadism, that she is emblematizing through projection a suffering to which she can then assent vigorously—reifying the opposition within herself as an opposition between herself and another.[34] Both passages seem to me unconvincing in their claim to unequivocal coldness, though this may be wishful thinking.

The attempted cultivation of indifference is a flight from the renewal and prolongation of grief, from its seemingly endless reopening, but it is nonetheless a *moment* of grief because it represents a preliminary and inadequate stage in separating what will turn out to have been a self from the lost world. In the procedure of mourning it is a rest stop and a first draft. But as a preliminary simulation, it proves especially vulnerable, like the feeling of worthlessness, to appropriative sublimation by dogma, which bids to pervert it into the end of mourning. David Stannard proposes that various Puritan social practices such as putting one's children into other homes at an early age to be educated by others may have been reactions to sorrow, attempts to forestall its revival by restraining affection in advance of disaster, so that, even if disaster could not be controlled, disastrousness could be:

> For children, despite the natural hold they had on their parents' affection, were a source of great emotional discomfort for them as well, in that there was a very real possibility, if not probability, that parental affection would be rewarded by the death of the child before it even reached puberty. The "due distance" kept by Puritan parents from their children might, at least in part, have been an intuitive response to this possibility, a means of insulating themselves to some extent against the shock that the death of a child might bring.[35]

It has become something of a commonplace when contemplating what appears to us as the harshness of Puritan attitudes toward child rearing to contend that "the child" as we know it does not appear in Western discursive forms until the nineteenth century, and thus that the appearance of a lack of tenderness is a naive anachronism. Stannard's argument seems to me superior because he assumes the tenderness, and then views the harshness as a real response to both the physical circumstances of seventeenth-century New England death and the ideology that responds to and avails itself of those circumstances. This desirous apotropaism was amplified and codified by Puritan thought with the premise that we are afflicted by loving too much—if we don't restrain affection, it will be done for us, a formula that legitimates the moment of indifference, disguises its status as inadequate prolepsis for the end of grieving. If a full heart then asks, what *can* we love fervently, answers are ready, and the process attains to ideological allegiance. The remaining work of mourning is consigned to its melancholy underground, a reservoir that keeps us loving the substitutes that have been proposed because the alternative is too horrid.

It is therefore not a random juxtaposition when, between the account of the dead papoose and the account of the tasty fawn, Rowlandson deploys her most extended and self-merciless discourse on the clear and proper connection between her sin and her punishment, an unusually precise expression of dogma that veers from the general tone of the narrative but is almost a piece with the frigid appetitive zest of the episodes that precede and follow it. This is Rowlandson close to making good on her best intention:

> Now had I time to examine all my ways: my conscience did not accuse me of unrighteousness toward one or another: yet I saw how in my walk with God I had been a careless creature. As David said, *Against thee, thee only have I sinned;* and I might say with the poor publican, *God be merciful unto me a sinner.* On the Sabbath days, I could look upon the sun and think how people were going to the house of God, to have their souls refreshed; and then home, and their bodies also: but I was destitute of both; and might say as the poor prodigal, *he would fain have filled his belly with the husks that swine did eat, and no man gave unto him,* Luke 15. 16. For I must say for him, *Father I have sinned against heaven, and in thy sight,* verse 21. I remembered how on the night before and after the sabbath, when my family was about me, and relations and neighbors with us, we could pray and sing, and then refresh our bodies with the good creatures of God; and then have a comfortable bed to lie down on: but instead of all this, I have only a little swill for the body, and then like a swine, must lie down on the ground. I cannot express to man the sorrow that lay upon my spirit, the Lord knows it. Yet that comfortable scripture would come often to my mind, *For a small moment have I forsaken thee, but with great mercies will I gather thee.* (346–47)

This passage, with its putatively unforced acknowledgment of the justice of the case, with its employment of the emblem of the prodigal and its expression of trust, is commonly taken as a piece of prime evidence by those who would contend that the narrative as a whole is true to the type. But such an opinion fails to notice the extraordinary and heartbreakingly direct plangency of the longing that comes forward here, and extracts the passage without noticing either the autosadism of the surrounding context or the discordant and utopian elements within it. First, though confessing sin, she is careful to classify her sin as minor, as sins go, not especially heinous because it did not harm others. If her religion was somewhat "formal," as Increase Mather might say, she might make use of Mather's contention that this was a general condition before the war in order to suggest that the special severity of her punishment was not in proportion to her ordinary sin, was perhaps motivated more by the Lord's need for an emblem of the working of providence than by her specific demerit. In this case her use of the emblem of the prodigal would have the character of begrudging submission rather than of acknowledgment in the fullest sense. Contrition would then be subtended by a resentment that does not quite become accusation, thought it nears the surface again when she informs *us* that he made her live like a pig.

Before this resurfacing of acrimony, however, she meditates on the life she had been living, but only, surprisingly, for the sake of contrast with the present misery, not to search out the minutiae of her laxness. On the contrary, the earlier assertion that hers had been only a common turpitude becomes an affecting memory and defense of what Hamlin Garland called "the clear water of Christian marriage." And, even now when that water is tears, the missing things are strikingly encircled with pleasure—God and the sunlight, souls at home, "and their bodies also." This memory has insufficient rigor for a moral meditation: mourning moves past the simplicity of indifference into more complex recollection, refuses to stop with rather than only pause with the derision of love. If the intolerable contemplation of the present misery threatens to restore contempt, the final expression of hope for recollection in life as well as memory intervenes *pragmatically,* to allow mourning to continue its advance, the dream of a future happiness making bearable the fuller thought of the happiness that is destroyed. Moral meditation invites her to recollect what she was and what she had, but loses control over what it prompts; and the apparent recontainment effected by the promise of relief in fact preserves rather than terminates fond memory because it renders the thought of loss tolerable. The best intention mutates: and recriminatory accusation evolves into demand, into a stipulation of the circumstances in the midst of which she will agree to reconcile, because to gather Rowlandson would be to find her parts and put them back together, rather than to supply a new and abstract coherence that will lead her to forget what has been scattered. Once again, the tenacious utopian fidelity of an impossible demand, because one key part of herself, Sarah, is, barring the sort of miracle that doesn't occur in the postbiblical epoch, gone.

In this decisive passage, therefore, Rowlandson takes the measure of a coldness that, however alluring, is in the end too easy.

My mistress, before we went, was gone to the burial of a papoose, and returning, she found me sitting and reading in my Bible; she snatched it hastily out of my hand, and threw it out of doors . . . (340)

Such a refusal, which she here emblematizes as an Indian's rather than as her own, might enable a more expansive sympathy for the plight of others, even including that of Indians, because it obviates the need to practice a heart-lessness:

They had turned [John Gilbert, a young captive] out of the wigwam, and with him an Indian papoose, almost dead (whose parents had been killed), in a bitter cold day, without fire or clothes: the young man himself had nothing on, but his shirt and waistcoat. *This sight was enough to melt a heart of flint.* There *they* lay quivering in the cold, the youth round like a dog; the papoose stretched out, with his eyes and nose and mouth full of dirt, and yet alive, and groaning. (344; emphasis mine)

But neither contempt for love nor self-preservative hope can annul the gone-ness of what is gone, which continues to remain outside the circle of postwar theocomic reunion at the end of the narrative. Because both disaster and griev-ing are still outstanding, she must remain apart from the social arena in which those debts are overlooked as a matter of policy:

I was not without sorrow, to think how many were looking and longing, and my own children amongst the rest, to enjoy that deliverance that I had now received, and I did not know whether ever I should see them again. Being recruited with food and raiment we went to Boston that day, where I met with my dear husband, but the thoughts of our dear children, one being dead, and the other we could not tell where, abated our comfort to each other. (361–62)

This expression of lingering nonintegration at the reunion provokes a compen-satory protestation of gratitude:

I was not so much hemmed in with the merciless and cruel heathen, but now as much with pitiful, tender-hearted and compassionate Christians. In that poor, and distressed, and beggarly condition I was received in, I was kindly entertained in several houses: so much love I received from several (some of whom I knew, and others I knew not) that I am not capable to declare it. But the Lord knows them all by name: the Lord reward them sevenfold into their bosoms of his Spirituals, for their temporals! (362)

The gratitude is not feigned, but neither is it complete. Rowlandson's desire for an economy of restitution pervades the passage's deliberate symmetries: as much cruelty as there was, so much love; as cruelty came out of unexpected places (fright), so now does love (wonder); as she was unable to express her grief, now she is unable to express her pleasure; as they gave her temporals, so let the Lord reward them with spirituals. This is a celebration of reconstituted sociality, but there is a persistent disequilibrium: the shortcoming in her reciprocation ("I am not capable to declare it") will require a divine intervention to close the system ("the Lord reward them"), which is therefore, at the present time, still incomplete, owing to her inadequate repayment of the kindness. But perhaps the present disequilibrium is a kind of rejoinder to the previous disequilibrium of pain, a three-player economy in which one still owes, and she is not the one: in the captivity she was billed more then she deserved to be charged, so now she should pay the generous neighbors less than they deserve, and let the Lord make up the difference, since he was the beneficiary of the first overcharge, the one that initially disequilibriated the economy of God, person, and society. She gave, God took; they gave, she took; now God should give, so that they can take.

But, she warns them, if he does pay, it is likely to be with a different specie, spirituals in payment for temporals, which they will be expected to accept as payment in kind. She thus confronts her society with the credulity it expects from her, with an expectation that spiritual blessings shall be taken as making up for lost things. Rowlandson is insisting on meticulous bookkeeping, but at the same time there is a deeper problem with commensurability itself, rather than only with its incomplete realization. Though the friends' generosity may equal the Indians' cruelty, the temporals the friends have to give cannot equal the things the Indians took, because the Indians took things whose preciousness lay in their singularity rather than in their typicality or fungibility. The value of the lost properties lies at the greatest possible dialectical distance from both exemplarity and monetary value, both of which, reducing singularity to generality, are insufficiently distinct from the simple rot that Rowlandson fears was the fate of Sarah's corpse, neither of which opposes the horrid ubiquity of the dead with a sufficiently faithful and meticulous dignity. She refuses to let the dead subside or decompose into categories such as "common calamity." Grief is an intractable refusal of numerical appraisal, an irony at the heart of the community's earnest and eager attempt to prove itself well again by denying the fact of its various decapitations:

> We were now in the midst of love, yet not without much and frequent heaviness of heart for our poor children, and other relations, who were still in affliction . . .
> That which was dead lay heavier upon my spirit, than those which were alive and amongst the heathen; thinking how it suffered with its wounds, and I as in no way

able to relieve it; and how it was buried by the heathen in the wilderness from among all Christians. (362)

Though she again attempts to confine enduring grief to worry about the current status of living captives, it again moves inexorably toward the thought of the unransomable captive. Still haunted: the utterly lost is segregated from the still redeemable ("that which" / "those which") and made the focus of memory, from which position it will not stop announcing the vacuity of new things:

> We were hurried up and down in our thoughts, sometimes we should hear a report that they were gone this way, and sometimes that; and that they were come in, in this place or that: we kept enquiring and listening to hear concerning them, but no certain news as yet. About this time the Council had ordered a day of public thanksgiving: though I thought I still had cause for mourning, and being unsettled in our minds, we thought we would ride toward the eastward, to see if we could hear anything concerning our children. (362)

In this passage, she confesses having refused the public theology of the thanksgiving, but this candor is enabled by shifting attention from the dead child to the captive children. I held out *a while longer* on thanksgiving: the sadistic alternation of hope roused and hope crushed persisted somewhat longer for her than it did for the others, and so the unfolding of privacy into public celebration was in her case delayed, until the two living children "came in." Until they come in, she like the extruded Indian at the powwow, stays out: now—at the time she writes—they *have* come in, and, she implies, so has she. The reader should trust the best intentions. By shifting from the dead to the still captive, Rowlandson relegates her noncompliance to the noncontroversiality of something that was but is no longer. She thereby expresses it without fear of judgment. I *was*.

But this act of preterition is self-protective and opportune, and not wholly convincing. The passage represses the thought of the unburied *it,* but does so imperfectly: though she is chronicling worry over the living, she employs her phrase for grief, the satanic "hurried up and down," a code motif that joins with "unsettled minds" and with the assertion that she held back from celebration due to *mourning.* This is the emotion proper to what is completely lost, and is distinct from worry or fear, which are appropriate to what is *mislaid,* to what may yet be lost but is not necessarily so (though fear of renewed loss is of course amplified by having been powerless to prevent loss). Her standing off from the public social circle of declared thanksgiving, therefore, from acknowledgment that something blessed has been given, is not temporary due to waiting on something that can still come, but is rather a still-current project of acknowledging that something blessed has been taken, something that will never come in and that therefore still blights the acknowledgment and accommodation that thanksgiving requires. Such accommodation, judging from the intensity of her abiding imagination of the unburied *it* and the brusqueness with which she attempts to dismiss that thought in order to generate the illusion of acceptance *after the time described but before the time of the describing,* is still incomplete: despite best intentions, this passage says, I think I still have cause for mourning.

Rowlandson thus conceals the statement she also makes, in part in order to conform to a temporality of subjective development prescribed by Puritan theory. In the elaboration of the protocols of a confessional genre—the conversion narratives presented as a petition for admission to the circle of church membership—the ministry and the congregations seem to have decided that, though the confession of past defiance was not only a permissible but an almost formally mandatory aspect of the autobiographical act, the entry of non-compliance into the tone of the confessing voice was scrupulously interdicted. The speech act had to be pure: and the ability to speak about one's sin, to posit it as a clearly outlined object of contemplation, something past (even if only moments past) and therefore bounded, was a crucially useful article of evidence demonstrating that the speaker was competent to dissever himself or herself from impure areas of consciousness. If the future course of the life proved markedly or even secretly unholy, such lapse overrode the possibility certified by admission to the congregation, that it might have been otherwise, that it was not inevitable. But "I am" or "I have been" undoes the rectitude demonstrated by "I was" or "I had been," even by "I had been until shortly before I began to testify" or "I had been until I began to testify," because the extension of defiance into the present of the speech act reveals a marred or streaked voice, an inability to check one's darkness at the door of the church, a saboteur. In Thomas Shepard's compilation of his parishioners' narratives, for example, Nicholas Wyeth's testimony stands out for two reasons: it was followed by prolonged and suspicious interrogation, Shepard asking him more than twenty sharp questions, whereas such examination was absent or brief in all the other cases; and second the confession of sins extends into the present moment:

> And every sabbath day [in England] I went four miles to hear [Robert Selby's preaching] about a year but I went on very poorly as I have done ever since . . . The Lord's hand hath been much out against me and is so still . . . I think myself unfit to come into their society . . . I have a wandering eye not attending on the word but helped; since I saw it again I have not made use of God's people to get into their societies . . . I have had when sabbath comes great hopes to see what I have not seen for I and hence joyed and yet it hath been with a great deal of deadness. And I labor against it and have hoped that the Lord would then meet with me . . . I see cause enough in my own heart why the Lord should deny me. I

know many things in my practice. I have not so meditated on the word . . . I have
had continual strivings against it, but I have been of a very forward hasty nature.

Shepard does not tell why Wyeth was questioned at length. The sins he confesses are not egregious by contrast with those of others who were not so
questioned. But the "I am" in the midst of the others' "I was" distinguishes him,
makes his narrative leap out (for us) as a deeply candid account of not finding
the relief and clarity for which one longs and of knowing that the lostness is also
oneself and (for Shepard) as a very dangerous failure to cordon off sin with the
preterite. I should add that Wyeth's lostness hovers around the issue of grief for
things taken despite his having acted on his best intentions:

> Hence I came to New England being persecuted and courted for going from the
> place where we lived and hence I used means to come hither where we might enjoy
> more freedom. And I had much joy in going about this work though I had lived
> very foul yet my heart much convinced me and that I should live under means more
> powerful. And so I was much opposed by my friends, and enemies of God
> discouraging me, and the Lord helped me to withstand them that did oppose me,
> for I could not be content to live where I did and I went through many difficulties
> before and when I came to sea. Yet I went on and God took away my son, some
> telling me that the Lord was displeased for going on, but discouragements of
> natural friends I regarded not and I did not care though the Lord took away all I
> had. Yet I had many things to call me back, my wife all the time going through
> many afflictions.[36]

Having sacrificed much for the Lord, and having defended those sacrifices
against the sophistries of "natural friends" who would have had him resist the
call, Wyeth is rewarded with afflictions rather than happiness, with precisely
the sort of event that would seem to confirm the natural friends' theory. The
most likely reactions would seem to be either a sense of betrayal by God, or a
conclusion that the New England mission was indeed a desertion rather than an
exodus, or utter perplexity. The last of these is theoretically acceptable to
Puritanism, but hardly conducive to the sort of clear voice required by the
occasion of the narrative. Accommodation would therefore demand that he
postulate hidden sin—that *his* migration was not really holy, that it was im-
pelled by a simple and heinous restlessness, that he did not sacrifice properly
and thus had to sacrifice more. Shepard's diary account of the aftermath of his
wife's death suggests that Shepard understood the struggle Wyeth had to undergo to constitute the justice of his suffering, and perhaps also therefore offers a
clue to why he questioned Wyeth so stringently. Most important, Wyeth, unlike
Shepard, was unable and unwilling to allow a complete sublimation of his
grieving into a celebration of and thanksgiving for the display of divine justice,

so perplexity endured into the act of speaking. Some such anxiety over the tense of the utterance and its involvement in the underground power of grieving may have provoked Rowlandson's attempt to suppress *I am* with *I was* by shifting from the dead it to the still-captive children.

But, as with Wyeth, the desire for social normalization is for Rowlandson coupled with a longing for the end of mourning—the conjunction and surface analogy of the two, again, being precisely the reason why an ideological sublimation of grief can take place. The dead will never stop being so; alienation feels interminable. Fixing or fixating on the still-captive children permits a feel of restitutability; still-redeemable means hope; and the constitution of the dead, along with the grieving self, as extrinsic, as objects of representation, with the consequent extrication of the subject of representation from its chaos, at least alludes to the end of grieving, albeit with a radically different concept of the pace, manner, and result of mournful representation. The preterition that Puritanism required in these tortured and painful utterances by people who had lost so much is therefore a version of the alluring demand placed on them by the funeral sermon, which may be theoretically if not historically prior to the conversion narrative in the social ontology of Puritan genres.

But whatever the complex motivation that pushes Rowlandson toward the "I was," this move is unconvincing and unsustained, the repressed memory of the it surviving as an ironizing background to the reunions with the live children:

> When my heart was ready to sink into the earth (my children being gone I could tell not whither) and my knees trembled under me, and I was walking through the valley of the shadow of death: then the Lord brought, and now has fulfilled that reviving word unto me: *Thus saith the Lord, Refrain thy voice from weeping, for thy work shall be rewarded, saith the Lord, and they shall come again from the land of the enemy.* (363)

Most of them.

Perhaps the most significant part of Rowlandson's account of her reluctance to join in the day of thanksgiving, at least for this argument, is her modest assertion of her *right* to her reluctance ("I thought I still had cause for mourning"). *Having cause* signifies an order of legitimate obligation that is, at least on this occasion, distinct from the morality of the festival—mourning is a defensible *cause* for abstaining from participation in the general public construction of happy reality. In this quiet insistence on the rectitude of her grief and the separation it creates between her and the society's surrounding project, Rowlandson uses the dead child as a concrete synecdoche for all that was irreplaceable in the old life, for all that cannot be redeemed or gathered again. Certainly, there are reunions with the husband and the two live children, and these are matters of joy, but the revival of familiar elements in a new array does not mean that the old is reborn: the frame is different. Without "our house and home and all our comforts within doors, and without," the gestalt of possessions whereby the family not only met need but signified itself and its history to itself, the regathering is marred by strangeness, a persistence from the captivity and a new presence in the circle, occupying the location where Sarah used to be: "I thought it somewhat strange to set up my housekeeping with bare walls; but as Solomon says, *Money answers all things;* and that we had the benevolence of Christian friends, some in this town [Boston, not Lancaster], and some in that, and others: and some in England, that in a little time we might look, and see the house furnished with love" (364). Solomon's assurance (Ecclesiastes 10.19) is not exactly pertinent to Rowlandson's situation because it concerns money's power to *preserve* a house (and, figuratively, a kingdom), and thus underscores the fact that Rowlandson no longer has a house to preserve. Money does not create, produce, or generate all that is *worth preserving* in a house; and it can be said to be able to replace a house only if we confine the meaning of *house* to the concept of shelter. Shelter is no small matter for her after the recent misery, and the generosity of the *scattered* Christians (perhaps indicating that the Rowlandson family has already become something of a sacred or awful object) is not inconsiderable either, given all the malign stinginess she has suffered during the captivity. But the house considered as shelter (like the tree considered as lumber, to borrow from Emerson) is only a partial representation of a complex and concrete being, leaving out a welter of other aspects that are the lost house's specific history. Bradstreet, "Some verses upon the burning of our house, July 10, 1666":

> When by the Ruines oft I past,
> My sorrowing eyes aside did cast,
> And here and there the places spye
> Where oft I sate, and long did lye.
>
> Here stood that trunk, and there that chest;
> There lay that store I counted best:
> My pleasant things in ashes lye,
> And them behold no more shall I.
> Under the roof no guest shall sitt,
> Nor at thy table eat a bitt.
>
> No pleasant tale shall 'ere be told,
> Nor things recounted done of old.
> No candle 'ere shall shine in Thee,
> Nor bridegroom's voice ere heard shall bee.
> In silence ever shalt thou lye;
> Adeiu, Adeiu; All's vanity.[37]

Considered as the vehicle of the family history, the house is so intricate a vessel of intentions as virtually to qualify for subjectivity, as Bradstreet intimates when she addresses it by apostrophe, a trope that, by elevating thing to person, is especially suitable to ironization by mourning, with its fixation on persons that have been demoted to things. If it is absurd to address the house as "Thee," this absurdity is no greater here than is the general absurdity of the survivor's keen desire for continuing dialogue with the dead; recognizing that the dialogue is over is precisely what mourning has to do before going on to describe to itself what the dialogue was. But the poem dramatically defines a difference between on the one hand such private and eventual acceptance and on the other both Bradstreet's autosadistic negatives and the providential interpretation of the event that hovers as a possible future but not a present reality for the poem's voice, both of which are emblematized by the fire that levels the house without warning, mercy, or consideration.

The simplifying force that Bradstreet emblematizes as conflagration is for Rowlandson signified by money, which can represent the house only in its aspect as shelter, and which therefore acknowledges only the first of the four properties Rowlandson lists: "our house and home and all our comforts within doors, and without." If money *answers* all things, it hears only that feature of them that is least specific to them. It leaves out what is crucial to feeling, which is what is central for mourning—a stern insistence on the value and valor of what the family did in its inconspicuous creative labor of physical, symbolical, and ritual self-establishment. Insofar as the new house does replace what is replaceable, therefore, she is grateful, but insofar as it does not do what it cannot do, she is estranged from it: the simultaneity of gratitude and estrangement is not a sign of confusion, but a phenomenological measurement of the new. The expression of estrangement is a result of grief, a representation alien to the theological notion that the reimbursements that arrive are *wholly* adequate, that the singularity of what was before is either inconsequential or a mark of its inferiority, and that gratitude should therefore be the sole emotion. Estrangement, even if it is only a temporary placeholder for the new home that will eventually be compiled, is an apostasy, an ingratitude rather than an accompaniment to gratitude, a sign that Rowlandson is still, despite all that has descended on her, a mixed thing. Despite Puritanism's hostility to bourgeois acquisitiveness on the level of social regulation, the relentless logic of exemplification, which would relegate houses to the category of *physically necessary possession enabling the saints' labor* (as Per Amicum relegated the horror of her captivity to the category *common calamity*), is analogous to the fetishism of exchange value in one of its effects, the erasure of historical complexities with a hermeneutic of fungibility (a point I will explore further in Chapter 4). Such a subsiding of the world is for mourning insufficiently different from nature, from death's obliviating wash. Rowlandson's expression of estrangement, there-fore, does not retract the sincerity of her gratitude, but it does give voice again to the part of her that does not accept the new as total recuperation, that is unwilling to reenter the circle by means of the forcible self-suppression that underlies Bradstreet's painful attempt to effect a transition from fondness to contempt for fondness, from death's victim to death's surrogate: from "Adeiu, Adeiu," the apostrophe, the house as dead friend, to "All's vanity." Such laying-to-rest is finally no more adequate to what has to be done than was the Indians' brusque trashing of Sarah's body. The confession of estrangement from the new consequently inserts an ironic background behind the quotation from Sol-omon—"Money answers all things"—making it echo with earlier caustic re-marks on the Indians' easy love of monetary exchange: "[My daughter Mary] was about ten years old, and taken from the door first by a Praying Indian and afterward sold for a gun" (329). As Howe remarks in one of this chapter's epigraphs, Rowlandson and two of her children have been commodities, an experience that would tend to make one sensitive to the nature of commodifica-tion. If the convergence of theological and pecuniary meanings in one of her keywords—*redemption*—signifies for her the similarity of effect between the two orders of representation, then the Praying Indian's sale may have been less a proof of his hypocrisy than a sign that he has learned his lesson.

What would be, to echo the title, *the restoration of Mrs. Mary Rowlandson?* As writer, she does not know what this would or will be, but, like Antigone, she shows signs of knowing what it is not. By contrast with the intentional facticity of theological and monetary transcendances—their bad infinity, Hegel might say, the night in which all cows are black, both the live ones and the dead ones—grief emerges as loyalty and fidelity. She is once again confronted with an oblivion, this one a human project, warm and subtle in its invitation rather than cold like plain violence, a project codified as a system and society of the good. Hers is therefore a careful estimation of her chances, a conclusion that the postcaptivity life may turn out to be desirable, but that it is not a restoration of what was, which is utterly gone, and therefore not a restoration of what was known as Mrs. Mary Rowlandson.

Kathryn Zabelle Derounian calls Rowlandson's disinclination to stop look-ing back a symptom of "the survivor syndrome." Noting that David Minter and others have discerned a "curious and double present-mindedness" in the nar-rative, Derounian contends that its "duality arises not merely from [the] con-trast between participant and observer, but additionally from a clash of codes between Rowlandson's psychological and religious interpretations of her expe-rience. I contend that during and immediately after her captivity she suffered from psychological trauma akin to what is now termed the 'survivor syndrome' . . . but that she tried to minimize the symptoms to conform to the Puritan doctrine of providential affliction." The "symptoms" include "unresolved grief" and a special intensity of memory devoted to crucial episodes rather than a general memory that looks at the experience as if at a whole from above: "patients with hypermnesia do not necessarily recall their entire experience so vividly; often they select particularly traumatic incidents," and their memory of these, according to Derounian's theoretical source, William G. Niederland, is "overly sharp, distinct, and virtually indelible." I agree with Derounian's perception of the text, especially with her focus on the sharp concretion of Rowlandson's memory, which gives the text its power: *episode* is for Rowlandson almost always *nexus,* a knotting of motifs that embodies the contradiction between the alluring demand of ideology and the need for mourning. But I also think that it is precisely this power of the text that tends toward being erased by Derounian's recourse to the language of clinical psychology, which imports perhaps a certain defensive deafness. This language universalizes "society" as an abstract entity and thereby resists inquiring into how a given society represents return to the survivor, how it stipulates the conditions of renormalization and pursues its own interest in that act of stipulation. This tends to establish reunion as an indubitable value, and therefore to consign the survivor's resistance to categories of the "psychological," the traumatized, the mentally ill, at which point noncompliance is a pitiable derangement rather than a critical reflection on the renewed world. Once we accept Derounian's implication that Rowlandson's memory is "*overly* sharp," we inevitably conclude that the narrative is "the psychological commentary of a deeply troubled person," but by so doing we repeat (albeit in the mode of therapeutic solicitousness rather than moral denunciation) the Puritan-Creonic identification of the social with the rational, which exiles "deep trouble" to the tenebrous status of wilderness or incoherence. Thus the sympathetic shrewdness with which Derounian charts the "symptoms" is replaced by an analysis that denies their status as reflections to which we would listen, rather than offer treatment.[38] My point is that the language of the clinic occupies roughly the same status in Derounian's text that the language of typology does in Rowlandson's. Though illness replaces animal naturality as an explanatory gesture, the language of the clinic here perpetuates the ideological gesture of representing the plural rationality of exemplarity and mourning as a simple opposition between the clear and the confused. This gesture becomes self-fulfilling prophecy if the repressive power it exerts successfully enthrones itself within the survivor's thought, if grief fails to realize that is is not obligated to accommodate itself to the public time of treaties and redemptions, that it is entitled to survey the new world under construction, to deliberate on the worthiness of representations that would lay the horror to rest by explaining what was lost and what the meaning of the loss is—that it "has cause."

The constitution of a peacetime, like exemplarism in general, is a project of legitimating sociality in a determinate mode, and thus can be a moral equivalent of war if it makes its way by attempted exploitations of grief's longing for rest or by derisory *effacements* of notions of rationality, ethics, and value not cut to its measure:

> Now I was full of joy, and yet not without sorrow: joy to see such a lovely sight, so many Christians together, and some of them my neighbors: there I met with my brother, and my brother in law, who asked me, if I knew where his wife was? Poor heart! He had helped to bury her, and knew it not; she being shot down by the house was partly burnt: so that those who were at Boston at the desolation of the town, and came back afterward, and buried the dead, did not know her. (361)

The sister, presumably, who had "much trouble upon spiritual accounts" when she was young, who wished to die during the attack and had the wish condemned and granted in one moment.

4

The Strangers

The stream was swift, and so cold
I thought I would be sliced in two.
But he dragged me from the flood
by the ends of my hair.
I had grown to recognize his face.
I could distinguish it from the others.
There were times I feared I understood
his language, which was not human,
and I knelt to pray for strength.
                    —Louise Erdrich, "Captivity"

A word that is almost deprived of meaning is noisy.
                    —Maurice Blanchot

Oh that we could believe that there is nothing too hard for God!
                    —Mary White Rowlandson

Despite Augustine's assurance that the sequel to the loss of the sacred is simply an agonizing vacuity, Rowlandson discovers that when one thing goes another appears, or perhaps that the second thing was already there but unseen because hidden by the light of the first. The monotheistic insistence that there is no other real thing but God is an attempt to preserve the supremacy of the first thing even in its vanishing. This second thing, therefore, would be *something that gets in her eyes.*

> At this place (the sun now getting higher) what with the beams and heat of the sun, and the smoke of the wigwams, I thought I should have been blind (337) . . . In this place on a cold night, as I lay by the fire, I removed a stick that kept the heat

from me, a squaw moved it down again, at which I looked up, and she threw a handful of ashes in my eyes: I thought I should have been quite blinded, and have never seen more: but lying down, the water run out of my eyes, and carried the dirt with it, that by the morning, I recovered my sight again. (342)

For Rowlandson, the destruction of settlement, and with it the array of functions that defined the site called Mary White Rowlandson, provokes two questions rather than one: not only, where has what I always saw gone (and why)? but also, what is this that I see now (where is what is left of me)? More specifically: who (rather than *what*) lives in (rather than *is*) the woods? and, do I? ("for a long space of time . . . in ye woods from ye meanes [of grace].") An exile is also a sojourn: the urgent perturbation of these questions, rather than what we might decide on as the degree of accuracy in her variable and desirous answers, is one of the marks of the real that this narrative transmits to us. Rowlandson is one of the very few American Puritans to have recorded the fact that she discovered another being, or rather had it discovered to her. If we almost always have only hints of authentic history, of *second things first,* at least here there are hints.

The simple overwhelming presence of the Algonquian captors was not of itself sufficient to compel Rowlandson to perceive them as persons, as cultural subjects, rather than as retributive or malign force: we are familiar with ideology's power to prompt admiration for the emperor's new clothes, and Puritan representation was especially adept at subduing fact with category. The presence of the Algonquians is a necessary but not sufficient condition for what happens in the composition of the narrative: only with the incapacitation of typology by grief does a human Indian figure come into view at the margin of perception. And this glimpse out of the corner of the eye, to use one of Poe's favored tropes, is subject to revocation when the constructive allure of typology once again swamps the narration; but the revocation is itself often again revoked in a revival of the glimpse, when the thought of typology's oppressions once again takes precedence over the thought of its allure. The representation of the Indians is caught up in mourning's ranging up and down between the longing to believe and the refusal of comforting dissolutions of the real, a ranging that *is* Rowlandson's voice, a voice that is closer to the whole forum defined by Hegel's *Antigone* than it is to Antigone's or Creon's position within that field. Even when inclining most fervently toward Creon, this voice expresses reconciliations that have to be imagined, that are present as not-yet-if-ever, as a blank frontier rather than a ready dwelling. *For the time (of) being,* the shock of the raw fact endures and memories of the captors are allowed to stand at an open door together with memories of the dead child and the dead life. For the time being, mourning wanders between two ways of remembering, such nomadism being for Puritanism an *Indian* trait, a hunter-gatherer vagrancy unregulated by the temporal and spatial commitments of agriculture and animal husbandry, an Indianism whose vicissitudes can be most precisely measured at any single narrative moment by deciding which of four ways of viewing the Algonquians is at that moment in power. To see where she is in the field of grieving possibility in a given episode, I suggest we decide whether she is seeing the captors (1) as figures drawn from the repertoire of Puritan symbology; (2) as secular figures not included in that repertoire; (3) as figures *of* the attitudes that pervade Puritan symbology; or (4) as figures betraying the nomadism of incomplete mourning (as demons, as a culture, as Puritanism, or as versions of herself). If the Algonquians are always *figured,* rather than *seen,* her figuration is perturbed and heteroglot: representation succumbs to unrest in the zone of the stranger, rather than ensuring that the stranger settles into the clarity of a homogeneous representational space.

The general pressure and temptation of Puritan ethnic dogma, together with the special allure of heaping acrimony on those who destroyed her life, often draw Rowlandson toward orthodox and, for us, unpleasantly familiar typological portraiture in her memoirs of her dealings with the Algonquians. Her participation in such rhetoric joins her to a widespread campaign of postwar race vituperation. Stephen Saunders Webb cites a report on the war that Nathaniel Saltonstall wrote for the *London Gazette* that included, among many instances of Algonquian barbarity, the story of "'two poor Travellers, that had nothing but small sticks to defend themselves with,' who were attacked 'by a great number of Indian women.' The squaws 'beat out their Brains, and cut off their privy Members, which they carried away with them in Triumph.'" According to Webb,

> The dead left a living legacy of hatred behind them. As the descendants of the survivors of the Indian war of 1676 in Massachusetts and Virginia became the leaders of American opinion, the image of the Indian savage which this year's conflict confirmed became a racist stereotype. [Saltonstall] fostered this hatred among the Bostonians, most of whom, like himself, had been safe during the struggle and never saw what he described and they believed. Worse than the number of casualties among the colonists, [Saltonstall] wrote, was the barbaric manner of their deaths. The English were "destroyed with exquisite Torments, and most inhumane Barbarities, the Heathen rarely giving Quarter to those they take, but if they were Women, they first forced them to satisfy their filthy Lusts and then murdered them, either cutting off the Head, ripping open the Belly, or Skulping the Head of Skin and Hair, and hanging them up as Trophies, wearing Men's Fingers as Bracelets about their Necks, and Stripes of their Skins which they dresse for Belts."[1]

If the Algonquians did all these things, their choice of atrocities would signal a rather shrewd insight into the English Puritans' special nightmares concerning the body—castration, abortion, cannibal decoration. Rowlandson will confirm some of these indictments (necklaces of fingers) and repudiate others (rape). But whatever satisfaction such conventional representation affords her is tainted by a cost, because the condemnations she levels against the Indians would tend to include her as well. The greater the satisfaction, therefore, the more imperiled her defense of her own cause for mourning, because the scheme of depiction she taps into associates what it sees as the egregious anarchy of Indian life with what it defines as selfish antisociality in white society, not only the sort of laxness she feels convicted of having indulged before the war but also the grief that persists into the narration. The trope connecting the savage with the sinner, the use of the savage as emblem of white error, is hardly her invention: it pervades the historical figurations of Bradford and Winthrop, runs through the Pequot war narratives, and reaches what is perhaps its perfervid apex in Increase Mather's formula—you were punished by Indians because you had grown like Indians. Puritan rhetoric thus controlled the circulations of fear and hatred with a transitive conditional: if you detest the destroyer, then you must detest your own noncompliance, of which the destroyer is both an effect and an emblem. This trope would be still more coercive when it associated Indians and reprobate women, since for both discipline was a precarious *addition to* their natures, an extrinsic curb rather than a fulfillment of their intrinsic racial or gender telos, always regulative, never attaining to the historical splendor of the constitutive. Hence the jealous and voyeuristic interest in the question of the captive woman's rape or seduction that will come to prominence in later captivity narratives (an interest Rowlandson brusquely dismisses): if the woman's fidelity survives being surrounded by those who openly indulge an equivalent to her secret turpitude, this will testify not to her central fidelity but to the strength of the domestic discipline that constrains her from without even in the physical absence of the enforcers of the discipline. Like pornography or Tom Sawyer at his own funeral, the captivity narrative produces for one kind of reader the fantasia of being able to see behind one's back, assuring him of the extent of his power rather than of the basic decency of what his hallucinated vision beholds. Rowlandson simply ignores the question of sexual temptation, because openness to new love of all kinds is exactly what grief has disturbed— her noncompliance with Puritanism is a matter not of preferring other liaisons, but of comprehensive mistrust and skepticism. If, however, Puritanism in its jealousy misperceives her allegiance in suspecting attachments to anyone other than the dead, it is nonetheless correct in assuming that her love is out of its proper place.

The intensely typological representation of the Indians begins for the reader in Per Amicum's preface, which refers to "the causeless enmity of these barbarians," "the malicious and revengeful spirit of these heathen" (318), to these "atheistical, proud, wild, cruel, barbarous, brutish (in one word) diabolical creatures" (321). He conjures a specter so familiar that brief allusion suffices, the typological keyword, diabolical, marshaling and arranging all the other attributes beneath its explicatory aegis and obviating any curious attention to the incongruity between "causeless" and "revengeful"—a blending that causes the question of motive to evaporate in the sunlight of moral notation. In the early pages, as she begins to write, Rowlandson decides to avail herself of the power of this rhetoric, with no sign of dissent, summoning the horror of the first attack in order to denounce the enemy on Matherian grounds, which may at this point be the only representational paradigm she is aware of having at hand (though others will get loose as she goes along). As Slotkin notes,[2] the Indians first show themselves as a force of separation fragmenting society at its root, the family: "the Indians laid hold of us, pulling me one way, and the Children another . . ." (324). They are not so much a concerted military operation as a blind force, to be apprehended not in itself but in its trace or effect, a sudden concussion at the center of regularity. Their own sociality, which she witnesses shortly later, is hardly worthy of the name, is no more than an exuberantly terrible simulation or even parody of the social, an outbreak of appetite, devoid of remorse for the victims, of any sense of the gravity of their deeds, even of attention to their own future needs:

> This was the dolefullest night that ever my eyes saw. Oh the roaring, and singing and dancing, and yelling of those black creatures in the night, which made the place a lively resemblance of hell. And as miserable was the waste that was there made, of horses, cattle, sheep, swine, calves, lambs, roasting pigs, and fowl (which they had plundered in the town) some roasting, some lying and burning, and some boiling to feed our merciless enemies: who were joyful enough though we were disconsolate. (326)

The topic in this rather perfect generic vignette is heedlessness, the Algonquians' lack of constancy, their inability to abstain from whim in order to protect a continual allegiance to an abstract notion of the self's and the community's future. Selfishness, then, is emotional nomadism, a being so driven and captivated by the various gusts of instantaneous inclination as not to be properly human. Wandering up and down, consciousness is slave to the qualities of its moments. This judgment depends upon a severely restrictive conception of constancy as what Nietzsche calls the promise, a repetitious maintenance of an explicit transcendental commitment defined by normative codes, an interruption rather than a pursuit of ordinary vectors. Without such continual interruption and repetitious allegiance, consciousness is viewed as being not really consciousness at all but rather an incessant oscillation, thought decayed into radically disparate episodes of perception and fluxional desire. Thus the Algonquians cook all the animals even though, as Rowlandson discovers, there are very lean days ahead, a fact she seems to feel the Indians must have known but were constitutively incompetent to plan for. If this conclusion ignores other manners of constancy, such as mournful fidelity or the ceremonial propitiatory or sacrificial rites that connected the group with its past and sought to protect its future, such obliviousness is ideologically deliberate, because it defines Puritan constancy as the only constancy, relegating all others to the category of incoherence, decomposition, and failure, a judgment that seemed to be confirmed as the English power to destroy the continent's other occupants was gradually established.[3]

James Axtell argues that the representation of Indian inconstancy was a provocation to as well as a legitimation of the exercise of colonial power:

> While they shared certain characteristics with the rest of mankind known to Europe, [the American natives'] cultures were so strange, so numerous, and so diverse that the invaders found it impossible to predict their behavior. If the Europeans hoped to harness, or at least neutralize, the numerically superior natives, they could ill afford to tolerate behavior that was as unpredictable as it was potentially dangerous.[4]

The Indians "had to be rendered predictable to make America safe for Europeans,"[5] and this "rendering" would have to be a creation: rather than a deep look into the patterns of interaction intrinsic to Indian culture, a look that might discover regularities governed by disparate social ontologies, the European strategy was instead based on a preliminary positing of "irregularity," followed by an erasure of those patterns and a subsequent substitution of early bourgeois conceptions of exchange and commitment and Puritan conceptions of spiritual consistency and integrity. Axtell finds the English Puritans much less adept than others, for instance the French Jesuits, less wily at making destruction and reconstruction appear to their victims as a smooth and seamless transition, as an act of social empiricism, and he attributes this to certain institutional obstacles: for the Puritans, the minister's ministry existed by virtue of his having been called by a congregation, so the project of going out to create a congregation was structurally dubious, potentially renegade.[6] But it seems to me that Puritan rigidity goes deeper, into the root of Puritanism as a horrified and nauseated belief that Renaissance Britain had betrayed its own patriarchal values and thereby degenerated into base pursuits of what Bradford calls "giddiness" and "newfangledness." As Edmund Leites contends, following Max Weber, "the grand movement of morals, commonly called Puritan, began to transform 'merrie old England' into a more sober and steady world. The thoroughness of the Puritan demand for emotional and moral constancy in various areas of life—in all areas of life, finally—is remarkable, as is the degree to which this demand extended outward to all classes of society."[7] If, as Michael Walzer argues, Puritanism "was marked above all by an uncompromising and sustained commitment to a political ideal . . . and by a pattern of rigorous and systematic labor in pursuit of the ideal,"[8] then learning the other's language, even to engage in manipulative dialogue, was apt to seem too dangerously seductive, too liable to lead the saint into the land of the other rather than the other into the land of the saint—touch it not. But, though *representation with* the other was foresworn, *representation of* the other's language and culture as a species of abomination, as a kind of *roaring of black things,* was highly useful, as a contrastive term demonstrating the excellence and meaning of the discipline that spent life opposing the roar. Consequently, though individuals such as Roger Williams or Thomas Mayhew, Jr., rivaled the Jesuits in cultural perspicacity, they were rendered somewhat suspect among their peers, discursive halfbreeds. Puritanism was in the main internally inclined more to force than persuasion, whether through war or through the relocation of Indians to praying towns where their customs were simply interdicted, rather than studied or addressed as they were by the Jesuits in the field. American Puritanism was a collective and might-ridden gesture of refusal, first of the English church, then of England, with the result that its military and discursive bearing toward the Indians was less politically successful than was the Jesuits'.

But the Puritans' discursive objectification of the Indians was not simply erroneous. Though they were largely incapable of acknowledging forms of personal and social fidelity other than their own, the behaviors they saw as inconstant were real: the Indians practiced serial monogamy and in certain circumstances condoned multiple partnering; there was no explicitly designated magistracy, so that justice often took the form of familial revenge; the division of supply between hunting and agriculture resulted in a group's geographical circulation within a certain range rather than spatial fixity and in very complex arrangements for land usership rather than ownership;[9] and the primary bond tended to be with the tribe rather than the language group or race, at least before the English invasion necessitated larger coalitions such as Philip's, so that Indian-to-Indian commitments often seemed feeble (but only seemed so due to the fallacious assumption that such bonds should be automatic). We might imagine, for instance, the Algonquians turning the table by pointing to intercongregational, intercolonial, or English-French-Dutch rivalries as evidence of petty backwardness among the white people: whereas the Puritans took enmities among the Indians as evidence of a feeble sociality, they would have considered the idea of white racial solidarity as a primary bond preposterous and apostate, precisely the sort of repellent aggregation that led them away from England.

   My survey of Indian economy and society is very cursory, but I want only to
make the point that alternate regularities tended to show themselves as irreg-
ularities to the American Puritans, but that this is a result not of a fundamentally erroneous understanding of the cultural difference but rather of a laborious and deliberate manner of representing the significance of that difference.
This representational labor is perhaps more pronounced among the English
Puritans than among any of the other New World Europeans because Puritanism was founded on a highly restrictive conception of what qualified as true
commitment. Societies are in general rather sluggish about recognizing nor-
malities other than their own as anything other than abnormality, and seventeenth-century British thought was not in the main liberal, at least before the
Restoration. Intolerance was compounded in Massachusetts by the fact that, as I
argued in the first chapter, Puritanism arose as an explicitly theorized rejection
of the concept of plural decencies *("sola scriptura")* and by the fact that American Congregationalists had not been tempered by the need for cooperation to
the degree that the British Congregationalists who participated in the Commonwealth had. Having moved across the earth to avoid being interfused with
groups less different from them than were the Indians, how could they possibly
have become suddenly expansive in their understanding of the range of human
possibility? If therefore Indian social practices came to be seen as evidence of
inconstancy, the Puritan cultural bias shows itself in most cases in the conclusion drawn rather than in the primary perceptions of how Indian life was
different, perceptions that were often themselves quite astute, because Puritanism was scholarly.
   The correctness of the Puritans' perceptions of the profound difference
between their own and the Algonquian cultures is in fact confirmed by the fact
that the Indians lost the war. The ethnic difference between the two groups was
not only real but eventually disastrous for Philip and his allies because, as
Douglas Leach argues,[10] the crumbling of the Indians' early success was at least
in large part the result of their failure to develop the systems of storage and
supply necessary for the sort of protracted and tenacious war aimed at cultural
destruction—abstract war, rather than ritually constituted episodes of violence
exchange—that had been introduced into North America. The only advantage
offsetting this cultural blindspot was their knowledge of military techniques
adapted to forested and undrained land, and, once these skills were assimilated
by the ingenuity of Benjamin Church and others (an assimilation viewed with
great suspicion by Puritanism, because it depended on a willingness to leave
open space and enter darkness), the Indians' inadequacy was inevitable. Theirs
was not, however, abstract inadequacy, such as their bodies' inadequacy before
the English germs, but situationally specific inadequacy, an inability either to
thrive in or to turn their backs on a form of violence so completely foreign to

what they considered appropriate and decent that, though they commenced the work of counteradaptations such as Philip's coalition, they must have been, at the deepest level, stunned by the advent of a relentless and extraordinarily powerful transcendentalism. According to Axtell, the "ultimate being in the Indian pantheon, just as in the Christian, was an all-powerful, all-knowing 'Master Spirit' or 'Creator,' who was the source of all good but was seldom or never seen. More frequently encountered, *especially after the advent of the Hell-bearing Europeans,* was an evil god, a 'matchemanitou,' who purveyed devilry and earth if not appeased" (italics added).[11] The redoubled emphasis on such a being, as Michael Taussig argues, derives from an attempt to signify and there-by localize a danger to signification and the world it secures,[12] an attempt to delimit conceptually the white danger in the east and thereby to identify what remains of sense. A labor, therefore, not unlike mourning. Axtell: "What the Europeans did not recognize was that the native renaissance of grave offerings coincided with another growing tendency to align the dead on an east-west axis with the head to the west . . . The simultaneous popularity of heading the dead toward the 'land of souls' and providing food for the soul's journey seems to suggest that at least some of the tribes who were experiencing the indirect but powerful impact of the European presence in North America felt a need for some degree of cultural revitalization."[13]

The Puritans' belief that their victory resulted from their renewed commit-ment to identitarian constancy and from the Algonquians' persistence in suc-cumbing to the scintillating blandishments the moment presents is therefore a mystification rather than an invention, a mystification propped upon the fact that Indian culture did not conceive of order as a disciplinary and repetitional abstraction from ordinary social regularities such as ceremonies where sym-bolic propitiatory sacrifice takes precedence over pragmatic calculation of fu-ture physical need. Perhaps every ideology, as Freud remarked of neurosis, needs a fact to hide behind, has a rationality it encloses and redirects, in this case converting the Puritan's greater deftness in contexts generated out of their own assumptions into evidence of an opposition between the human and the heed-lessness of the animal: the sacrifice of the livestock is just waste, waste is a sin, and the sinners lose the war because they starve. The victory is a providential revelation that the palisade around the English Puritans is the border of the human, and Rowlandson, within the wall again, can take a certain pleasure, though not an unalloyed pleasure, in contemplating the meaning of her former captors' fate.

Philip's cause fails, in the Puritan view, because it is not a cause at all, really, but a temporary coalition of transient and dissimilar appetites for the pleasures of cruelty and waste. Though Philip and those with him are themselves un-aware of the wisdom embodied in typological thought, he is himself nev-

ertheless a clear type of the failure to develop and maintain an elevated attention to the future, a bestial determination to revel in the moment's storm and to
be governed by no more foresight than the vague and minimal resolve to stay
alive for the next moment. (The various accounts of the hunt for Philip in the
last days of the war and the descriptions of his beheaded and quartered body
show an especially ferocious obsession with locating and dismantling the source
or crucial locus of the disease, much like the 1988 media narratives of the hunt
for "Agent Zero," the putative first North American transmitter of AIDS. Both
narratives are allegories of the process of emblematization, of giving a body to
that which is of danger to the collective body, Philip's "nature" [di]splayed.)
But, again, whatever satisfaction Rowlandson takes from inflicting this available discursive blow on the memory of those who killed her daughter and
destroyed her life is offset by the tendency of the blow to ricochet. When she
thinks of her own lapses of faith—neglecting the Sabbath and smoking before
the captivity, heavy and unredeemed mournfulness during and after—she must
think of them as specimens of incipient Indianity, according to Mather's formula; when she remembers and detests the horror of the first assault, she is
encouraged to detest her own reprobation come to life and attacking itself,
traitorous as an Indian, bashing out children's brains against trees; and when
she contemplates the emotions and the physical needs that pressed upon her
with such urgency during the captivity, she must see them as of a kind with the
devils who laughed when she and Sarah fell off the horse.

This association of her own inner being with the diabolism of the Indians
may be the reason why she so frequently insists that, through the medium of
Scripture, God kept her alive though she contemplated giving up. There is no
reason to doubt that she experienced moments of despair so great that the
command to live and serve God proved effective when desire for her own future
could not; but it is also true that Rowlandson's sheer inclination to live, despite
the absence of completely credible emotional or religious reasons for doing so,
was wily and tenacious, and in excess of a pure and undesiring submission to
heteronomic compulsion. It is this excess of the desire for life, not only beyond
what she imagines life can provide again but also beyond what can be represented as diligent fealty, that motivates the frequent assurances that she survived
because she was told to do so, rather than because she desired to do so. These
assurances are so frequent as to reveal what they deny, a desire for life that
wants itself despite the worthlessness that comes from having lost all its cherished objects and despite the moral worthlessness of which it is held to be a
prime specimen—an unheeding selfishness, an Indian. Rowlandson's contention that she is alive now because she was told to be so is an evasion of shame
and a strong motive for writing: if she can compose the book that reveals the
work of providence she will have fulfilled the higher purpose that sustained her

when, or so she would have it, desire did not. But the degree to which she insists on attributing survival to faith rather than to desire, again, suggests what Freud calls *denegation,* a protesting-too-much that betrays the repellant vitality of what it seeks to deny, the degree to which she desired to live and mourn, to maintain her life as its own purpose, a desire that has become for her mysterious, haunting, and grotesque:

> Then I went to another wigwam, where there were two of the English children; the squaw was boiling horse's feet, then she cut me off a little piece, and gave one of the English children a piece also. Being very hungry I had quickly eaten up mine, but the child could not bite it, it was so tough and sinewy, but lay sucking, gnawing, chewing and slobbering of it in the mouth and hand, then I took it of the child, and ate it myself, and savory it was to my taste. (350)

The figural association of Indian with reprobate woman transfers the ethnic slander she has directed against the Algonquians into her own self-conception: as the captors' society is judged to be no society because it does not display Puritan norms of constancy, so her personal commitments to her own life and to the memory of her dead are judged to be no commitments, only tempests of self-indulgence, because they do not conform to sanctioned forms of commitment, because they overwhelm even a white child's need to eat. If ethnic prejudice originates in part in an attempt to project difficult parts of oneself onto the being of a racial other, Rowlandson follows a returning curve that discovers what is called the Indian at the heart of herself, a returning curve traced by the thesis that a white woman is much more like an Indian than is a white man. The more she views the Indian as apostate, the more she must come to view her own survival and grief as episodes of nature, as horrifying and repulsive movements of something in her which had been unacknowledged, but which is avowed in the text despite whatever shame this might entail. If she therefore comes close to confirming for the Puritan reader certain prejudices concerning the craven souls of Indians and women, she also expresses for us an astonishingly candid human truth, that lurking beneath the desire to live for God, community, or family there is this commonly unknown being, simply a desire to *live* rather than to *live for.* In unprecedented and unsanctioned counterconversions such as her startling discovery of her desire to sit all night with Sarah's corpse, Rowlandson comes across a Rowlandson she can hardly recognize, but which she does acknowledge, one that eats hoof, bear, fetus fawn, and enjoys:

> The first week of my being among them, I hardly ate anything; the second week I found my stomach grow very faint for want of something; and yet it was very hard to get down their filthy trash: but the third week, though I could think how

formerly my stomach would turn against this or that, and I could starve and die before I could eat such things, yet they were sweet and savory to my taste. (333)

There came an Indian to them at that time, with a basket of horse liver. I asked him to give me a piece: What, says he, can you eat horse liver? I told him, I would try, if he would give me a piece, which he did, and I laid it on the coals to roast; but before it was half ready they got half of it away from me, so that I was fain to take the rest of it and eat it as it was, with the blood about my mouth, and yet a savory bit it was to me: *for the hungry soul, every bitter thing is sweet.* (335)

But I was fain to go and look after something to satisfy my hunger, and going among the wigwams, I went into one, and there found a squaw who showed herself very kind to me, and gave me a piece of bear. I put it into my pocket, and came home, but could not find an opportunity to broil it, for fear they would get it from me, and there it lay all day and night in my stinking pocket. In the morning I went to the same squaw, who had a kettle of ground nuts boiling: I asked her to let me boil my piece of bear in her kettle, which she did, and gave me some ground nuts to eat with it: and I cannot but think how pleasant it was to me. I have sometimes seen bear baked very handsomely among the English, and some like it, but the thought that it was bear, made me tremble: but now that was savory to me that one would think was enough to turn the stomach of a brute creature. (339)

As in religious conversion, extremity drives her to discover something in herself that she did not know or perhaps fearfully suspected, but these conversions from disgust to the ability to savor prompt an astonishment that does not have providence as its object, but rather a self that has been in the cellar all along, a self that exults in the amoral purity of its survival. This is an astonishment that she might have gone through life without experiencing had it not been for the captivity, an astonishment so great as to make her forget shame over her Indian heart in favor of wonder at this cohabitant. She penetrates successive layers of prohibition—interdicted categories of food, rawness—to witness in herself the blasphemously autotelic and splendid foundation of organic life sustaining itself, a sphere of experience that will reenter American literature most power-fully in *Moby-Dick*.

However anomalous and unprecedented, though, this sphere has for her a cryptic familiarity, because it is the area of being where the body of the dead it still is, the site for an eater's vengeance on the other eaters, or even for a phantasmal and hideous reassimilation of that which has been torn from her. The death and physical decay of the loved one opens to her gaze a place where her life is and has always been, a previously occluded place where she imagines the Indians always are, a place where the dead it might be taken back into safety. But eating cannot fulfill any more than longing can; appetite, like mourn-ing, is an infinite rictus.

> I cannot but think what a wolfish appetite persons have in a starving condition: for many times when they gave me that which was hot, I was so greedy, that I should burn my mouth, that it would trouble me hours afterward, and yet I would quickly do the same again. And after I was thoroughly hungry, I was never again satisfied. For though it sometimes fell out, that I got enough, and did eat till I could eat no more, yet I was as unsatisfied as I was when I began. And now I could see that scripture verified (there being many scriptures we do not take notice of, or understand till we are afflicted) Micah 6. 14. *Thou shalt eat and not be satisfied.* Now I might see more than ever before, the miseries that sin hath brought upon us . . . (348)

The verse from Micah, together with two other verses cited shortly after, intervenes to circumscribe appetite, to reveal it as a providential message: as you have done nothing but desire, so you shall do nothing but desire without cessation—the punishment, as with the Indian attack, is an aggravated intensification of its cause. Rowlandson's declaration that she was *never again satisfied,* however, rather than that she was never satisfied during the captivity but has been satisfied by the redemption, echoes with her confession of enduring grief, extending into the present tense of the writing and rupturing the encirclement of appetite and the restoration of dogmatic sense that the passage seeks to erect: though I have food, I'm still hungry; though I'm safe, I still lie awake at night full of anxiety; though I have been generously given a new world, I still dwell with the dead. Hunger and mourning are both still unsatisfied longings at the moment of the telling, and the theology that would arrest them with its concept of justice is a food indiscriminately seized upon in desperation, and a food that is no more enough than are the others.

The passage on insatiability is thus, like the text as a whole, a kind of field of suspension between the plenitude of theology and the experience of wanting that has come to seem to her to be herself rather than an interruption of herself. At several points, when dogma is almost entirely ascendent, Rowlandson presents her mourning as well as her hunger as a piece of selfish Indianism, as an irresponsible, weak indulgence of antisocial mood, a petty forgetting of emotional nobility, an inability to govern and learn the lesson of the vacuum now discovered where happiness had been. This fear that her grief is selfish leads her on occasion to test her power to sympathize with the griefs of others, because sympathy would be evidence that mourning has at least a small social component. In the episode of the grieving Indian mother, she had gloated, but concluded that this was an appropriate return for the way she had been treated. In other cases, she seems to herself to have proven capable of exchanging sympathies: "As I sat amongst them, my son Joseph unexpectedly came to me: we asked of each other's welfare, bemoaning our doleful condition, and the change that had come upon us" (336). Her ability to feel together with another (white) person implies that her mourning is not a purely Indian defection from social existence. And, she assures us, whenever she encountered someone who had recently been among the free English, she eagerly inquired after her husband's well-being and the state of his feelings: "I asked [Thomas Read, a recent captive] about the welfare of my husband, he told me he saw him such a time in the Bay, and he was well but very melancholy" (343); "I asked [Tom and Peter, two Indian negotiators] how my husband did, and all my friends and acquaintance: They said, They are all very well, but melancholy" (353). She worries, though, that her solicitous gestures may only conceal selfishness: the Indians have been telling her that her husband is dead or that he has remarried (perhaps to disconnect her from her past and reconcile her to the captivity, rather than, as she believes, to indulge cruel humor), so her eagerness to hear that her husband is alive and concerned for her may be more mindful of her own welfare than it is of his. When it comes to considering his suffering per se, rather than as evidence of abiding love for her, she is distressed to find and to have to admit to a coldness that echoes with her lack of response to the grief of the mother of the dead papoose or with her lack of concern for the hunger of the child gnawing desperately at the horse's hoof, or, worse, to have to admit to a petulant insistence on the prerogative of her own grief, as if there were room in the world for only one grief:

> Hearing that my son was come to this place, I went to see him, and told him his father was well, but very melancholy: he told me he was as much grieved for his father as for himself; I wondered at his speech, for I thought I had enough upon my spirit in reference to myself, to make me mindless of my husband and everyone else: they being safe among their friends. (344)

A moment of unpleasant emotion, based on the assumption that everyone totals up his or her amount of suffering, and the winner gets the spotlight, a moment in striking contrast with her son's selflessly munificent sentiment. But of course we have only what the son says about himself to her, not the sort of extraordinary candor we get from Rowlandson's testimony, from her determination to tell how it is with grief rather than to construct the noble face, a determination that dictates her decision not to conclude the anecdote by declaring that the contrast between how her son said he felt and how she knew she felt made her ashamed. All she says is, there was this difference between us. It is at such moments that we see the troubled and profound sincerity of Rowlandson's attempt to respect the religion of Increase Mather, her agreement to entertain the premise that her performances of sanctioned love are only disguises or "formality," her search for instances of such hypocrisy, her willingness to lay what she finds before a judging eye, to confess that piety is hypocritical, like those "barbarous creatures" who are "so like . . . to him who was a liar from the beginning" (344). "So unstable and like madmen they were" (352): not a form of constancy or loyalty, grief recognizes nothing but its own irresistible ephemera.

But confessions of one's particular shortcomings can mutate rather easily into innuendoes about the general nature: if Rowlandson's experience of extremity has led her to a demon whose subtle cogency infects the purity of higher purposes, her singularity may lie in having had to confront that being directly, intensively, and without mediatory rationalizations, rather than in having it within her in the first place. Confession reverses into the defiance of one who has known herself, and bespeaks the rigor of the mourner's refusal to evade the thought of loss by consoling herself with the pretense that the family is intact. The husband and the other friends are elsewhere, "safe," that is, at home: she is here in the no place of the cold ground which may some place else hold the dead it. If her claim to greater suffering fails to respect their suffering, it also measures the distance of her isolation and refuses stipulated proprieties of the sort her son voiced. This is how it was with me; something *has* happened. In its loyalty to the fact of the dead, grief does refuse the inadequate consolations of present communities, not because it is intrinsically antisocial, but because the social is destroyed: the grieving Algonquian Master lives in a social nexus that is not hers and that cannot suffice as a frame for shared commiseration; and, though her husband is alive, he is an element left over from a world that is dead, a present part of a world elsewhere that is not hers, and a potential part of a world that is not yet and may never be. There is love in her desire to learn that she is still loved, but the knowledge that she is still loved across this distance cannot annul the experience of the distance, however much she ought to say it does, because their bond is ambiguated and estranged, stranded in anomaly, the two of them even after the redemption wandering through an astonishingly littered wilderness: "About this time the Council had ordered a day of public thanksgiving: though I thought I still had cause for mourning, and being unsettled in *our* minds, we thought we would ride toward the eastward, to see if we could hear anything concerning our children"; "We were hurried up and down in *our* thoughts . . ." (362; italics added). During the captivity, the bare thought of a way back to him was almost enough to make her cease:

> The swamp by which we lay, was, as it were, a deep dungeon, and an exceeding high and steep hill before it. Before I got to the top of the hill, I thought my heart and legs, and all would have broken, and failed me. What through faintness, and soreness of body, it was a grievous day of travel to me. As we went along, I saw a place where English cattle had been: that was comfort to me, such as it was: quickly after that we came to an English path, which so took with me, that I thought I could have freely lain down and died. (335)

A trace or spoor of mercy in an awful land: "As we went along I saw an Englishman stripped naked, and lying dead upon the ground, but knew not who it was" (350). "Oh that we could believe that there is nothing too hard for God!" (356).

The verdict against grief's selfishness, therefore, like the reduction of Algonquian culture to selfish impulse, is a mystification of a truth rather than simply a falsehood, a representation of the mourner's refusal of inadequate consolation as a refusal of love and community per se. Such a discouragement of grief thrives on what it distorts, but Rowlandson is at best unevenly willing to lend consent, at other times alert to the slippage from fact to representation, to the opportunistic equation of the refusal of present surrogates for what has been lost with a comprehensive antisociality, to the correlation of grief with petty selfishness. She discovers this systemic and utilitarian misprision, and separates emotion from its imposed facade, when she remembers that grief is a memorial fidelity, the preservation of what otherwise have been obliviated in war or in the expediencies of construing a peacetime.

The emblematization of the Indian as force of chaos, then, has considerable appeal for her, because it accords with her experience of a destroyed family and because it allows an outlet for expressing retroactive vilification. But the emblem of the diabolical savage dominates only the first few pages of the narrative—when the beginning or best intention would have been most fully in control, before the investigation of experience revealed that the woods is a complex network of pathways and intersections—reappearing fitfully, but never really sustaining itself as a clear ethnographic position. I think that there are two reasons for the waning of the emblem. First, the emblem would have been, during the captivity, a cognitive obstacle to her attempts to secure food, milder treatment, more advantageous shelter, and information from the Indians. During the eighth remove, Rowlandson begins to participate in an economy, trading various pieces she has sewn for various kinds of favor, acquiescing now in order to claim a prerogative later, and so on: "Philip spake to me to make a shirt for his boy, which I did, for which he gave me a shilling: I offered the money to my master, but he bade me keep it: with it I bought a piece of horseflesh" (337). The Algonquian leader relieves her from having to depend on the whims of gift givers and provides her with social agency, with effective means for securing her own well-being. Her entry into exchange lifts her out of the abjection of being on the dole, and thus creates a measure of equality between herself and the captors, with whom she can now barter, that is, set terms, rather than only accept. But if she is in this way raised out of abjection, the Indian is also set loose from the emblem: Philip enters the narrative not as archbeast, but instead as trading partner, as desirer-of-shirt and as possessor-of-shilling. If these traits offer us rather less of Philip's personality than we might like to know, they are nonetheless conspicuously distinct from typology. In the sequence of exchanges recounted in the ensuing narrative, this de-diabolization of the Indian continues, reflecting a process that would have been at the time of the captivity *necessary:* to be effective in exchange, she had to discover a measure of pragmatic calculability, if not deep comprehension, a provisional ability to predict what a *particular captor* will want that she can provide, the likelihood that this particular trade partner will pay what he promised, and so on. This task is for her especially difficult, because the captors' economic behavior seems to her frequently to be bizarre and eccentric, so they are neither devils nor trusty bourgeois, but something in between, each one seeming to have his or her own quirky relation to the promise. Assuming that the captors were uniformly and generically chaotic and unstable would therefore seriously impair her fledgling economic life, since negotiation must assume some sort of regular behavior and recognize the individual character of the other participant. Such recognition does not of course credit the Indians with true rationality—a hunter also assumes the regularity of certain animal behaviors—but it does move her away from contemplating them as an undistinguished and unknowable outbreak of pure force. Economic engagement, therefore, pries her loose from the sequestered clarity of typology, which thrives only where it can manage not to hear (whether through avoidance or destruction) the voice of what it labors to construe as a represented object. Since Rowlandson must deal with them, and since she cannot single-handedly do what Axtell claims English culture was attempting to do, "reduce" the Algonquians to European patterns of contractual promise and accounting-book exchange, she must *learn their language,* in both the literal and figural senses, their pattern of weird economy. She must learn a pragmatic minimum as travelers do, what is necessary to make her way through the other rather than lay hold of the gist of the other culture which, though it remains unknown on the most abstract level, is nonetheless concretely known in several aspects that border on her need. Laurel Thatcher Ulrich[14] and Lyle Koehler[15] contend that Puritan women regularly participated in extramural exchange, disbursing what was produced in domestic industry and procuring what was necessary for domestic maintenance, so we can assume that Rowlandson brought certain skills to the task of trading with the captors. But in her earlier economic activity she would have been able to rely on English norms and protocols that were absent during the captivity, so the dealings with the Indians would have required considerably more perspicacity and ingenuity, both of which would have been weakened by maintaining allegiance to the tone of the emblem; and her dealings with the English in Lancaster would always have been subaltern, in the name of the husband, putatively if not really subordinate to his vision and direction, whereas the dealings with the Indians were in her own name, and openly testified to her exceptional capacity to thrive as an independent economic unit. Rowlandson's explicit and functional public autonomy might in Puritan eyes suggest a likeness to her sometime mistress Weetamoo, the woman sachem of the Pocassets, whose name is rarely mentioned in the literature of the war without a disdainful implication that the Indians' acceptance of female monarchy, like the female testimony encouraged during Quaker services, betrays an elemental derangement. Though Rowlandson does not merge with the Algonquians' social and political values or absorb their cultural practice, her restricted economic integration into the life of the tribe would nonetheless seem to evidence, once again, an incipient Indianity, both a forgetting of the captors' true nature and an expression of a woman's pride in her cleverness and autonomy. The moral dubiousness of this arrogance would have been compounded by the motive for her economic activity, which was not the glory of the Lord, who might have been more worthily worshiped had she remained abject, like the prodigal among the pigs, dependent on what His dark-skinned minions happened to provide, but comfort—better food, lodgings, and treatment—in other words, the affections of the self that brought on the captivity in the first place.

The waning of the emblem in the act of telling the story as well as in the experience recounted, therefore, requires a second motive in addition to practical necessity, about which it would have been judicious to remain silent. Her accounts of her dealings with the Indians are not only uncoordinated with the narrative's uneven dedication to exemplarity, but even implicitly antithetical, both in their waiver of the emblem of the Indian and in their celebration of her shrewdness. Thus they come into being as textual entities only as part of the general counterlegitimation entailed by her defense of mourning. If grief refuses specious compensations for what is lost, then it resolutely maintains an alienation from the values that pervade those false comforts: however mystically horrifying Rowlandson's abiding vision of the littered terrain may be, its emotional power over her memory provokes a restless skepticism, an unwillingness to adapt her mind and heart to less than compelling proprieties. If, therefore, she is not even distantly tempted toward a defense of the Algonquians, toward becoming the sort of "white Indian" that Axtell claims became an increasingly common figure during the next century,[16] she is just as disaffected with the value system that produces the emblem. She will measure out her own disgust or distaste where appropriate, and render appreciation where it is due.

In reading the stories of her exchanges, then, we begin to witness a spiral rather than just a ricochet: prejudice projects certain dreaded traits onto the other, but the fact of being the other's victim means that Rowlandson is herself convicted of those traits, which therefore return to her (ricochet); but, as with her contention that her mourning had cause, the narrative exploration of her motives and actions tends to release them from typological judgment, a release that then travels back across the bridge to the others, releasing them from typology, allowing them a more complex mode of being than moral infraction, permitting a Philip who wants a shirt for his son and has a shilling. Rowlandson's mourning leads her toward recognizing Indian society *as a society,* rather than as lawless animality: if the resulting perceptions are still recognizably English, rather than either Algonquian or scientific, this Englishness does not have either the coherence or the clarity of typological rendition, but rather displays an eclectic and pragmatic searching among the disparate paradigms and commonsenses of English culture in order to engage more successfully with a complex and sophisticated alien cultural entity. The real left its mark on her practice, and mourning's defense of the reality that concerns it spreads out to let these other episodes of the real stand in the narrative. Her recognition of the Indians' sociality proceeds in part from her actual encounters, the construction of exchange relations demonstrating the existence of functional and ongoing structures, rather than only an aggregate of pure impulses. But this concrete recognition is fortified by the defense of mourning, which introduces a perversion into Puritan logic, the black light of the irony at the heart of the community: if the grief of the captive woman is a normal, defensible, and even mandatory homage to the decent ordinariness of the life that is lost, and if the grieving woman is analogous to the Indian, then the Algonquians, no longer cloaked by the emblem, may also be engaged in the elaboration and preservation of a structure; if vilifying the Indians rebounds against herself, then defending herself can rebound the other way. If there are several orders of permissible memory, then perhaps there are several kinds of society, rather than the binarity of the Puritan division between Christian order and the license of the beast. Hesitation before ideological assent can (and, in Rowlandson's case, does) provoke ethnological reconsideration, as William Simmons observes:

> Persons who were alienated from the dominant orthodoxy of Puritan society tended to view the Indians in a more positive light and identified with them to a greater extent. Roger Williams, for example, was fond of pointing out ways in which Indians exceeded Europeans in their natural qualities, and was sympathetic to the ways in which Naragansett religious and political interests resembled his own: "They have a modest religious perswasion not to disturb any man, either themselves *English, Dutch,* or any in their conscience, and worship, and therefore say . . . *Peace, hold your peace.*"[17]

A variation on Simmons' thesis is played in the first person in an extremely powerful essay, "Grief and a Headhunter's Rage," where the anthropologist Renato Rosaldo argues that his own anger after the sudden accidental death of his wife Michelle led him to reject extrinsic interpretive paradigms based on the axiom that the Philippine Ilongots were not conscious of their motivations and instead to listen, to take at face value their statements about the interrelationships between grief, anger, and the desire to go searching for someone to behead.[18] Having like Williams lost his world, Rosaldo notes that, if the vindication required for mourning to proceed requires one to emancipate oneself from explicit public canons of emotional propriety, this emancipation from stipulated perspective may not confine itself to the case of oneself, but instead diffuse outward to become an attitude toward the world, a pervasive secularity. I should add, though, that neither Williams nor Rosaldo was taken captive by the people he describes. At the time of experience, the struggle for a measure of comfort did not require them to attend closely to the minutiae of daily life, so they could select aspects of experience that were imaginatively useful, disregard evidence of the other culture's abiding foreignness, and suppose themselves to have experienced a conjunction with the spirit if not the letter of the other's law. Furthermore, at the time of writing, they are not burdened by anger at the other, so the positing of an abstract cross-cultural oneness is not impaired by resentment. I am suggesting not that they were either more imaginative or more naive than Rowlandson, but that her situation was such as to inflict on her the raw shock of the other, a shock that endures despite her assemblage of a pragmatic competence and that confines her identifications to a more sporadic and limited status, such as the structural and logical equivalence between barterers for the duration of the act of exchange. "Then in came an Indian, and asked me to knit him three pairs of stockings, for which I had a hat, and a silk handkerchief. Then another asked me to make her a shift, for which she gave me an apron" (351–52).

The practice of exchange, the disaffection with Puritan values, and the burgeoning capacity to recognize Indian society as such, then, culminate in representations of the Algonquians that markedly depart from moral symbolization after the initial pages of the narrative, perhaps because in the course of writing she discovers layers of significance in experience that she is reluctant to cover over. At some points, she dismisses stereotypical assumptions curtly and directly, for instance when she testifies that only on one occasion did she see an Indian drunk or that she never felt threatened with rape. Such challenges to Puritan commonplace make her report from the field into something other than what Per Amicum called it, a concrete application or demonstration of abstract principles. On the contrary, her attempted instantiation of principles results in a medium where topoi wane and an otherwise invisibilized way of life comes into view, in passages where mimetic accounting wanders off from ostensible moral purpose:

> And yet how to admiration did the Lord preserve them for his Holy ends, and the destruction of many still among the English! Strangely did the Lord provide for them; that I did not see (all the time I was among them) one man, woman, or child die with hunger.

Though many times they would eat that, that a hog or dog would hardly touch; yet by that God strengthened them to be a scourge to His people.

The chief and commonest food was ground nuts: they ate also nuts and acorns, artichokes, lily roots, ground beans, and several other weeds and roots, that I know not.

They would pick up old bones, and cut them to pieces at the joints, and if they were full of worms and maggots, they would scald them over the fire to make the vermin come out, and then boil them, and drink up the liquor, and then beat the great ends of them in a mortar, and so eat them. They would eat horse's guts, and ears, and all sorts of wild birds which they would catch: also bear, venison, beaver, tortoise, frogs, squirrels, dogs, skunks, rattlesnakes; yea, the very bark of trees; besides all sorts of creatures, and provision which they plundered from the English. I can but stand in admiration to see the wonderful power of God, in providing for such a vast number of our enemies in the wilderness, where there was nothing to be seen, but from hand to mouth. Many times in a morning, the generality of them would eat up all they had, and yet have some further supply against what they wanted. It is said, Psalm 81. 13-14. *Oh, that my people had hearkened to me, and Israel had walked in my ways, I should soon have subdued their enemies, and turned my hand against their adversaries.* But now our perverse and evil carriages in the sight of the Lord, have so offended Him, that instead of turning his Hand against them, the Lord feeds and nourishes them up to be a scourge to the whole land. (359)

This nonnarrative passage interrupts an account of the Indians' satirically named General Court in the midst of deliberating over whether to allow her to return. Rather than proceeding directly to the chronicle of redemption, she pauses for this longish and abstract disquisition on the "remarkable passages of providence" in the course of the war as a whole, rather than in her specific experience. Writing general history rather than personal history, then, she foreshadows the redemption, passing as writer from the self's perspective to a broader rumination on the meanings of collective experience, just as in the narrative she will shortly pass back into the bosom of white generosity. She is instigating a denouement, wrapping it all up, commencing closure. And, of course, the means of closure is providential explication, the resolution of the apparent paradox of divine generosity toward evil beings. The surprising thing for me is the length to which she goes to make her point, which would have been received wisdom in postwar Massachusetts, something to which she could allude briefly, citing for authority the eventual victory of the whites. Instead, she interrupts her recollection at the point of incipient redemption, and shifts to an expository mode unprecedented elsewhere in the text. She delays moving on to the story of her reunion, a story that will require her to acknowledge both the justice of her affliction and the complete satisfaction of her new life. Instead she dissolves personal experience in the grander view, a frame in which the acknowledgment of providence is perhaps less full of problems because it does not require her to be thankful for her special affliction.

The awkward distention of this section (pp. 358-60) seems to me to indicate another denegation, the subterranean presence of a resentment of what closure is going to require in the pages ahead. If the explication of the benignity of the general providence implicitly affirms the justice of what happened to her as a small element of large historical movements, it does not do so directly and explicitly, and it does not affirm her singularly excruciating lot. If staving off this denegated resentment requires extraordinary rhetorical means, a recourse to the abstract artillery of the treatise or sermon, the intruder nonetheless leaves its trace on the surface of the discourse in the representation of Indian techniques for eating. Beginning the passage and compelling it to end with a general description of the ways in which the Lord arranged a minimum supply to maintain the bearers of his message (the delivery of which would therefore be their surplus value), Rowlandson's account of amazing food forgets its purpose midway, lapsing back into personal recollection and citing a wholly nonprovidential amazement at how the Indians lived, the vaguely repellant but still "remarkable" frugality and ingenuity they marshaled against scarcity. If at the beginning of the narrative she saw wastefulness and heedlessness, and if through the middle of the narrative she had seen an obscene taste for wrong foods, she here sees an eclectic and economical competence, a collective knowledge about how to preserve the bodies of the members of the group in what would to untrained eyes appear to be an inimical physical setting. Her "admiration" for the wonderful power of God that sustained them through the war is an admiration not at New World manna laid in front of unintelligent eaters who would otherwise starve, but at a knack or resourcefulness that, if it comes from God, is nonetheless theirs, is nonetheless *them,* and that is perhaps even more deft than the complacent and habitual eating patterns of the English. Their pursuit of food is not proud, it acknowledges necessity, in smart ways. If rationalized fields, herds, and storage seem to her still smarter, she seems also to understand that this kind of war has made the Algonquians desperate: the flaws emerging in their life-style are produced by external intrusion rather than intrinsic defect. The advantage of English means of supply exists in a context created by the English, rather than in the order of nature—it is a situational and pragmatic rather than an ontological or moral advantage. (Losing in someone else's game means only that it is his game rather than yours; and the Algonquians did rather well, even in the other's game, perhaps despite a fear that the better you get at the other game the more rusty you get at your own. To save our lives, we must risk our culture, adhering strictly to our culture we risk our lives, in which case an intact culture is of little matter. Though this historical quandary generated by the European incursion would allow no actual synthesis, the openness to risk for the sake of preservation demonstrates precisely the humanity that the representation of Indian animality was designed to hide.) Most important, the ingenuity Rowlandson admires in the Indians has been hers as well as theirs: she too found the agility to survive in unpromising environments, to overcome dietary chariness in order to be able to recognize nutrition where it is rather than where she would have liked it to be, to endure in situations remote from what she would have chosen. The account of providence therefore mutates: rather than closing off the defense of the mourning self and what it did in a moral *denouement,* the treatise voices admiration for and therefore defends her own and the captors' talent for survival, a *talent* or cultural *technique,* not an unheeding appetite. Becoming-an-Indian here means acquiring a virtuosity that, if it is not clearly subordinated to Protestant virtue, is nevertheless quite recognizable.

Rowlandson's secularized perceptions of the Algonquians occur most frequently, however, not in general statements about the vices they did not display or about their manner of life, but instead in the mode of individual characterization she chooses. She disassembles the collective representation of the Indians that dominates Puritan discourse, the image of an undifferentiated conglomerate of identical specimens of pure vice. She introduces real plurality into "them." To be sure, many of the captors are cruel or capricious, and she reacts sometimes with exasperation or contempt:

> When we came to the place where they intended to lodge, and had pitched their wigwams, being hungry I went again back to the place we were before at, to get something to eat: being encouraged by the squaw's kindness, who bade me come again: when I was there, there came an Indian to look after me, who when he found me, kicked me all along: I went home and found venison roasting that night, but they would not give me one bit of it. Sometimes I met with favor, and sometimes with nothing but frowns. (340)

> As I was sitting in the wigwam here, Philip's maid came in with the child in her arms, and asked me to give her a piece of my apron, to make a flap for it. I told her I would not: then my mistress bade me give it, but still I said no: the maid told me if I would not give her a piece, she would tear a piece off it: I told her I would tear her coat then, with that my mistress rises up, and takes a stick big enough to have killed me, and struck at me with it, but I stepped out, and she struck the stick into the mat of the wigwam. But while she was pulling of it out, I ran to the maid and gave her all of my apron, and so that storm went over. (344)

> I told [one of the Indians] when my husband came I would give him some [tobacco]: hang him rogue (says he) I will knock out his brains, if he comes here.

And then again, in the same breath they would say, That if there should come an
hundred without guns, they would do them no hurt. So unstable and like madmen
they were. (352)

and sometimes with humorous disdain:

There was a squaw who spake to me to make a shirt for her sannup [husband], for
which she gave me a piece of bear. Another asked me to knit a pair of stockings,
for which she gave me a quart of peas: I boiled my peas and bear together, and
invited my master and mistress to dinner, but the proud gossip, because I served
both in one dish, would eat nothing, except one bit that he gave her upon the point
of his knife. (337)

Then I went home to my mistress's wigwam; and they told me I disgraced my
master with begging, and if I did so any more, they would knock me in the head: I
told them, they had as good knock me in the head as starve me to death. (350)

Taking the rather surprising position of being *less* delicate than those she
elsewhere likens to animals, Rowlandson is developing a mode of portraiture
that stands upon her own commonsense practicality rather than upon moral
judgment, and that therefore betokens a considerable departure from her initial
agglomerations: "The Indians were as thick as trees: it seemed as if there had
been a thousand hatchets going at once: if one looked before one, there was
nothing but Indians, and behind one, nothing but Indians, and so on either
hand, I myself in the midst . . ." (334). The delineation of petty vanities, of
petulances, whims, and peevishnesses, moves well beyond the broad tableau of
mass deviltry:

Oh! the outrageous roaring and whooping that there was: They began their din
about a mile before they came to us. By their noise and whooping they signified
how many they had destroyed (which was at that time twenty-three). Those that
were with us at home, were gathered together as soon as they heard the whooping,
and every time that the others went over their number, these at home gave a shout,
that the very earth rung again: and thus they continued till those that had been
upon the expedition were come to the Sagamore's wigwam; and then, Oh, the
hideous insulting and triumphing that there was over some Englishmen's scalps
that they had taken (as their manner is) and brought with them. (330)

As the narrative moves away from such large sketching (where the only differentiation is spatial—the group here, the group there coming toward it) and
toward portraiture, Rowlandson comes across a fracture in the representation
of the Indian as both incessantly changeable and unchangeably abominable.
She continues to allude to the first of these maxims ("So unstable and like

madmen they were"), but the recitation of dogma fails to arrest a transformation in the significance of inconstancy. The Algonquians are not constant in providing an emblem of vice, because some are kind and some are cruel, some are charitable and almost Christian sometimes and malicious at other times. Such reversals overtax the emblem's capacity to account for experience in terms of an abiding heinousness, so its authority wanes, and this waning is further expedited by Rowlandson's developing perception of the existence of Algonquian protocols that at least partially regulate such reversals. If the mistress gets haughty when Rowlandson mixes the bear meat and the peas, this is the result of Rowlandson's having been unaware of a culinary prohibition—a prohibition she may neither comprehend nor admire, but of which she will be aware in the future. As she thus comes across pieces of Algonquian culture, the purpose or spirit of the practices frequently eludes her, but she nonetheless begins to apprehend its presence, to apprehend a coherent entity that may be bizarre in itself, or may only seem so because her contact with it is partial, sporadic, and extrinsic. If therefore the moral interpretation of inconstancy gives way to character portraits of eccentricity, there may be a third motivating force in addition to mournful disaffection and a taxing experiential density, the suspicion that the unusualness of this awkward world may be an undiscovered pattern's mode of manifestation, the way it shows itself to one who has accustomed herself only to its outer precincts. Under these three pressures, the thematic of inconstancy escapes the simplicity of the emblem and bears the message of a perceived but only partially comprehended sociality, the message of the complexity and mystery of an alien culture that reveals itself always to have been there where had been the propaganda of fright and disgust. Rowlandson's ability to acknowledge this alien's furtive cultural subjectivity is perhaps fortified by her growing familiarity with the condition of grieving, because sensed-but-not-possessed is also the mode in which the not-yet-adequately-mourned are present, always just turning the corner ahead of us.

Were there a sufficient remainder of Algonquian culture, ethnological study might reveal that Rowlandson's exasperated and bemused representation of the Indians' instabilities should not be accepted as an explanatory hypothesis, a conclusion she herself seems on the verge of reaching when she takes note of the interdictions against begging or against bear and peas mixed together: though both of these seem bizarre because they run contrary to commonsense practicality, they are rules, and therefore evidence not of individual eccentricity, but rather of culture, of structural opposition to impulse in service to collective self-definition. But, though she at times tends toward this perception, the portrait of individual bizarreness is more common, and her depictions of Indian caprice with their aura of characterological realism are therefore a kind of vestibular or boundary account of the structure of Algonquian life, registering without comprehending its specific difference from American English life. This is especially clear in her accounts of Indian economy, where the disparity is sharpest, where any form of exchange not aimed at the simple acquisition of concrete use value or exchange value is viewed as a specimen of mild dementia. A product of what Marcel Mauss calls "the stage of pure individual contract, the money market, sale proper, fixed price, and weighed and coined money," Rowlandson fails to understand that the "perpetual economic effervescence" of Algonquian society results from a comprehensive and self-regulating practice of "total prestation": "Thus we see that a part of mankind, wealthy, hard-working and creating large surpluses, exchanges vast amounts in ways and for reasons other than those with which we are familiar from our own societies."[19] I am not faulting Rowlandson for having failed to anticipate Mauss, but rather trying to specify the character of what I have called her realism, which is the result not of an adequate representation of the object—of either the absent it or the present strangers who show themselves there where the dead it was—but rather of a disordering of representational conventions that is not (yet) replaced by a satisfying hermeneutic *cure*. We might resume Slotkin and Folsom's terminology by calling this a "psychological" realism, true to reality as she experienced it, but that term carries condescension because it presumes an objective or empirical realism by which we measure the lesser glory of psychological realism. Certainly, ethnology after Mauss supplies such a superior conceptualization of Algonquian exchange, but I consider Rowlandson's distress at death and consequent shock of encounter to be closer to history as "what hurts," in Jameson's formulation, to the real as what Lacan calls the "missed encounter," "*die Idee einer anderer Localität,* the idea of another locality, another space, another scene, *the between perception and consciousness* . . . the place of the real, which stretches from the trauma to the phantasy . . ."[20] than are retrospective conceptual formulations demonstrating not that our knowledge is no longer traumatized but that for some of us the place of the real is elsewhere. I leave this conception of realism as my axiom, an axiom that I *hope* is largely faithful to Rowlandson's decision to describe what she calls "the wine of astonishment," to record the impinging force of baffling things:

> There was one Mary Thurston of Medfield, who seeing how it was with me, lent me a hat to wear: but as soon as I was gone, the squaw (who owned that Mary Thurston) came running after me, and got it away again. Here was the squaw that gave me one spoonful of meal. I put it in my pocket to keep it safe: yet notwithstanding somebody stole it, but put five Indian corns in the room of it: which corns were the greatest provision I had in my travel for one day . . . here lived a sorry Indian, who spoke to me to make him a shirt. When I had done it, he would pay me for nothing. But he lived by the riverside, where I went often to fetch water, I would be often putting of him in mind, and calling for my pay: at last he told me

if I would make another shirt, for a papoose not yet born, he would give me a knife, which he did when I had done it. I carried the knife in, and my master asked me to give it to him, and I was not a little glad that I had anything that they would accept of, and be pleased with. (338)

Nothing stays in the pocket long here, neither the dead it nor the spoonful of meal, but rather everything keeps moving at a dizzying and indescribable velocity: the pocket like the self is this empty concavity through which things rotate in a manner over which control is a rare victory.[21] Passing from confusion and resentment at theft and nonpayment to a pragmatic compliance with the master's demand for tribute, Rowlandson is *taking everything down,* chronicling behaviors where rationales—objects as bearers of symbolic prestige, objects that exchange does not completely alienate from the first bearer, giving or taking rather than selling or bartering, the obligation to keep gifts moving on to new bearers ("Indian giving")—are not available to her, studying the captors, seeking at least pattern where reason is wanting, a kind of urgent assiduousness that may very well also have been practiced by the "sorry Indian" during those confusing conferences with the Englishwoman who would never simply fetch her water but always insisted on making incomprehensible demands. If he was also lacking rationales—an exclusively numerical appraisal of two objects with only extrinsic relations to their initial bearers, a confinement of social relationship to a cell of two participants in the segregated moment of delivering with one hand and receiving with the other—we can imagine, paraphrasing Freud, the vexed reciprocity of shared befuddlement: what *does* an Indian/ Englishwoman *want?* (I leave aside the historically insoluble possibility that the Algonquians may also have found the man who lived by the river to be a peculiar or sorry Indian.) We can also see why British money proved as efficaciously destructive as British war and British liquor: as Axtell argues, the disastrous effect of putting a bounty, or *price,* on scalps was not limited to those who lost their scalps, because it substituted an extrinsic and accidental conjunction between the vessel and what it bears (exchange value) for a singular and intrinsic relation between the scalp and the honor or prestige of the victim.[22] During the century after Rowlandson's narrative, motivated by disasters such as the outcome of the war, the Indians would *study* the whites with more diligence than the whites studied them, mastering alien paradigms, but with a mastery that ultimately proved as erosive as what they were attempting to stave off was destructive.[23]

Rowlandson cannot afford the arrogance of failing to study the other during the captivity, and abiding alienation during the writing leaves her disinclined to subside into complacent ethnic slander. Instead she preserves the tone of enigma and partially successful resourcefulness, ensuring that even her rare vilifications have the intimacy that Hawthorne found in truly personal hatred. It may even be that Rowlandson's failure to investigate the rationale rather than only the patterns of Algonquian exchange results at least in part from her alienation from Puritan spiritual economy, which would call Sarah's death the price exacted for her smoking, pleasurable Sabbaths, and so on. If the space she creates for grief is defended by reducing production, consumption, and exchange to the level of meaningless circulation of physically necessary but spiritually inconsequential objects (a sphere in which she comes to participate with a notably adamantine vigor, like Beckett's Molloy circulating his sucking stones between his mouth, hands, and pockets, controlling a process and keeping it from controlling her by depriving it of deep consequence), then her conclusion that Indian economy is bizarre, rather than an emanation from a cosmology, may result from a desire to see this way, rather than from an inability to see otherwise. Exchange is kept clean, it does not embroil her. If this were so, then grief would have emancipated her from the Puritan spiritualization of the Indian but also left her unwilling to investigate the symbolic armature of Indian exchange, seeing instead perverse thrift, petty delays or refusals of payment, nonsensical prolongings of negotiation, or inconsistent, pointless and sporadic generosity— an emblem not of a cosmos but of the blank reversibility that is the nonface that the earth presents to mourning. Where ethnohistorians such as Simmons, Axtell, or Neal Salisbury see an extensive and coherent system aimed at conserving prestige, defining prerogative, and maintaining an overall homeostasis or ecology of goods and powers, as well as providing for individual need,[24] she sees an irregularity that, however frustrating or irritating, does not presume to communicate the meaning of her loss. In this frame of life, money does not answer all things, but only moves them around. Conversely, we should note, she seems not to have been even tempted to take Bible in hand and pursue the work of conversion: neither absorbing nor disputing, she leaves their spirituality alone, trades knitting for food.

Rowlandson's mode of characterization anticipates certain generic traits of the novel, for example the depiction of eccentricities in some of Dickens' more or less peripheral characters, a resemblance that suggests that the representation of such virtually allegorical automatons in the novel may function as an ideological device for repressing what Ernst Bloch calls nonsynchronisms: "Not all people exist in the same Now. They do so only externally, by virtue of the fact that they may all be seen today. But that does not mean that they are living at the same time with others."[25] Cultural logics operating from radically different premises from those that underpin the bourgeois worldview appear in the sunlight of today as areas of irrational grayness, as perversity (or neurosis), laziness, slow-wittedness, *peculiarity*. Their specific rationalities are annulled so that they can be assimilated to the humanism of ordinary bourgeois reality by means of literary supplementation with a post-Protestant literary type, the grotesque or bizarre, which by Dickens' time had become as common a region of the literary map as that charted by sentimentalism. By this device, the plain fact that alternate realities are still extant is acknowledged, its impact is registered; but at the same time they lose coherence as worldviews and are reduced to automatisms, to an unaccountable repetitiousness that fails to recognize obvious advantage. However frustrating or humorous the gray area may be, then, it has no power to prompt reflection on the light, only provides an opportunity to behold the spectacle of a folly that is so regular as to be predictable, and that can therefore be factored into a rational equation no matter how irrational it is in itself. The supplementary representation of peculiarity assures the bourgeoisie that, if it cannot pervade the human field completely, its ingenuity will nevertheless not run aground in those areas where its reason is not affirmed. Such at least is the implicit argument of "Bartleby the Scrivener," where the employer's genial tolerance for Nippers' and Ginger Nut's routinized perversions of office routine proves inadequate in the face of an absolute and intransigent oddity that comes to the center. To make the immobile Bartleby a peripheral being you have to move your office elsewhere, but in the process lose your sense that center and periphery are anything more than spatial and relative. Bartleby is a near-mute near-robot that disables the liberal hermeneutic, drives the desperate employer back toward theology, toward consulting Edwards' *Freedom of the Will,* and flags the vigor of a submerged and incomprehensible preference, of what Melville in *Moby-Dick* called "the Divine Inert," a figure that reappears in Billy Budd's thoroughly strange innocence. To "prefer" in the way Bartleby prefers is to express an elemental and unrationalized inclination that simply *is* ("I prefer apples"). Introductory writing textbooks tell students that such a statement should not furnish the thesis for an expository essay because the contrary statement ("You do not!") is untenable. Preference of this kind can be rationally challenged only by an imperative ("You will not!"), by a recourse to the mandatory that Bartleby's employer finds unacceptable because it would compromise his genial self-image. But the difficulty with Bartleby lies solely with the negativity of his preferences: positive preferences ("I prefer ginger nuts") can be factored into a routine ("Every day, at exactly 2:15, he goes to the window and looks out") without any explication of their origins or purposes. Bemused realism thus preserves an intact system despite the alterity of its components without having to engage in deep dialogue with those components. Though Rowlandson's representations of her trading partners foreshadow such a strategy of humorous accomodation, her purpose is not an example of ideological conformity because in the Massachusetts of the last quarter of the seventeenth century the representation-of-choice for noncompliance was sin. Her portraits of eccentricity therefore do not hand the Algon-

quians over to dominant paradigms but rather reflect her attempt to find a way
to see differently. Despite some resemblance between her accounts of the Algonquians and the wit of Restoration drama (or the cynical "characters" popular in the salons of La Rochefoucauld's Paris), she is not the promoter of a
bourgeois ordinariness, which does not exist in her society in its liberal form:
rather than defending a socially articulated array of capitalist *idées reçues,* she
is instead cultivating a moral sparseness that holds spirituality at a distance to
prevent it from contaminating mourning. More like Bartleby than like the
employer, she is a gray area rather than a dominant light, engaging in nonsignifying mechanisms in order to resist the allure of confusions and distractions—preserving (what is left of) herself.

Rowlandson's narrative cannot be taken as a forerunner of bourgeois realism, as a project of wrestling reason loose from the grip of faith, because,
though "pure" exchange appeals to her as a practice, the abstract premises of
the bourgeois system meet with some of the same objections she directs at
Puritanism.[26] The distinction between monetary and spiritual economies is not
absolute in the abstract, because money takes to itself an aura of transcenden-
tality, and Puritanism and mercantile capitalism compete precisely because they
lay claim to the same area of desire. The antagonism between them, which
emerges explicitly in Puritanism's anticommercial bias and in the young Franklin's decision to make Puritanism his first object for antithetical self-definition,
draws its intensity and focus from their similarity, from their common postula-
tion of an absolute entity that concretely dissolves the world's opacity and
renders all objects commensurate within a lucid sphere that has no outside.

Though Rowlandson frequently in practice availed herself of the antagonism, using exchange to hold spirituality at bay, her authorial reflections
sometimes venture into exploring the resemblance that invigorates the antagonism, the resemblance between the protocols of monetary and religious symbolization. We can trace this meditation through her comments on the Algonquians' attitude toward money:

> [My master] was dressed in his holland shirt, with great laces sewed at the tail of it,
> he had his silver buttons, his white stockings, his garters were hung round with
> shillings, and he had girdles of wampum upon his head and shoulders. [My
> mistress] had a kersey coat, and covered with girdles of wampum from the loins
> upward: her arms from her elbows to her hands were covered with bracelets; there
> were handfuls of necklaces about her neck, and several sorts of jewels in her ears.
> She had fine red stockings, and white shoes, her hair powdererd and face painted
> red, that was always before black.

Their attire displays the eclectic assimilativeness that Axtell finds characteristic
of Indian society,[27] a diffuse heteroglot amalgam that is the narrative's inadver-

tent but perhaps most apt synecdoche for the social totality of seventeenth-century New England, though without a sign of war between the parts. But Rowlandson sees profanation and degradation rather than eclecticism, and her purpose in this portrait is to return to the emblem, to put the diabolical on view by awaking a loathing for the licentiousness of undue ornament, perhaps recalling Mather's contention that many of the captives were stripped by the captors in order to be a memorandum concerning their taste for fashion. The Indians' apparel bespeaks a love for the created thing that goes beyond the purpose for which it was created, keeping the body warm, like loving language without regard for the pious message it was designed to bear. (Her attention to the theme of the perversion of the producer's intention may in this case have been intensified by the fact that her knitting was the major item the Algonquians sought from her: the episode arouses a specter of unwitting complicity, which may account for the emphasis in her disdain.)[28]

Rowlandson's employment of the Master's and Mistress' attire as an emblem of licentiousness continues with the Master getting drunk—a rare event among Indians, as she remarks, as rare as the harshly prejudicial tone she takes on in this episode. Inordinately enjoying liquor beyond its purpose—health and temperate civility—he then pursues sexual pleasure, intemperately again, and apparently without regard for the creation of offspring:

> My master after he had had his drink, quickly came ranting into the wigwam again, and called for Mr. Hoar, drinking to him, and saying, He was a good man: and then he would say, Hang him, rogue: being almost drunk, he would drink to him, and yet presently say he should be hanged. Then he called for me. I trembled to hear him, yet I was fain to go to him, and he drank to me, showing me no incivility. He was the first Indian I saw drunk all the while I was amongst them. At last his squaw ran out, and he after her, around the wigwam, with his money jingling at his knees: but she escaped him: but having an old squaw he ran to her: and so through the Lord's mercy, we were no more troubled that night. Yet I had not a comfortable night's rest: for I think I can say, I did not sleep for three nights together. (357)

Here the representation of eccentric inconstancy veers back toward the emblematic Indian: the master's decision not to molest her is attributed to divine intervention rather than to any Algonquian hesitation over or sanction against rape, and his oscillations in attitude are segments of behavior that is abominable rather than bizarre. Perhaps the anxious sleeplessness she mentions, a premonition of what she still suffers five years after the redemption, accounts for this socio-epistemological severity: "The night before the letter came from the council, I could not rest, I was so full of fear and troubles, God many times leaving us in the dark, when deliverance is nearest: yea, at this time I could not rest night or day" (357; immediately after previous quotation). If deliverance from captivity has still not brought her deliverance from fright as she writes in 1677 or 1678, then her attempt to locate the beginning of sleeplessness in this glimpse of the demon's true character may also be an attempt to identify the source of and thereby mitigate the disembodied pervasiveness of anxiety, and her recourse to the emblem would in that case be not so much an affirmation of Puritan wisdom as a confession that life among the Puritans has failed to lay the horror to rest.

But, whatever the motive for this recurrence of prejudice late in the narrative, my point here is that she includes a perverted attitude toward money among the many degenerations and collapsed proprieties that the master carries about his knees. When seeking to move representation to a plateau of disdainful clarity, she mingles bourgeois disgust with Protestant disgust, and thereby reveals her awareness of the theoretical resemblance between the two paradigms. Indictment invokes two authoritarian standards, but in the process suggests that they are not, in the deepest sense, really two, rather than variants of one. As the master's pleasure in clothes, drink, and sex can be made to epitomize inadequate spiritual sublimation, so too the ornamental use of wampum and shillings reveals an inordinate love of the vehicle—of money used for display rather than exchange or savings. If exchange and savings are not synonymous with spirituality, their transcendental structure is nevertheless analogous with that of spiritual transcendence, because it requires the constitution of a contrastive degeneracy, and because it calls that degeneracy, in the present instance, the Indian (in other instances, the woman). From the perspective of Puritan dogmatics, the use of money as ornament, even when dropped to the knees in heat of lust, would be not intrinsically worse than making the accumulation of a fortune one's life motive, but instead simply another manifestation of the same kind of thing. Rowlandson's willingness to draw such a disgusted distinction and to blend that disgust with orthodox Protestant disgust therefore reveals her awareness that, whatever doctrinal tension may exist between the dogma of faith and the dogma of capital, the two share highly compatible forms of self-defining disdain for what they create as the lower. And if, in the account of the Master's wild night, she voices both kinds of disdain, then bourgeois transcendence is vulnerable at other points to the same sort of mournful mutation that befalls typological abstraction: if mourning is the low for the bourgeois view as well as for the Protestant view, because it affixes itself to singularity rather than to interchangeability and commensurability, then the defense of mourning would tend toward a critique of the euphorias of Puritanism's imminent successor as well as of Puritanism proper, despite the utility of exchange as a manner of effective deportment in her dealings with the captors.

The missing insight in Rowlandson's account of the Master's wild night,

missing perhaps precisely because she wants to vilify him as an outbreak of
purely unheeding license, is a recognition that his decorations are *cosmetic,* not
in the Western sense of a painted disquise of truth, but *cosmoi,* allegories that
define his place in a socio-ontological hierarchy. Such a recognition would
entail a second recognition, that the difference between sartorial tastes that
comes to the fore in this episode is a difference between disparate systems of
social self-presentation rather than a difference between system and unthinking
heedlessness. According to Mauss, societies such as that of the captors do not
recognize the utter alienability or abstractability of the object from the identities of its producers and possessors. They do not base themselves on the concept of the autonomous commodity; even the individual piece of money is
named, signified as a singularity. Its intrinsic gravitation toward blank interchangeability, which is recognized, since it is money, is circumscribed or ward-
ed off as the danger, perhaps, of *mana,* the undifferentiated threat that being
poses to social life,[29] or perhaps more simply as the decay to which bodies go.
The master's pecuniary apparel, therefore, may be a specimen of a systemic
antichaoticism, of a social intention, that Rowlandson does not, will not, or
cannot see, rather than a decline into chaos. It may be a determination not to let
the referent—abstract value—secede from the complex order of the sign and all
the cosmological and social discriminations that that order sustains in its ecology, rather than a crude or childlike inability to distinguish between the referent
and the sign. Rowlandson does, will, or can see only the latter, and her disdainful gaze presages the modern judgment that those who wear too much gold or
silver are vulgar (presages also the chic frisson to be gotten from doing just
that), that is, they are insufficiently abstract, the abstraction of the cosmos
having become for us a nonabstract grossness—our anorexia of the sign. But,
for Rowlandson, they are sinful rather than vulgar, because apprehending the
abstract purpose of a thing and not getting lost in the confusions of its phys-
icality was the duty of piety.

But not really sinful either, again because a proper attitude toward gold and
silver was not intrinsically pious. As Weber argued in *The Protestant Ethic and
the Spirit of Capitalism,* bourgeois and Calvinist thought share certain assumptions about the method and nature of signification, a bridge that would enable
the transcendentalization of the bourgeoisie despite its self-origination in opposition to faith as the essence of social unity. But in the discourse of Rowlandson's culture, the two are opposed to the point of being an absolute either/or:
the love of accumulation, according to Mather, was one of the provocations of
the divine anger that brought on the war. Faith *or* fortune. When Rowlandson
likens sin and wastefulness, establishes both of them as instances of the violation of transcendent orders of commensuration, therefore, she steps out of an
either/or that both the Calvinist and the bourgeois would wish to maintain.

She attains to an insight that is more abstract than these systems of abstract rationalization, an insight that shows how Weber could use the word *and* rather than *or* in his title. Barring the possibility of genius, and asking where this aberrant insight could have come from, I can think of only two possibilities: Indian culture, with its extraordinarily disparate attitude toward symbolization and exchange, a difference so great as to diminish the apparent difference between the pious and the frugal; and/or mourning, for which the attachment to the singularity of the dead is so focal as to throw all systems of confident belief in interchangeability and adequate compensation into the same pot.

Experience, then, in the radical form in which it descended on Rowlandson, provided the necessary condition for unprecedented insight, though Rowlandson's writerly imagination and intelligence are required in addition as the sufficient condition for such an exploration of the consequences of experience, an exploration that drills into two key words, *restoration,* from the title, and *redemption,* from the last pages of the text. Though she recollects with some satisfaction the ingenuity and diligence she displayed in her transactions with her captors, she remembers also that, along with her son and daughter, she was *sold* by the Indians and *bought* by the English, and that a new home was *bought* for her, to replace the home that, along with the life it contained, along with Sarah, was, in another register, *sold* in order to be able to *repay* her debt to God, who then *paid* her the sum of a new life as a *just price* for the vanished life, perhaps because her repayment quantitatively exceeded the original debt. All of the best things of life, including the life itself, have been things of a kind with the various shirts, pieces of meat, corns of grain, and so on; as they rotated through her possession, so too she and her best things have been rotated through a pocket indifferent to what it holds for a short time. In the black light her potent bitterness emits, the two strands of transaction, providential and commercial, become so intertwined and snarled that they emerge as one, a smug and aloof balance book in which the conjunction of providence and commerce in the one word *redemption* degrades neither because the distinction between the two has perished in the abyss between mourning and what she shows to be the offensive belief that there could be anything like redemption of either kind, a belief that would require indifference to the thing relinquished, a perception of its interchangeability, an anamnesis of grieving knowledge. If a slight innuendo of difference remains between providence and commerce, it is the *more explicit* coldness of commerce, which allows her to derogate the pretense that redemption could be anything but cold: "Money [like providence] answers all things," but with a reply that contributes to their perishing, that seeks to appropriate their perishing as its might and means of operation. Rowlandson insists every time she writes that such a person was *owned* or *sold* rather than "held captive" or "ransomed." Rowlandson has been a commodity:

and if theology tells her that her error lay in taking pride in the deluded thought that she had ever been anything else, how then can she recover from this most primal insult and degradation to trust that she has been *restored* or *redeemed* as a person, since redeemability is a property of things in the very state she is said to have escaped? If, as I argued in Chapter 2, she is for the English a sacred object, she is still an object or precious commodity, a thinking thing. The imputation of preciousness does not revoke the ontic degradation, and Per Amicum's is therefore a confusing praise. If in her transactions with the captors she is a kind of capitalist trading post, advance-guard, or (to recall Axtell's contention about the effect of setting prices on scalps) virus, the narrative is nonetheless not an early statement of the new social ethic, but rather a radical defense of mournfulness that will retain its antitheticality into the age of Franklin and beyond. I do not mean to claim for Rowlandson's vision a super- or subhistorical authenticity, but instead to contend that within the circulations of history there are currents not confined to what a society sets as its either/or.

Perhaps the sharpest irony of Rowlandson's narrative is her inability, failure, or refusal to contemplate directly affinities between her mournfulness and Indian culture, an irony rendered most acute by what seems to have been the explicit and socially sanctioned emphasis on the singularity of the dead in Indian mourning ritual. Though exemplarism was certainly practiced, for instance in the vaunting of martial heroism, practices such as the embalming of the dead, extended burial ceremonies, the placement of cherished personal possessions in the grave and their consequent removal from availability to new ownership, the encouragement of long and prolonged expressions of misery (noted by many contemporary European observers), the prohibition against speaking the name of the dead by others outside the family during the period of mourning, and the continuing mantic conversation between the dead and the survivor through the shaman all suggest not a social appropriation of mourning but rather the social definition of a boundary around mourning, a collective gesture of respect protecting mourning against opportunistic or meddlesome encroachment—like the awe of the taboo-point on the border of mana,[30] an arrangement with certain structural resemblances to the pre-Protestant attitude toward mourning that John Bossy describes.[31] The powwow ceremony, for example, unlike the thanksgiving day from which she abstains shortly after her return, openly recognizes and represents the individual's desire or right to stand apart from social fusion. Rowlandson's close interest in the dramatic structure of the powwow may arise from a kind of rudimentary comparative ethnography, from a perception of the difference between the powwow and the day of thanksgiving as a difference between two symbolizations of alienation, rather than between blackness and light. Seen as a symbolic act, the powwow comes to seem rather more rational than it would have otherwise; seen the same way, the day of thanksgiving may seem to her rather more like a peculiar rite, like one of the possible manners of human ceremoniality, than like action in pure accord with the desire of the divine nature. Though Indian grieving practices may have been so alien that Rowlandson simply failed to recognize their similarity to the mourning for which she felt herself to have cause, we may at least speculate (but no more) that the Algonquians *taught her how to mourn*, as *Antigone* almost taught Hegel, and that her failure to acknowledge the origin of the lesson results from the fact that such an acknowledgment would also be a confession that she *had* become what Axtell calls a "White Indian," not because she indulged a heedless selfishness nor because she would have preferred to live among the captors, but because her narrative imported into the heart of white textuality an exorcised principle of memorial signification that was antithetical to the ideological machine governing the production of New England texts. This importation would be much less easily compartmentalized than were the extrinsic assimilations Axtell finds common, such as moccasins, snowshoes, techniques for forest warfare, and new words for new things, like *succotash*.[32]

Though Rowlandson either did not experience or refuses to admit such deep modeling, there are furtive moments of attention, for example her cold but nonetheless intrigued remembrance of the "mourning and howling" that followed the death of the papoose, or her close study of the performance of the varying distances between the individual and the group in the powwow, a socially sanctioned exploration of the permissible limits of society. In her expository treatise on the general providences revealed in the course of the war, she makes a suggestive remark that may have inspired the unexplored contradiction between "causeless enmity" and "revengeful spirit" I noted in Per Amicum's preface: "the enemy came upon our town, like bears bereft of their whelps, or so many ravenous wolves, rending us and our lambs to death . . ." (358). Though the clause referring to wolves uses sheer appetite to revoke the possibility of grief raised in the clause about bears, and though the use of bears as a figure for grief animalizes it, this double negation is another of Rowlandson's denegations bespeaking what it denies: the vengeful grief of one causes the grief of another, a symmetrical violence (bereft of their whelps / rending us and our lambs to death) that makes first cause and last effect recede to their respective temporal horizons and leaves the land strewn now with two types of entities, not the Algonquians and the English, but the dead and the mourning. In the frame of this infinite spectacle, those who are mourning are perhaps distinct only positionally, in the moment of exchanged murder, but akin in the abstract, in which case noncanonical identifications become possible, identifications with the Indians' anger, despite the fact that the Indians caused her anger, or fledgling recognitions that the fright of incomprehensible reversal and the destruction of the world had been a constant of Indian experience for some time, and that it had provoked the war that introduced those factors to her. She is unlikely to have been oblivious to the fact that, according to Francis Jennings' estimate, Indian populations declined at the general rate of sixty to ninety percent during the first century of white contact, the largest losses coming early on due to disease.[33] Rowlandson's remark concerning the Algonquians' vengeful grief, and even the whole treatise exploring the meaning of reversals of fortune between the two sides during the war, seems to me to arise not only from the chronicle of adequate redemption she feels compelled to write next but also from the baffled fascination with Indian melancholy she expressed four pages before:

> When they went [to the attack on Sudbury] they acted as if the devil told them they should gain victory: and now they acted, as if the devil had told them they should have a fall. Whether it were so or no, I cannot tell, but so it proved, for quickly they began to fall, and so held on that summer, till they came to utter ruin. They came home on a sabbath day, and the powwow that kneeled upon the deerskin came home (I may say, without abuse) as black as the devil. (354)

Black here refers to melancholy, not race: if she sees melancholy as diabolical, such a judgment would include the narrative in which it occurs, and, remarkably, she openly confesses that diabolization on the grounds of race is abusive, rather than simply true. The difference between those who mourn and those who don't supersedes the difference between cultures. According to Slotkin and Folsom, the Algonquians may have been depressed not because they had a premonition of later defeat, but because, lacking a "statistical notion of victory" (368-69), they considered the battle at Sudbury a defeat despite the fact that fewer Indians than English died. This interpretation is consistent with Jennings' persuasive contention that the Indians did not practice abstract or exterminative war, but Rowlandson's suspicion that they had an intuition of the final outcome may not be completely erroneous if their success in battle showed them that they had acquired competence in a world that meant the death of their own, no matter what the final body count. The recourse to mournfulness upon return may have been an attempt to disconnect from the sickening premises of their recent violence and to forge a reconnection with their cultural past. Whether this is the case or not, Rowlandson is here neither exuberant nor vindictive, but rather obliquely and cautiously interested in those who will lose their world, in how they apprehend that loss, and in what they do to survive it. At such fugitive moments, she seems to view Massachusetts as the barren land of an utter reciprocal destruction, and to gaze with fascination, but without abuse, on the black mourning of the other, on the mystery of what he does.

According to Simmons, the "cosmological beliefs of seventeenth-century

Europeans were so different from those of the Indians they encountered that the English could only dimly comprehend any logic in Indian thought."[34] Rowlandson's careful attention to Indian grief, significant enough in retrospect to deserve inclusion in the narrative, may intimate a furtive conjuncture, a leap or flash from her experience to the meaning and importance of behaviors seen no longer as bizarre but rather as trenchant and more adequate for them than what her society provides for her in its attention to mourning. But she does not announce herself as having learned from what she saw, and, though we may speculate on all the reasons she might have for not saying such a thing, the fact remains that we can only wonder about the possibility of a comprehension that is dim because the sunlight of the type will not tolerate it.

Even without such a *profound intuition* of the Algonquian sociosymbolic order and its structural motives, however, the narrative does not simply rehearse prejudice: the binaristic division between culture and animality is present in the narrative in the manner in which the authoritarian word (of which it is a function) is present, as an element in a turbulent ambience, offering both the solace and the demand of a demarcated clarity, and therefore not entirely *immanent* throughout the text. Though she does not annul her experience of the difference between English and Algonquian cultures by affirming a discovery of fundamentally common values, she reworks, transposes, and worries over her understanding of the difference, moving away from theologized difference (which recurs sporadically, in response to emotional need), into a secularized and protonovelistic distinction between the individualized eccentricities of the captors and the ordinariness of her own not-especially-pious dependability, even toward a proto-ethnological recognition of a difference between ontologically equal systems of social convention and signification.

Even in the episode of the Master's and Mistress' ornamentation, for instance, in which the theological reasserts itself and fuses with bourgeois disdain, the intended effect, depicting the Indians' heinous naturality, is marred by an earlier version of the event. In the course of the previous remove, five pages earlier, Rowlandson had been granted an audience with Philip, who chose to show her how far she had sunk from civility: "He asked me, When I washed me? I told him not this month, then he fetched me some water himself, and bid me wash, and gave me the glass to see how I looked . . ." (351). Like disaster and the Bible, which present her with a moral mirror in which to see clearly what has become of her in the eyes of God, this Indian mirror compels her to witness what has become of her during the infinite days of grief. The passage is striking and even shocking in its presentation of Philip, elsewhere in the writings of Rowlandson's contemporaries represented as the locus of degenerated civility, here as an agent of recollection, as calling her back to herself, as reminding her of the need for civility. If Philip's gentle reproof does not recall her to piety, it also does not seek to induce a complete defection from composure. Philip's mirror, like the biblical mirror, despite the different standard of civility, is a social injunction, and thus differs from the biblical mirror as a variation within a field of possibility rather than as an utter opposite.[35] Jane Tomkins finds it "remarkable" that Rowlandson's memories of Philip do not focus on Philip *as* "the leader of the Indians who captured her and mastermind of the campaign that devastated the white population of the colonies." I agree that remembering Philip as a man who asked her to make a shirt for his son, who offered her a pipeful of tobacco, and who showed her herself in a mirror is quite remarkable, but this conclusion contradicts Tomkins' general contention that Rowlandson "saw what her seventeenth century English Separatist background made visible." On the contrary, Rowlandson seems to be holding the dominant representation of Philip at arm's length, in order to permit the emergence of a representation of a "person," an entity that may be shaped by certain historically determined mimetic codes, but that is certainly not an immediate emanation from Puritan typology as it was inflicted on the memory of Philip—decapitated and cut in quarters, the head kept as a trophy, the Polyneices of theology's social self-reconstitution. It is entirely consistent with Rowlandson's developed understanding of mourning that, though she does not champion Philip, and probably has little desire to do so, she dedicates herself to recounting the disparate minutiae of what happened, while avoiding completely the Matherian construction of Philip as a beast of apocalypse.

If there is animality in the episode of the mirror, it is Rowlandson's dishevelment, which is immediately afterward contrasted with the elaborate self-decoration of Weetamoo:

> My master had three squaws, living sometimes with one, and sometimes with another, this old squaw, at whose wigwam I was, and with whom I had been those three weeks. Another was Weetamoo, with whom I had lived and served all this while: a severe and proud dame she was, bestowing every day in dressing herself neat as much time as any gentry of the land: powdering her hair, and painting her face, going with necklaces, with jewels in her ears, and bracelets upon her hands: when she had dressed herself, her work was to make girdles of wampum and beads. (351)

In other contexts, this passage might serve to emblematize Indian sensuality. But the immediately preceding report of Rowlandson's slovenliness prevents an opposition between piety and sensuality because the contrastive term to Weetamoo's vanity would have to be a plain and clean garb, not an unwashed and neglected self that, as in the parable of the prodigal son, would tend more toward emblematizing sin than the modesty of contrition. The contrast, then, is

between the unkempt naturality into which Rowlandson's self-consuming grief
has led her and Weetamoo's ornate and carefully maintained civility. Rowlandson's portrait of Weetamoo's vanity avails itself of a secular and comic typology
("severe and proud dame") that likens Weetamoo to civilized if not especially
zealous Englishwomen ("as any gentry of the land"), an association that rela-
tivizes the sartorial normativity of both the cultures compared and contrasts
them both with Rowlandson's own sloppiness—which may have resulted from
depression, from having been deprived of what she would consider proper
occasion to wash, or perhaps from the peculiar intensity of her hatred and fear
of immersion in the rivers. The shock of what the mirror shows is a sudden
intrusion of what is the case, emotionally equivalent to her experience of
running out of the wigwam thinking she is at home, and the subsequent contrast between her state and that of both Weetamoo and the Massachusetts
gentry discards the ontological difference between white and red in favor of a
difference between, on the one hand, those who keep to procedures of social
self-presentation, red or white, and, on the other, those for whom grief has
caused an imploded and recusant secession from such ritual announcements of
place and participation. Once again, as so often for Rowlandson, the extreme
difference that grief introduces into English meaning here renders the opposi-
tions that that meaning requires less than compelling.

Both the episode of the mirror and the portrait of Weetamoo's vanity follow
shortly after the account of an event I discussed in Chapter 3, but to which I
would like now to return:

> In that time came a company of Indians to us, near thirty, all on horseback. My
> heart skipped within me, thinking they had been Englishmen at the first sight of
> them, for they were dressed in English apparel, with hats, white neckcloths, and
> sashes about their waists, and ribbons upon their shoulders: but when they came
> near, there was a vast difference between the lovely faces of Christians, and the
> foul looks of those heathens, which much damped my spirits again. (349)

Though the aestheticized citation of an indubitable difference between white
and red bodies here sums up Rowlandson's intensest desire to derogate, the
confusion over the properties with which bodies equip themselves prepares for
the cultural relativizations that come to the fore in the pages that follow. If what
seems white can turn out to be red, and destroy the hope of rescue, it is also the
case that what has been thought red can turn out to be analogous to white two
pages later, and reveal that rescue is not a passage across a rift in human being.
Her mournfulness is the major counterpoint to civility per se in this section of
the narrative, rather than the Indians' manner of life, which passes into the
category of ephemeral and estranged socialities. Thus reversibility—the inter-

changing, without pattern, of things that seemed completely divided—reappears as a property of relative cultures, rather than as a principle of blind force, of divine tutelage, or of Indian inconstancy.

Rowlandson's grieving ethnography hovers in the anomalous discursive zone she has secured in her writing, not only horizontally between two civilizations, but also vertically between two ways of perceiving the ethnic difference, between, on the one hand, theological clarity and, on the other, the sort of puzzlement that arises from an astonished recognition of unsuspected structure and a consequent reduction of her own culture from sole structure to member of a group of possibilities:

> In the morning they took the blood of the deer [whose embryo fawn they had eaten the previous day], and put it into the paunch, and so boiled it; I could eat nothing of that, though they ate it sweetly. And yet they were so nice in other things, that when I had fetched water, and had put the dish I dipped the water with, into the kettle of water which I brought, they would say, they would knock me down: for they said, it was a sluttish trick. (347)

Moving from repulsion toward intrigue and pragmatic study, Rowlandson's ethnological realism is not an affirmation or even a full perception of the alien, but rather a mixture of confusion and piecemeal useful insight to which the old notion of the demon is plainly inadequate at the time of the experience, and unsatisfying at the time of writing. She has lived among inklings: if those who are sometimes "nice" at other times eat blood boiled in paunch, this may be evidence, not of Indian inconsistency, but of inconsistency between English and Algonquian canons of niceness. When, having moved away from the emblem toward individual characterization, Rowlandson returns to group portraits, as in her descriptions of the powwow and the aftermath of the Sudbury fight, she introduces a feel of internally consistent structure or pattern more or less beyond her circle of English comprehension, rather than beyond the circle of the human. Rather than an anarchic outbreak of unregulated impulse such as she thought she saw in the woods that first night of captivity when the animals were slaughtered, Algonquian need, desire, and thought move in channels, reach relays, represent themselves, observe strictures. Though Rowlandson retains the aversive wariness and hovering nausea of incomplete assimilation, her representation of the experience of ethnic difference also expresses occasional respect and partial acknowledgment, thereby resisting a full collapse into the reductive clarity of typological insult, and, at least in principle, resisting also what Jennings sees as the real consequence of Puritan ethno-epistemology: "To call a man [or woman] savage is to warrant his death and to leave him unknown and unmourned."[36] During the time of the captivity, the setting-aside of typological obliviation, again, would have been hastened by practical concerns such as food and shelter; if one persists in viewing a social environment as a uniform expression of an abstract trait it becomes a blank wall, and the chances for effective concrete interaction are accordingly impaired. As Simmons remarks, the weaker tend to know the stronger much better than the stronger know the weaker because they must maneuver their way through the world as it is defined by the stronger.[37] Simmons refers to the Indians' familiarity with the procedures of English society, but his insight pertains equally well to Rowlandson's unusual situation, where she was the weaker and therefore the studious party. The setting-aside of the emblem transforms a hypostatized reality into an *actuality,* converting the world that confronts her from blind concussion and the abjection of concomitant passivity—the barren absence of possibility, taking whatever food goes by on the current of pure force, dishevelment—into an array of social practices that, though their ultimate reason remains elusive, can be studied, known in part, probabilistically, and that she can therefore affect with her language and labor. It is at least possible that she would have survived had she maintained the catatonic or eremitic passivity of grief, relying on what manna God sent her way, in which case her decision to generate an intersubjective actuality—an at least functional if not entirely heartfelt *us*—would represent an advance in mourning, a refusal to remain in what Deleuze calls a world without others:

> What happens when the other is absent in the structure of the world? only the brutal opposition of sky and earth reigns with an insupportable light and an obscure abyss: "the summary law of all or nothing." The known and the not-known, the perceived and the not-perceived confront each other absolutely in an unconditional combat . . . Raw and black world, without potentialities or virtualities: it is the category of the possible which has collapsed. Instead of relatively harmonious forces arising from a ground and entering the world to inhabit it in accordance with an order set by space and time, nothing more than abstract lines, luminous and wounding, nothing more than a without-ground, rebellious and grasping. Nothing but the Elements. *The without-ground and the abstract line have replaced the model and the ground.* Everything is implacable, having ceased to stretch and bend towards each other, objects rise up meanacingly: we then discover cruelties which are no longer those of man. It is as if each object, having surrendered its model, reduced now to its hardest lines, slaps us or strikes us from behind. The absence of others is when one bumps into things and when the stupefying speed of our movements is revealed to us.[38]

If this is the way the world looked to Rowlandson at the beginning of the narrative, it is also the way it looks all the time to Puritanism, which is an intentionally isolated culture, severed from its social media or neighborhoods, self-enclosed and self-generated, fed out of its own libidinal interior. Removing herself beyond Puritanism's sacralization of collective loneliness, Rowlandson is coming across conditions that might in other circumstances have permitted interchange and creative cultural evolution more profound than the information about cultivation, combat, and liquor that passed both ways across the Indian/English line. Studying the Algonquians brings possibility, virtuality, actuality into being, rehumanizes the world, discovers models for the course of events, which, if it is still cruel, is cruel following certain patterns. Rather than unconditional combat between the sparsity of the known and the looming blankness of the unknown, there is now a heterogeneous mixture of the known-for-sure, the might-be, and the unknown-but-not-necessarily-incomprehensible, episodically blended rather than segregated in uncommunicating zones. Such a pragmatic intersubjective actuality can be brought to life without entailing the sort of total assent that Puritanism demanded from its adherents or suspected in those who dealt with the Indians, and the lingering of the gist or rationale of Algonquian culture in the shadow of mystery may even be for Rowlandson desirable, because it allows purposive action to proceed while deferring the question of deep acceptance or rejection—transaction without full assent, spare pragmatism, the social at a distance, which leaves room for the work of mourning. When Rowlandson, in the process of writing, waives the temptations of a retroactive curse by way of the emblem, therefore, her willingness to allow the experience of cultural relativity to burgeon into a motif amounts to a reproof of all that a recourse to the emblem would entail, a sign of incomplete *reassimilation,* a decision not to step back into passivity before a blank wall, and a determination to preserve a residue of her transactional rapport with a society that no longer encloses her but which is not congruent with what is said about it by the society which now encloses her, partially, and once again provisionally. Perhaps she remembers how to participate without assimilating in order to replicate that achievement in the new circumstances of redemption.

Rowlandson's persisting difference from Puritan values motivates a third manner of representing the Algonquians, a counteremblatization. Puritan stereotypings of the Indians sometimes concentrated on despotism rather than selfish licentiousness, but more rarely, and the two traits were not theoretically integrated, because the Puritans were not liberals. Though they had had abundant experience with oppressions such as those handed down by Archbishop William Laud, they nevertheless conceived of proper authority as sovereign command: their task was to rehabilitate and divinize the model of patriarchal authority that Filmer advances, not to go over to the model of fraternal and immanent authority with which Locke challenges Filmer. Representing the inclination to command as a *passion,* therefore, combining tyranny and license (as in the eighteenth-century revolutionary period or in the abolitionists' portraits of the slaveholders), was too dangerous, too apt to misfire as a critique of their own strategies of governance. But antidespotic rhetoric survived in the popular imagination, despite and perhaps often because of its potential critical force in the midst of specifically Puritan patriarchies. When Rowlandson represents the Indians as the source of sovereign demands or compulsions, therefore, rather than as instances of heedless license, she is at least in part using socially permissible expressions of anger at the despotism of her captors as a vehicle for ventilating socially interdicted anger at Puritanism, especially its prohibition of grieving. Having grown to believe that she is not a pure specimen of the traits that were called "Indian," Rowlandson can turn to imply that the domineering and insensitive brutality of the Indian Master is analogous to (an emblem of) the commands and compulsions of Puritanism. At such moments her alienation from the society of the emblem that vilifies the Indians proves consonant with certain of her vilifications of the Indians. Annette Kolodny sees such disguised outrage in several captivity narratives written by women:

> The anger such women felt (but dared not express) toward the husband who had staked the family's future on the availability of rich lands on the frontier might thus, through the captivity narrative, vicariously be displaced onto the dark and dusky figure of the Indian, a projection of the husband's darker side.[39]

I am not proposing that Rowlandson is using the narrative to let loose her resentment over her childhood relocation to New England or Lancaster, but I abstain only because there is no suggestive evidence, since she does not mention her childhood: but, again, it is not impossible that the narrative bears revived traces of this archaic trauma, of the child being dragged across the face of the world, or rather, of the child dragged out from the world into the woods, without assent or comprehension. Rather, I am proposing that her portraits of Indian despotism, expressed caustically in her snidely subversive willingness to use the terms *My Master* and *My Mistress,* of the fact of her having been property to be used at (another's) will, voices a resentment of theology's exploitive intrusion into mourning's privacy. As an *object of exemplary representation,* she is *still* of use—if she were not, the production of the narrative commodity would be pointless, because it would gain no place in the apparatus of printing and distribution.

Rowlandson's diatribes against the Algonquian Master concentrate not on his sensuousness or selfishness, but rather on his uncontrovertible demand for motion in another direction than hers and on his interruption of her rest. Grief wishes to stop, to collect remembrance, not to proceed to any future place other than that which it will generate out of its own work. Without destinations, motion is senseless, but the Master keeps them moving. Immediately before associating herself with Lot's wife, for instance, the command to move on comes from the Indians—"On Monday (as I said) they set their wigwams on fire, and went away" (334). If the Indians burn what has been to her a place to pause and compel her to walk, then they are typologically analogous to Lot, or, more pertinently, Lot, the dutiful executor of the divine command to restrict mourning in order to realize destiny, is like an imperious Indian. This hint echoes with the episode on the hill overlooking Lancaster the first night, where the Algonquians' derisive question—"What will you love English men still?" (326)—reprises the Puritan chastisement of inordinate fondness for destroyed pleasures when that fondness threatens to inhibit progression. At one point, she apostrophizes the Indians in terms Job used to rebuff those who would shame him out of his grief ("miserable comforters are ye all, as he said" [328]), likening them to a theology that would placate the mourner with an explication of the meaning of her suffering; and, shortly afterward she associates them with one of the heroes of Old Testament holy war: "Like Jehu, they marched on furious-ly . . ." (332). Because Rowlandson's emphasis is on the furious marching, her connection of the Indians with Jehu, anointed king of Israel by Elisha and charged with destroying the family of Ahab, seems to me to associate the destruction of her family, and of her attempt to mourn her family, with a specifically *zealous* violence, an identification that tends toward indicting divine legitimations of destruction, enforced forgetfulness, and compulsory marches toward a mandatory future. If, as Bercovitch contends, the saga of Israel was the American Puritans' preferred image for their own historical mission,[40] then Rowlandson's association of Jehu with the Algonquians amounts to an incrimination that travels first back to Jehu then forward again to the saints who saw themselves as *Israel redivivus*. This countertypological detour or innuendo implies that all of this violent sublimation of life in service to an exclusionary and unyielding socialization of the good is a form of savagery, rather than an overcoming of savagery. Having labored to emancipate her self-conception from the emblematic category of the selfish appetitiveness of the savage, she refills that category with new content, brutal and deaf demand, and throws it back upon the ideology that thought to indict her. Piety of this kind is an Indian, perhaps even the god of providence is an Indian: "Deut. 32. 39. *See now that I, even I am He, and there is no God with me; I kill and I Make Alive, I Wound and I Heal, Neither is There Any Can Deliver Out of My Hand"* (317); "Sometimes I met with favor, and sometimes with nothing but frowns" (340); "So unstable and like madmen they were." A hidden purpose, hidden not because it is ineffable but because it will not communicate with other subjective trajectories (*"there is no God with me"*), and, because uncommunicating, manifesting itself only as the force of pure whim; a purpose replete with power, adamant not only about its own movement but about the requirement that all must move

with it, and willing to do violence to ensure this conformity; a regime that
allows lulls that should never be mistaken for escape; if this is the horrid specter
of the Indian, then it is a specter from which both the god and society of Per
Amicum are *inadequately distinct.* That which has been the blank and blinding
force of nature, the ashes thrown in the eyes, reappears as the power of holy
resolve—the eyes recover after they have watered for a while.

Her hatred for the Indian *as master* is real, but it expresses more than that.
The last sentences of the narrative:

> It was but the other day that if I had had the world, I would have given it for my
> freedom, or to have been servant to a Christian. I have learned to look beyond
> present and smaller troubles, and to be quieted under them, as Moses said,
> Exodus 14. 13. *Stand still and see the salvation of the Lord.* (366)

The narrative manages a contrite denouement, a willing passivity, and how
could it not, given the closural requirements of her best intentions? But the
tranquility she assures us she has attained is rather flatly contradicted by the
insomniac anxiety she described on the previous page, a vigilance that is hardly
indifferent to the possibility of renewed trouble, that does not know whether it
will turn out to be small or not; and, looking closer, we notice that all she is
assuring us of is that her continuing contemplation of the events of salvation—
the captivity—takes precedence over the ordinary issues and domestic concerns
of her postredemption life. If her vital recollections of trauma have sufficient
force to "quiet" contemporary problems, to reduce them to the status of un-
threatening transactions, the present is therefore itself a time not of quiet, but
rather of lingering disquiet that dwarfs present business by contrast. Though
she is thus pragmatically accommodated to the redeemed life, she is not yet
reconciled on the deepest level to the new life's prices and its preconditions and
to what the rhetoric of salvation calls its essential equivalence with the old life.
The durable reserve of unprocessed fright expresses itself in the equivocation of
the second-to-last sentence: "I would have given it for my freedom, or to have
been servant to a Christian." Is the redemption an emancipation and a compensation, or a favorable exchange of masters that leaves the abjection of servitude
intact? *"Neither is There Any Can Deliver Out of My Hand."*

The tradition of Christian thought on spiritual liberty—or at least the strain
that strongly informs Puritanism—holds that freedom is gained through submission to divine law, a submission so heartfelt, thorough, and entire that the law is
experienced not as constraint or compulsion but simply as a kind of adequate
paraphrase of the Christian's intrinsic and spontaneous being. Winthrop:

> [Civil or federal liberty] may also be termed moral, in reference to the covenant
> between God and man, in the moral law, and the politic covenants and constitu-

tions, amongst men themselves. This liberty is the proper end and object of authority, and cannot subsist without it; and it is a liberty to that only which is good, just and honest . . . This liberty is maintained and exercised in a way of subjection to authority; it is of the same kind of liberty wherewith Christ hath made us free. The woman's own choice makes such a man her husband; yet being so chosen, he is her lord, and she is subject to him, yet in a way of liberty, not of bondage; and a true wife accounts her subjection her honor and freedom, and would not think her condition safe and free, but in subjection to her husband's authority. Such is the liberty of the church under Christ, her king and husband; his yoke is so easy and sweet to her as a bride's ornaments . . . [41]

Winthrop excludes certain considerations here for polemical reasons. He would not include, for instance, the Algonquian powwow among those "covenants and constitutions" that should elicit a Christian's consent. On the contrary, such political affiliations belong to his contrastive category, "natural liberty," the liberty of the beasts. The Christian's internally unanimous assent to *true law* would entitle and even require her to refuse any compliance with such simulacra: it would be right and proper to perceive false law as coercive force. Rowlandson's representations of Indian tyranny are therefore not controversial. But when she transfers attributes from that tyranny to Puritanism, she implicitly likens the world of redemption to a form of bondage that offers no avenue for affectional identification. When she *thinks twice,* equivocating over whether redemption is freedom or simply a kind of upgrade in servitude— better food and quarters, etc.—she is briefly and cryptically allowing her abiding alienation to infect the narrative's denouement, to signify the degree to which she is still wavering outside the circle of the English powwow, still ingeniously finding her way across a terrain governed by authority that does not correspond to/with her. The Christian is always subject to the divine law no matter what the condition of her heart, but experiencing that law as servitude rather than as freedom and fulfillment indicates an at least residual nonalignment between law and heart, and perhaps more, a law that is an unholy compulsion, and therefore not different in kind from the despotism out of the midst of which she was purchased. The fundamental equivalence of the two cultures I described as an effect of Rowlandson's portraits of Algonquian eccentricity here reappears as an essential equivalence between two orders of opportunistic enslavement, one of which is more comfortable and familiar than, but not therefore intrinsically different from, the other.

But if Rowlandson's resentment of external compulsion, whether that of the captors or that of the redeemers, arises from a desire to be free to mourn, this does not mean that mourning is quiet and easy, that it is not compulsory in its own way. The mourner, seeking to rest with the various preliminary memorial draft representations of the dead one, is continually pulled forward, each renewal of memory challenging the formulations that have been composed to that point and provoking the "second deaths" of revision. These second deaths are losses, not of the dead again, though they feel like that, but of the as-yet-insufficient ventures into adequate recall that have been constructed. Her sleeplessness, for instance, may be, in addition to a fear of what disaster might occur while she sleeps, a way of resisting the state of being helpless before the presentation of images in dreams, the unconscious playing the part of master compelling her to move on. Mourning, like Puritanism, is a law and an obligation—an abstract demand that precedes and transcends the intentions and wishes of its subject, a law that will be experienced as an onerous regulative burden that seems to earn no affirmation from the dead heart that wishes only to be left alone. Mourning is never a constitutive paraphrase of spontaneous desire, because the mourner's desire wishes to stop here rather than to move, to not have to undergo further encroachments of memory into the museum it has built and in which it has chosen to spend the days and nights that remain. Thus though the command to continue the work is internal to the mourner, it is external to her desire to control fright and save love; and if this sovereign command itself emanates from a desire to revive her life and future, such a life would be so incommensurate with the past, so *disloyal* to the dead, that the desire that aims for them can only be experienced as a cold compulsion alien to what is called the self, such an extrusion of the will to live seeming to be a way to avoid complicity in the revisionary infidelity of being herself still alive. Rowlandson's resentment of the shocks that always launch her from her sparse shelters—Lot, Jehu, the river, forced marches—is therefore figuratively overdetermined, directed against both what would coerce mourning and the coerciveness of mourning; and, insofar as theology seems, in the last sentence of the narrative, to present her with the opportunity to "Stand still *and see the salvation of the Lord,*" its coercion of mourning still has the allure of seeming to be an escape from mourning's own and proper coercions—to be a freedom. Mourning and theology are binary stars in rival orbits, each accusing the other of being a species of bondage, and the fact that their rival claims are not adjudicated in these final sentences suggests that mourning is not finished for the writer, precisely because *foreclosure* has considerable allure.

The pious equipoise of Rowlandson's last word, therefore, is forced, not fully complete, because it cannot resolve, subsume, or account for the durable anger of the remark concerning the Christian Master, but also because it cannot forswear the temptation of the Christian resolution, because it acts prematurely on the desire to close the case, to arrest mourning's forward motion, not only for the sake of being orthodox, but also for the sake of finding peace. I think that the most powerful evidence for the text's prematurity can be found in Rowlandson's consistently intense and pejorative scorn for the Praying

Indians, those converted by John Eliot and others to a profession of English culture and Congregationalist religion, some of whom defected to join Philip's cause, others of whom remained only to suffer harsh winter internment on Deer Island in Boston harbor and near-execution at the hands of those to whom they chose to remain loyal. Several ethnohistorians see the program of Indian conversion as an arm of the Puritan search for political sovereignty because its major purpose seems to have been the erasure of Algonquian cultural integrity and its power of resistant coherence.[42] Eliot's rhetoric rather wishfully declared that the Algonquians were blank slates ready to have Puritan wisdom written on them, but in point of fact whatever ready blankness there was was a result of procedural erasure rather than original readiness. Extensive and meticulous regulations enforced in "praying towns" such as Natick prohibited the use of body grease, the killing of lice between the teeth, the segregation of menstruating women from the group, ritual gaming, communalist architectures, vocally demonstrative mourning, and so on. The Algonquians, in other words, were to be *made into* blank slates through the practice of etiolated cultural disassembly, a disassembly that would function most smoothly if it were based on a correct identification of the compository foci of Algonquian culture. Those who sought supremacy through assimilation rather than through the force of war, therefore, came to know the Indian social structure and language with an ethnological depth that surpassed Rowlandson's, but for the general purpose of supplanting rather than of transacting business.

The project of conversion, like the project of war, is eradication, and it reveals succinctly the externally directed dialectical negation Perry Miller passed over. Rather than Miller's mystical negativity directed against its own institutionalization, Puritan New England was a society almost completely confident of the divinity of its objective institutionalization exerting the force of negation against what it posited as a pure antithesis, the crude or nonexistent form of its competitors' sociality. This is, as I argued in my second chapter, a difference of focus within Puritanism. Miller's decision that the passion of Roger Williams, for instance, represents the truth of American Puritanism is not demonstrably wrong on the theoretical level because he is speaking of what he considers the vital philosophical and affective center of value in American Puritanism, its durable legacy, rather than describing the central premises of American Puritanism's *actual* and historically dominant form. This form, as Miller argues, exerted itself *against* Williams and thereby revealed the internal contradiction between the negative transcendentalism of Puritanism's early oppositional phase and the theopolitical positivity of its institutional form. Miller's preference is clearly for the first of the two positions in this homegrown confrontation between Kierkegaard (Williams) and Hegel (Winthrop et al.), and he is erroneous only when he projects this preference onto the American Puritans in general, for example when he calls the jeremiads a lamentation over the loss of the purity of the negative in the act of institutionalization, rather than a lamentation over the fall from the splendid institutions accomplished by the first generation. For Miller, institutionalized Puritanism rather than its waning is the melancholy event, and he therefore pays relatively little attention to what is for him a rather distasteful, parasitical, and extrinsic form. But, though he therefore fails to capture Puritanism's own sense of institutionalization as an advance into historical actualization, his rare discussions of the political effect of institutionalization do not lack insight into the violence of negation directed against the other: "the theology of the covenant inevitably bred a contempt for lesser breeds outside the covenant, and no federal theologian, not even Eliot, could have treated the Indian way of life courteously enough to have written the *Key*." Williams' larger apprehension, however, is for Miller rooted not really in "courtesy," but rather in his skepticism toward Puritan society's sense of its own sufficient dogmatic accomplishment:

> But Williams could do it because he believed that in all human history there had been only one nation in covenant with Jehovah, only one chosen people, and that this unique federation had vanished from the earth on the morning of Christ's resurrection. From then until the end of the world, nations are no more than civil contrivances for getting along with a minimum of law and order. No country as a country—least of all New England—has a divine blessing peculiar unto itself, and consequently none can exercise such spiritual power in political affairs as did Israel. Thus Narragansett and Mohegan are intrinsically no worse than French or English. There might be more "civility" in Europe, but such amenities are relative.[43]

Thus though Miller's work does not *focus on* the sort of intercultural subjugation that concerns Francis Jennings, it is not incompatible with such study, and it frequently provides an analysis of the origins of violence that is more subtle than Jennings' often blunt (but not therefore incorrect) portraits. In fact, according to Miller, Williams' greater receptivity to the other derives precisely from his disaffection from the mainstream of American Puritanism: in a world from which the fusion of the divine and the social has utterly vanished, there are a variety of societies that, for all of their procedural differences, are ontologically equivalent in their common lacking of absolute foundations. Miller's Williams therefore resembles my Rowlandson (though for her the earth is a lacking of the precaptivity life rather than of Israel), a resemblance that makes her strident excoriations of the intrinsic perfidy of the Praying Indians all the more striking and perplexing.

In making such remarks Rowlandson comes close to the war-heightened jingoism of those who believed that the Indians could not be converted, that their professions of acceptance were the pretenses of saboteurs. Once again, we are in the presence of an ideological judgment that has some correspondence to fact. Even before the war, according to Salisbury, the conversion of the Indians enjoyed at best modest success because the Puritans failed to realize how deeply culture informs subjectivity, and how difficult erasure is without psychosis. Where they hoped to *replace* they often only *overlaid,* and "backsliding" was common in the praying towns, especially among the members of tribes such as the Nipmucks that had been less thoroughly decimated by English germs, commerce, and war than had the Massachusetts. Defection was in large measure fueled by Indian funerary practices, which constituted a reserve of culture: Salisbury agrees with Axtell that Algonquian mourning rituals, already culturally central before the English invasion, reached still more elaborate expression in response to the invasion. And the liability to defection was if anything enhanced by the segregation of the Indians in the towns. After partial deracination, they were not then integrated into Puritan society, and so were left suspended in a nowhere, an interregnum that could only encourage clarification by movement back where movement toward was blocked: "While encouraging the Indians to reject their own culture and to emulate the English, [Puritanism] denied the possibility of either assimilation or revitalization. The converts were left suspended between two cultures, with their own cultural expression carefully controlled from without."[44] Even among those who did not defect, the persistence of the parent culture often expressed itself in a revisionary eclecticism, in the assimilation of items of white culture into the context of red culture (like Rowlandson's master's heterogeneous apparel), rather than vice versa. Less precise and obsessed with homogeneous purity than the Puritans, the Algonquians included the English god as a new and impressively powerful member of a pantheon, or joined enthusiastically in the portions of Puritan liturgy that preserved a dwindled public ritualism, such as group singing. Whereas the Puritan attempt to assimilate the Indians failed for the reasons Salisbury describes, Indian attempts to assimilate whites during the course of the eighteenth century would, as Axtell contends, prove disturbingly successful,[45] perhaps because of a greater collective competence for inclusive eclecticism, a competence that would, by some political and aesthetic standards, suggest the superiority of Indian culture despite its vulnerability to single-minded assault. Hybrid formations such as those that sprang up in the praying towns, like the defections, though less drastically, revealed to the Puritans the inadequacy of their assimilative technique, a perception that emerged, after ideological garbling, as the doctrine of the fundamental intransigence or intractability of Indian nature. Those Puritans who demanded that the Praying Indians be interned or executed, therefore, operated from a correct appraisal of the likely outcome of the attempts to convert.

It is therefore not surprising that the majority of the English were either indifferent or hostile to the program of conversion, that those Praying Indians who remained politically loyal were treated like the politically loyal Japanese-Americans during World War II, and that conversion attempts largely ceased after the war. Rowlandson's vilifications are far more typical of English vindictiveness than are Increase Mather's exhortations to revive the cause of conversion, which seem to me to result from a fideistic commitment to the programs of the first generation, especially those of Richard Mather, which were themselves in large measure the result of a desire to legitimate the Congregationalist errand in the eyes of a suspicious home government, rather than of a theoretically consistent concern for the souls of the red. Though Mather's commitment can in this way be explained away, and though we might attribute Rowlandson's opinions to a desire to *épater les Mather,* it is nevertheless disturbing, especially to me at this late point in my argument, to have Rowlandson affirming an ugly general sentiment to which Increase Mather takes exception: as Rowlandson knew, such abrupt reversals are *not a pretty sight.* Her conformity with public opinion is shocking because it runs against the grain of her hesitation about heartfelt accord with the divinization of Puritan social and political policies and her hesitations about deploying the emblem of Indian apostasy. Whereas the individual Indians who were directly responsible for the death of Sarah and for the miseries of her captivity are exempted from the type and permitted to appear in the secular register of character portraiture, a subgroup within the Indian whole is subjected to a categorical denunciation despite the fact that their commitment to Philip's cause was much more equivocal than was that of the rest of the Indian whole, despite the fact that she knew only a few of the eleven hundred or so Praying Indians during the captivity, others not at all. The intensity and univocality of these diatribes, and their impermeability with respect to the hesitations that structure the text outside their area, constitute a black space in the text's crepuscular/matinal gray, a sealed atmosphere or crypt of traumatized symbolization, something (not yet) approachable.

A fixation of thought, therefore, a device meant to be forcibly clarifying in desperate circumstances where clarity does not seem to be arising in the ordinary course of things: martial law, revealing exactly the fact of the text's prematurity and foreclosure with respect to its undone work. There are two things to note about Rowlandson's deprecations of the Praying Indians: first, because her invective is not directed against all the Algonquians remaining alive at the end of the war, not even against those who were cruel to her and to her family in particular, the object of her ire is not wartime deeds or past military opposition, but rather the potential *future* perfidy of those living Algonquians who do not merely submit to English superiority but who also *pretend* to affirm the values of the rejuvenated Puritan regime; and second, this conclusion that the Praying

Indians are without a doubt pretenders reduces all potential ambiguities of commitment—indecision between cultures, hybridism, expedient bicultural-ism, intercultural anomie—to an unequivocal intransigent redness overlaid by a cynical and dangerous posture of whiteness. Her hatred is directed not at the fact of past Indian violence but at a present and future unclarity clouding the time of redemption, and it arises from a desire that the true be forcibly divided from the feigned, in order *to prevent misguided trust,* a version of which anxiety Philip himself confessed before the war in a conversation with several Rhode Island Quakers, in the course of which he remarked that the Indians "had a great Fear to have any of their Indians should be called or forced to be Christian Indians. They said that such were in everything more mischievous, only Dissemblers, and then the English made them not subject to their Kings, and by their lying to wrong their Kings."[46]

In the early pages of the narrative, pejorative commentary on the Praying Indians is only a subordinate part of the general indictment by emblem: "little do many think what is the savageness and brutishness of this barbarous enemy, aye even those that seem to profess more than others among them . . ." (326). Later, however, her ire turns specifically against posturing itself, rather than primarily against what the posture conceals:

> Towards night, I gathered me some sticks for my own comfort, that I might not lie a-cold: but when we came to lie down they bade me go out, and lie somewhere else, for they had company (they said) come in more than their own: I told them, I could not tell where to go, they bade me look; I told them, if I went to another wigwam they would be angry, and send me home again. Then one of the company drew his sword, and told me he would run me through if I didn't go presently. Then I was fain to stoop to this rude fellow, and to go out into the night, I knew not whither. Mine eyes have seen that fellow afterwards walking up and down in Boston, under the appearance of a friendly Indian, and several others of the like cut. (341)

As her conviction that she can predict what would happen should she go to another wigwam suggests, Rowlandson considers this episode of cold unhous-ing to be almost tediously familiar. The rude fellow is singled out, therefore, not because of his cruelty, which he shares with the others, but because he disguises it after the war and receives hospitality he does not deserve. When she mentions "others of the like cut," she reveals that the tenor of the anecdote concerns those who pretend, rather than those who threw her out that night. If pretense continues to flourish, then the boundary that was breached in the attack on Lancaster and the other towns of the periphery, the boundary be-tween terror and home, has not been resecured. The comfortable presence of the rude fellow and others of his ilk in Boston, at the center, divulges the information that victory has not drawn a line between cruelty there and hospitality here with sufficient success: the war is not over, but has instead gone underground. By attempting to use the knowledge gained during the captivity to identify and expose residual pretense, Rowlandson is trying to finish the war, to close what is thought to be closed but is in fact not. Hence the need to indict those of the "like cut," a need that later blossoms into a poisonous philippic:

> There was another Praying Indian, who told me he had a brother, that would not eat horse; his conscience was so tender and scrupulous (though large as hell, for the destruction of poor Christians). Then he said, he read that scripture to him, 2 Kings, 6. 25. *There was a famine in Samaria, and behold they besieged it, until an ass's head was sold for fourscore pieces of silver, and the fourth part of a kab of dove's dung, for five pieces of silver.* He expounded this place to his brother, and showed him that it was lawful to eat that in a famine which is not at another time. And now, says he, he will eat horse with any of them all. There was another Praying Indian, who, when he had done all of the mischief that he could, betrayed his own father into the English hands, thereby to purchase his own life. Another Praying Indian was at Sudbury fight, so wicked and cruel, as to wear a string about his neck, strung with Christians' fingers. Another Praying Indian, when they went to Sudbury fight, went with them, and his squaw also with them, with her papoose at her back . . . (352–53)

Beginning with an episode that arises in the course of narration, Rowlandson digresses with a certain tenacity into iterative citation, identifying with a liturgical regularity those who may subsequently have escaped correct perception and even now perhaps be walking the streets of Boston.[47] Her hunt for the hypocrites is unlike the hunt for Philip because her concern is not with the magnitude of what is hidden but with the fact of hiding: if the deeds denounced above are largely unremarkable items in the catalog of the enemies' cruelties, their perpetrators are worthy of note because, unlike, say, Philip or Weetamoo, they do not display their truth. The task in such passages is to *mark* them, to rehabilitate the line.

The issue in these passages is therefore not the nature of the Indian but the nature of the war's denouement: killing and captivity have ceased, houses and towns have been built or rebuilt, days of thanksgiving have been proclaimed and celebrated, all the living members of the families have been brought back together—but in the place of the dead one or it, there are two strangers who are new at the festivity of the table. First, there is anxiety, fear of fright, a need to foresee the sort of disaster that vigilance failed to foresee or forestall last time:

> On the tenth of February 1675, came the Indians with great numbers upon Lan-
> caster: Their first coming was about sun-rising; hearing the noise of some guns,
> we looked out; several houses were burning, and the smoke ascending to heaven
> . . . We had six stout dogs belonging to our garrison, but none of them would stir,
> though another time, if any Indian had come to the door, they were ready to fly
> upon him and tear him down. The Lord hereby would make us the more to
> acknowledge his hand, and to see that our help is always in him. (323, 324)

Whereas fear precedes an event, fright always follows: "we looked out; several
houses were burning . . ." Fright is condemned to begin *too late, it already has
happened.* Anxiety tries to transcend this awful suddenness and belatedness
with the help of a general and ubiquitous vigilance that does not repose trust in
unreliable aids—don't think that because the dogs aren't barking tonight that
. . . If February 10, 1676 (new dating), indelibly associated waking up after
sunrise with the temporality of fright, it is no surprise that she lies awake at
night, mentally testing all the locks on all the points of entry, trying to remember any unsecured apertures. Her sleeplessness may be taken as *contrite* vigilance, as lingering doubts about herself that prove her humility, her lack of
arrogance concerning her holiness, and Per Amicum and others may have read
the confession of insomnia this way.[48] We should notice, however, that she lies
awake when "all are fast about me" (365): if her anxiety is simply doctrinal
correctness, then either she is overscrupulous or the others remain in pride, in
which case they will bring on renewed attack even if she does not. However, I do
not think that the fastidiousness of self-doubt accounts fully for her sleeplessness, because the next passage shows her unpersuaded by the efficacy of
contrition, about its power to secure things:

> I have seen the extreme vanity of this world: one hour I have been in health, and
> wealth, wanting nothing: but the next hour in sickness and wounds, and death,
> having nothing but sorrow and affliction. (365)

This allusion to the world's vanity suggests that what keeps her awake at night
is not her own sin but rather the world's proclivity to jump its groove in
spontaneous and sudden reversal—the matter of fright. Such skepticism jeop-
ardizes the chances for renewed affectional satisfaction after the redemption
because it originates in the supposition that all bonds will be undone *incessantly,* with only brief interludes, regardless of preventive moral labor—including quitting smoking, diligent Sabbaths, and sleepless nights. But, though the
price of skepticism is reunion, the gain would be the transcendence of fright
through alert fear, and the corollary disappearance of anxiety. If she assumes
that the reversals of disaster and redemption and disaster and redemption are an

inevitable aspect of the world's circulation of event, she will not experience them as frightening interruptions of what she has unwisely come to believe to be the ordinary: a sparse and melancholy world, but a *world* nevertheless, rather than an unprogressing succession of naive worlds uncontrollably demolished without warning; a prolongation beyond the quotation mark of one of the narrative's epigraphs, "I kill and I make alive again," and I kill again, and I make alive again . . . As I argued in Chapter 3, I do not believe that Rowlandson has achieved such skepticism, because the sleeplessness bespeaks continuing fear of fright rather than a demystified accommodation to vicissitude. Skepticism is something only aimed for here. Control is at this moment more desirable than pleasure: skepticism, were it within range, would sacrifice happiness to gain freedom from fright—a bargain, it seems to a still-grieving self, because the better part of happiness lies back in the past anyway. The vessel is secured at the cost of its content.

But skepticism directed toward a specific area of the world, the Praying Indians, rather than toward the world as a whole, offers the comfort of fear, of having an object in view *before* the arrival of disaster, the comfort of transcending fright without having to pay the price of general affectional disengagement. If one zone of the world is designated the point of reversal's entry, then one knows where to look, and the other zones can be thought of as secure. As with Ahab, the desire to belong to a competent world converts a view of general vicissitude into a compulsive attention to an area of demarcated danger and an insistence that the truth of ambiguity is pretense, malignity cloaking itself in benign atmospheres. If in this way Rowlandson tries to force reengagement, she does so by employing the Praying Indian as symbol of all that she suspects about the font of future pain, including perhaps a suspicion that the solicitous religiosity of the English is as false and agile as the chain of reasoning whereby the Praying Indian persuaded his brother to eat horse. Such sophistical scripturalism has its corollary in being instructed to accept (ingest) typological representation as a sufficient view of the dead it. The tropological means for this symbolization is synecdoche, part of the world's potential for reversal standing in for all of the world's potential for reversal. This act of symbolization, however, unlike the figuration of the Indian as demon, conceals itself: whereas Increase Mather was eager to point out the correspondences between Algonquian life and the corruptions of the English, Rowlandson's denunciation of the Praying Indian is designed to make him absorb within himself all of the world's vanity, the rest of the world then being cleansed, distinct from him, without pretense, at peace. This sort of synecdochic localization—fetishism or scapegoating—does not expand outward from the vehicle to illustrate the tenor, but on the contrary imports the tenor's trait into the vehicle, declares the vehicle to be the sole embodiment of the tenor, and denies the figural bridge between the two, thereby purging the tenor. Such a sanitary project requires a scrupulous quarantining of the goat, ostensibly because he might infect, but really because resemblances might be discovered. This need to sequester may explain why Rowlandson's diatribes are so tonally dissevered from the general ambience of the narrative, their ferocity and vigor indexing the intensity of her desire to cleanse the world, and, therefore, by denegation, her conviction that despite the victory over Philip the world is not yet clean. The sullying force of sudden surprise is still at play across the face of the earth, reversals are still imminent, including the memories that mourning will present to her, compelling her to relinquish whatever provisional representations of the dead she has to this point constructed, compelling her yet again to emerge from the wigwam to see what is there: "When all are fast about me, and no eye open, but His who ever waketh, my thoughts are upon things past, upon the awful dispensation of the Lord toward us . . ." (365)

But if the world offers fair pretense to her, so too does she to it, in the very best intentions that are one aspect of her whole story. Guilt sits at the table with fright at Sarah's place, not just guilt for a sin that once was and that precipitated the disaster, but the guilt of an abiding fracture in the heart. If the paragraph on vanity suggests that her sleeplessness cannot be assigned solely to worry over her own sin, that mistrust of the world is present, the worry over sin is also present. The two are not mutually exclusive, because Per Amicum says sin brings on reversal, and because her own wavering allegiance to the culture of redemption, like the wavering and stumbling of the man outside the circle of the powwow, is a key part of the world's promiscuous reversibility. She may very well be frightened by herself. If so, then the passages that express anxiety and harsh skepticism indicate a split self, one that worries, and one that is worried over, the latter a furtive specter, the saboteur or underground. Are the diatribes against the Praying Indians even now walking freely through Boston an exculpatory projection of her own waywardness as well as a scapegoating of the world's waywardness with respect to human desire? Such a projection would be the most desperate manifestation of the force that propels Rowlandson's best intentions, the desire for a reintegration that, precisely because it is so fervently longed for, is not present, a forcible closure secured by a self-righteous dedication to detecting and exposing the external duplicity of the Indian who prays. Closure secured this way proves that neither Rowlandson nor her narrative is synonymous with the best intentions, that the best intentions can be taken as the whole story only by burying an early American Antigone alive, rather than by raising experience into a lucidity without the shadow cast by the dead it. It is still an *awful morning*. Whether anxiety and guilt presage a renewal of affliction or not, for *we who read* they flag the stumbling eloquence of the pillar, tears long gone but not without a trace—the salt:

Lot's wife was salt and barren, because she was full of loss and mourning, and looked back. But here rare flowers would gleam in her hair, and on her breast, and in her hands, and there would be children all around her, to love and marvel at her for her beauty, and to laugh at her extravagant adornments, as if they had set the flowers in her hair and thrown down all the flowers at her feet, and they would forgive her, eagerly and lavishly, for turning away, though she never asked to be forgiven. Though her hands were ice and did not touch them, she would be more than mother to them, she so calm, so still, and they such wild and orphan things.[49]

5

Afterword: Rowlandson's Future

Rowlandson's narrative was probably written during the two years following the redemption, in 1677 or 1678. In November of 1678, her husband, Joseph, died, and his final sermon, *The Possibility of God's Forsaking a People,* was published as an appendix to the first edition of his godforsaken wife's book, in 1682. Did the publication of the manuscript wait five years until its supporters, such as Per Amicum, found what they took to be its message politically useful or comfortable to other projects? To what degree does the Rowlandson of 1682 maintain the desires and resistances she voiced in 1677–78? Kathryn Zabelle Derounian implies that the time between composition and publication may have been sufficient for Rowlandson to have recovered:

> I contend that *during and immediately after* her captivity, Rowlandson suffered from psychological trauma similar to what we now term the "survivor syndrome," but that she tried to minimize the symptoms to conform to the Puritan doctrine of providential affliction. In writing her captivity account, Rowlandson therefore performed a personal and public service. Articulating her experience was therapeutic (personal) because she confronted her past journey outside conventional society, yet it was also devotional (public) because she documented her present reentry into it. (Italics added)[1]

But how can we do more than hope (or fear, as the case may be) that such reintegrations came to pass, in five years' time or longer? What is the schedule of mourning?

Though at the end of her narrative Rowlandson's desire for resolution is still open, this uncompletedness is not entirely without precedent in her society's discourse, because there is a Puritan genre for which the prematurity of the ending is decorous and appropriate rather than aberrant: the preparatory meditation, which reached its aesthetic apex in Edward Taylor's poetry. Taylor's poetic voice echoes through the vacuum of an anomalous psychic time, the time of the no-longer and the not-yet of fulfillment, of types and emblems mangled, not fully convergent with divinity, an interlude in divine being during which Taylor readies himself for what he hopes but is not sure will arrive again. More directly than Rowlandson, Taylor draws his voice from a more or less original wrinkle that New England theologians introduced into what Edmund Morgan calls "the morphology of conversion."[2] In their concern to steer a course between Pelagianism and Arminianism on the one hand and antinomianism on the other, according to Norman Pettit, the American Puritan morphologists of conversion, most prominently Thomas Hooker, Thomas Shepard, and Peter Bulkeley, contended that, though the will could not summon the event of grace, which is something that happens only unaccountably and unpredictably if at all, it can nevertheless with some success clear away the obstacles and blocks to receiving the event that makes its own moment, should it at some future time do so. As Pettit puts it,

> Those who preached preparation and believed it to be consistent with predestination were concerned with the problem of a possible period in time before conversion that was neither wholly the work of the Law nor entirely beyond man's control. Although natural man, under the Law, did not have the power to make the Gospel effectual or to choose Christ out of the power of his nature, he could respond to the Law in a gradual way and need not be constrained all at once. By preparation they meant a period of prolonged introspective meditation and self-analysis in the light of God's revealed Word. In this process, man first examined the evils of his sins, repented for those sins, and then turned to God for salvation. From conviction of conscience, the soul moved through a series of interior stages, always centered on self-examination, which in turn were intended to arouse a longing for grace.[3]

The social valence of the notion of preparation, its contribution to Puritanism's legitimacy, is ambiguous. On the one hand, it defined resistance to the infusion of an imposed order of representation as evil to be systematically uprooted, it facilitated the demand for emulation of exemplary types by allowing the minister to delineate concretely and specifically defined patterns for the chronology of saintliness, and, in Shepard's case in particular, it provided a model with which to decide the worth of individual experience as recalled in the testimonies of congregational applicants—a concrete criterion for deciding what kind of subjectivity merited social inclusion. But, on the other hand, it sponsored patience and hope in a time of waiting and misery after the comfort of a way of life had been destroyed, it reassured those who were troubled that the fact that they had not yet found peace did not necessarily mean that they were defective, it prompted thought and emotional work in the interest of a new future, and the at-least-perfunctory reminder of the mystery of grace's arrival reduced regulations to the level of suggestions.

Preparing is therefore in its second aspect not unlike mourning, which is also, to echo Pettit's phrasing, concerned with the problem of a possible period in time before a restoration of peace; which lives under an inability to make a new life effectual immediately by force of resolve; which is also a period of prolonged introspective meditation and self-analysis, a movement through a series of interior stages, always centered on the examination of self as it was shaped through its involvement with the dead, which in turn arouses a longing desire for grace. It may be that the near-homology between preparation and mourning means that preparation was Puritanism's most alert approach to the power it wished to appropriate (which would account for the double legacy of control and perceptive solicitousness), but the closer the resemblance between the simulacrum and the interdicted procedure of mourning, the more likely a misfire in the strategy of sublimation. Rather than absorbing the energy of subterranean grief, a proximate and delicate restatement of grief's implicit logic could end by pointing the way to exactly the kind of thought it was designed to prevent. The better the paraphrase, the closer it is to being simply a restatement from which all opportune revision is absent.

But, though preparation may in this way bring her too close to mourning, the last step still belongs to Rowlandson, whose narrative, if it is a preparatory meditation, is a creative transformation of the genre, akin to her counter-typology: once again, her writing is a zone that bends genre, stretches it in unprecedented ways, puts it to uses for which it was not designed. If the mournful narrative shares certain formal resemblances to the chronology of subjectivity outlined in the notion of preparation, it pares away the values affixed to that model of consciousness by theorists such as Shepard. Prolonged introspective meditation and self-analysis are for Rowlandson performed not in the light of God's revealed Word, but rather in the odd light of memory's struggle to construct a specific *was* that will be revealed at the end of the struggle. The revealed Word of theology is for Rowlandson precisely one of the obstacles to revival that her preparation has to clear away, and the grace that is longed for is not the plenitude posited by a representational order whose premise is that nothing has really vanished, or any plenitude for that matter, but a specific and personally adequate knowledge of what is gone and what is left, of what kind of crater the self and its world are, of the line between the dead and the strangers who remain in the place of the dead. Insofar as the unrest, anxiety, and unpersuasive closures that surround the ending of the narrative show that Rowlandson is at that moment still in mourning, her narrative is a preparatory meditation rather than an account of completed conversion, a removing of obstacles from the path to a still-enigmatic and indescribable denouement—but a preparatory meditation that exerts itself against the ideology that the genre of the preparatory meditation was designed to reinforce. Any genre predicated on a structure of transformative reversal in self-conception can in this way have its points of commencement and conclusion reversed: the movement toward conformity with canonical value can become a movement away, what was taken to have been the goal of an aversive motion of self-emancipation instead becoming the point of departure. Per Amicum was correct in his suspicion that the devices in the Puritan arsenal can, in the wrong hands and sometimes despite the best intentions, become a potent enemy: his fear presciently foreshadows the complex and volatile part that Protestantism has played in American political and social history. By laying out a model for grueling and minute emancipation, Puritanism cuts a path out of its own woods, assisting Rowlandson to see that what has been thought good corn and peas are in fact weeds that must be cut away to make a clearing in which anomalous or mutant instances of grace (a curtain moving in the breeze, rather than an arrow or rock coming through the window next to it) may one day appear.

In a 1985 essay, David L. Greene argues that Rowlandson did not die sometime during the decade after the redemption as is commonly assumed. Rather, Greene contends, her *name* vanished: her husband having died in 1678, shortly after the redemption, and therefore perhaps already among the dead when she wrote of their reunion and shared grief, she married Captain Samuel Talcott, who had been an assistant administrator of Joseph Rowlandson's estate, in 1679. Talcott died in 1691, and Mary White Rowlandson Talcott did not marry again before her death in 1710 at the rather extraordinary age of between seventy-two and seventy-five.

As Greene notes, the new information adds little to our knowledge of her life after the war that engulfed her, though the fact of her having remarried and lived so long does confirm the tenacious vitality she confesses so uncomfortably in the narrative. There is, however, an intriguing moment, a courtroom episode, the documents from which exude the inadvertent mysteriousness or frustrating partiality, the focus on what for us is *not* the essence of the event, that characterizes the genre of legal writing. Rowlandson's son, Joseph, taken captive by the Algonquians shortly before his fourteenth birthday, confined apart from his mother, though as you will recall, short visits were permitted during which they shared grief and he announced his noble sympathy for his father's grief, redeemed several weeks after his mother, was arrested in 1707, when he was fifty-five:

> According to the Hartford County Court Records . . . a man claiming to be Nathaniel Wilson appeared in September 1707 before the Hartford County Court

and alleged that in June 1702 his brothers-in-law, Joseph Rowlandson and David Jesse, had gotten him drunk in Boston and put him on a ship to Virginia, where he was sold as a servant. As a Bostonian, David Jesse was outside the court's jurisdiction, but Joseph Rowlandson was arrested. Although he denied the charge, the court considered him "Strongly Suspected to have been privy & Accessary to the transporting the said Nathaniel Wilson to Virginia and Selling of him there . . . ," and the court bound him to answer further to the complaint.[4]

Greene suggests that Joseph Rowlandson stood to acquire a considerable sum by way of his wife, Hannah Wilson Rowlandson, sister of Jesse's wife, should Nathaniel Wilson have been judged dead. This suspicion is complicated, however, Greene contends, by the fact that, eleven years after Wilson's return, Joseph King, now husband to Jesse's widow, claimed that the supposed revenant was not Wilson at all but an imposter, "one Joseph Clements, an utter stranger." Why did it take eleven years to discover this? Was this yet another attempt to defraud Wilson by obliviating him, this time with the aid of a sister willing to say he was not who he was? Shortly after his putative return from Virginia, the putative Wilson had been declared insane and his property "placed in the hands of the Hartford selectmen to be expended for his care." Perhaps, Greene speculates, the assertion that Wilson was not Wilson was a ploy to take over the money and see to his care themselves. The case was decided, then reversed, and then reversed again in the county court, whereupon it went to the Connecticut General Assembly, which concluded that "'the evidence on both sides is unusually strong and peremptory to the degree that certain truth is not likely to be gained by human testimony.' One can only agree with the Assembly that in this case 'the overtures of providence were strange, unheard of and unaccountable.' The mystery has never been solved."[5]

Though the Assembly's remarks concerning truth, testimony, and the strange overtures of providence would make good epigraphs for Rowlandson's narrative, she had died by the time of the imbroglio over the insane man who was not Wilson, and thus could not have savored their resonances. She was, however, not only alive at the time of the earlier charges against her son, but present in the court. Greene introduces the knotted thread of the Wilson story because the 1707 document mentions that Joseph Rowlandson's mother, Mary Talcott of Wethersfield, Connecticut, appeared in court to co-guarantee fifty pounds he had posted as bail, a fact that seems to prove that Mary Talcott was Mary Rowlandson. But for us the resolution of the mystery of her identity introduces another mystery deeper and more durable than the mystery of the man who was not Wilson, the mystery of what the mother thought about what she must at least have feared that her son had done, about the resurrection of violent and sudden captivity, the destruction of a person's life and identity, the reduction of a person to a price, this time with the former captive presiding as captor in a drama of his own devising. From the perspective of the narrative, the motive for the crime of which the son was accused dwindles in interest before the manner he was accused of having chosen, abduction without appeal, the careful arrangement of a pure vanishing. Did he do it? Whose idea was it, his or Jesse's? If his, what prompted him to devise *this* way of defrauding Wilson? What must she have thought?

> Whereas Nathanael Wilson of Hartford, hath been absent and Missing from his propper home and place of Abode at Said Hartford, for Severall years last past and now Vizt. on the first day of this Instant Month of September is returned to Hartford again, and appeared before this Court, and made Information and Complaint. That Whereas he the Said Nathanael Wilson Sometime in or about the Month of June -----"----- Anno: 1702, being at Boston in New England, in Company with his two brothers in Law, Vizt. Joseph Rowlandson of Wethersfield, and David Jesse of Boston, amongst other persons, was by them perswaded to drink Strong drink and Liquors until he was quite drunk and bereved of his Senses, and that while he was So drunk and Senseless the Said Joseph Rowlandson and David Jesse did Convey him Said Nathanael Wilson or cause him to be conveyed on board a Ship or Vessel then bound from Boston aforesaid to Virginia, and that he was transported in the Said vessel to Virginia, and there Sold a Servant for Several years by Some person or persons belonging to the Said Vessel, whose names he knows not, And that haveing lately been set at Liberty, he is now returned home again . . . [6]

> Hearing that my son was come to this place, I went to see him, and found him lying flat upon the ground: I asked him how he could sleep so? He answered me, that he was not asleep, but at prayer; and lay so, that they might not observe what he was doing. I pray God he may remember these things now he is returned in safety. (337)

Those who cannot sleep cannot be truly awake but remain in dreams throughout the day. What is the schedule?

> . . . but lying down, the water run out of my eyes, and carried the dirt with it, that by the morning, I recovered my sight again. (342)

Notes

Index

Notes

1. Introduction

1. Mary White Rowlandson, *The Sovereignty and Goodness of God, together with the Faithfulness of His Promises Displayed; Being a Narrative of the Captivity and restoration of Mrs. Mary Rowlandson, Commended by her to all that Desire to Know the Lord's Doings to, and Dealings with Her. Especially to her Dear Children and Relations* (Cambridge: Samuel Green, 1682), rpt. in *So Dreadfull a Judgment: Puritan Responses to King Philip's War, 1676–1677* ed. Richard Slotkin and James K. Folsom (Middletown, Conn.: Wesleyan University Press, 1978), p. 321. Henceforth, all quotations from Rowlandson's narrative will be cited in parentheses, as will various quotations from the editors' introductory essays. I have chosen to use Slotkin and Folsom's edition because it is currently the most commonly available and because it contains extensive commentary and notes. My readers might also wish to refer to the notes in the edition of Rowlandson's narrative included in *Puritans among the Indians: Accounts of Captivity and Redemption, 1676–1724,* ed. Alden T. Vaughan and Edward W. Clark (Cambridge: Harvard University Press, 1981), pp. 29–76.

2. Robert K. Diebold, "Mary Rowlandson," in *American Writers before 1800: A Biographical and Critical Dictionary,* ed. James A. Levernier and Douglas R. Wilmes, Q–Z, pp. 1245–47. See also Diebold's article on Joseph Rowlandson, immediately preceding. For a detailed history of the text, see Kathryn Zabelle Derounian, "The Publication Promotion, and Distribution of Mary White Rowlandson's Captivity Narrative in the Seventeenth Century," *Early American Literature,* 23.3 (1988), 239–61.

3. An impossible *if,* since the narrative includes remarks on her redemption and the victory, but an *if* that I nonetheless invite my reader to contemplate because Philip's culture was obliviated with nearly this degree of thoroughness.

4. For fuller accounts of the war and its context and consequences, see *So Dreadfull a Judgment,* pp. 3–35 (Slotkin and Folsom have compiled a useful chronology that appears on pp. 46–52); Douglas Edward Leach, *Flintlock and Tomahawk: New England in King Philip's War* (New York: Norton, 1966); Francis Jennings, *The Invasion of America: Indians, Colonialism, and the Cant of Conquest* (New York: Norton, 1976); and Stephen Saunders Webb, *1676: The End of American Independence* (Cambridge: Harvard University Press, 1985), pp. 221–44.

5. Webb, *1676,* pp. 221–44.

6. Derounian, "Publication, Promotion, and Distribution," pp. 240–41; Increase Mather, *An Essay For the Recording of Illustrious Providences* (Boston: Samuel Green, 1684), pp. 39–57.

7. On this point, I am indebted to Carolyn Porter, "Are We Being Historical Yet?" in

The States of "Theory": History, Art, and Critical Discourse (New York: Columbia University Press, 1989), pp. 27–62.

8. Georg Lukács, *Studies in European Realism* (New York: Grosset & Dunlap, 1964), pp. 11, 12, 21, 22.

9. Ibid., pp. 7, 1.

10. Paul de Man, *Blindness and Insight: Essays in the Rhetoric of Contemporary Criticism* (Minneapolis: University of Minnesota Press, 1983), pp. 51–59.

11. Boris Tomashevsky, "Thematics," in *Russian Formalist Criticism: Four Essays,* ed. and trans. Lee T. Lemon and Marion J. Reis (Lincoln: University of Nebraska Press, 1965), pp. 80–82.

2. The Society of the Example

1. Samuel Willard, THE HIGH ESTEEM Which God hath of the Death of his SAINTS. As it was Delivered in a SERMON Preached October 7, 1683. Occasioned by the Death of the Worshipful John Hull Esq: Who Deceased October 1, 1683 (Boston: Samuel Green, 1683), in *New England Funeral Sermons,* Vol. 4 of *The Puritan Sermon in America, 1630–1750,* ed. and introduced by Ronald A.Bosco (Delmar, N.Y.: Scholar's Facsimiles and Reprints, 1978), p. 16.

2. Sandra Gilbert and Susan Gubar, *The Madwoman in the Attic: The Woman Writer and the Nineteenth-Century Literary Imagination* (New Haven: Yale University Press, 1979), p. 55.

3. Wendy Martin, *An American Triptych: Anne Bradstreet, Emily Dickinson, Adrienne Rich* (Chapel Hill: University of North Carolina Press, 1984), pp. 58–59.

4. Anne Bradstreet, *Works in Prose and Verse,* ed. John Harvard Ellis (Gloucester, Mass.: Peter Smith, 1962), pp. 100–102.

5. See Karen Sanchez-Eppler, "Bodily Bonds: The Intersecting Rhetorics of Feminism and Abolition," *Representations,* 24 (Fall 1988), 34–35, and Louis A. Renza, *"A White Heron" and the Question of Minor Literature* (Madison: University of Wisconsin Press, 1984).

6. Slotkin and Folsom report that the pseudonymous author of the preface calls himself "Ter Amicam," "thy threefold friend." According to Kathryn Zabelle Derounian, however, he calls himself "Per Amicam" ("For a Friend") or "Per Amicum" ("By a Friend"). "The Publication, Promotion, and Distribution of Mary White Rowlandson's Captivity Narrative in the Seventeenth Century," *Early American Literature,* 23.3 (1988), 240. The difference may derive from different editions, or from different typefaces.

7. Derounian, "Publication, Promotion, and Distribution," p. 249.

8. Here and at several subsequent points in my argument, I draw on an unpublished essay by Anne Lackey, "The A and the Public Eye." Lackey contends that Hester Prynne decides to return to her scene of trial at the end of *The Scarlet Letter* because the stigma of the letter brought her from social nonexistence into the harsh light of public actuality, from invisibility into perceptible historical existence, however repellant that mode of existence is. For the woman in Puritan society, according to Lackey's reading, conspicuous ostracization is the sole and ineluctable avenue to being, a dilemma demonstrated

by the fact that virtually the only public woman's words we have from the Puritan period are Anne Hutchinson's. Hester's acceptance of the letter, therefore, is not simply a matter of contrition or masochism, but rather it stems from her acknowledgment of the narrow conditions under which her society is willing to allow her to become visible and from her determination to accept those conditions in hopes of being able to use that visibility to some historically positive end. Rowlandson says little about what her celebrity means to her, but all of her remarks about having been *singled out* probably carry with them a premonition that she will not soon recede into the background she inhabited before the attack.

9. This idea began in a conversation I had with Arthur Riss.

10. A glance below will reveal some long notes. In these notes, I attempt to situate the theory of mourning I derive from Hegel with respect to other theories of mourning and other readings of Hegel. These notes detail the axioms of my argument, rather than advancing it toward Rowlandson's narrative. I have therefore put these deliberations over axioms in notes to make them available to those who wish to turn aside without trying the patience of those who wish to move on to Rowlandson without digression in the body of my text.

11. G. W. F. Hegel, *The Philosophy of History*, trans. J. Sibree (New York: Dover, 1956), p. 415.

12. G. W. F. Hegel, *The Philosophy of Right*, trans. with notes by T. M. Knox (Oxford: Oxford University Press, 1952), p. 95.

13. Mary Fulbrook, *Piety and Politics: Religion and the Rise of Absolutism in England, Wurttemberg, and Prussia* (Cambridge: Cambridge University Press, 1987); Lawrence Dickey, *Hegel: Religion, Economics, and the Politics of Spirit, 1770–1807* (Cambridge: Cambridge University Press, 1987).

14. G. W. F. Hegel, *The Phenomenology of Spirit*, trans. A. V. Miller, with analysis of the text and foreword by J. N. Findlay (Oxford: Oxford University Press, 1977), p. 335.

15. Sacvan Bercovitch, *The Puritan Origins of the American Self* (New Haven: Yale University Press, 1975).

16. Cf. Karen Rowe, *Saint and Singer: Edward Taylor's Typology and the Poetics of Meditation* (Cambridge: Cambridge University Press, 1986).

17. In its most contemporary expression, this stance reappears as American Foucaultianism, with a similarly dismissive contention that the contemporary reader's identificatory involvement with books from periods other than his or her own is a naive obstacle to be surpassed on the way to a scientific historicism. The antinomy to this new historicism is a new pragmatism that claims that identificatory involvement is the *only* possibility, that reading cannot even be said to exercise a reductive force against the text because there is no text except insofar as it is construed in its readings. The perfect symmetry of these positions, stressing the impotence and omnipotence of the reader's identification, suggests that they are partners in a system designed to appear to exhaust the field of possibility—to repress the notion of interchange between reader and text, of identification gratified but also blocked, the reader changed by the encounter with the blockage, then returning for a different kind of identification, in a cycle whose repetition is not necessarily terminable. The mutual exclusivity of the two poles in the antinomy

seems to sterilize the possibility of reading as dialectical education, a process with several points of resemblance to mourning.

18. My typology of critics of typology is overly simplistic, I hope only heuristically: individual critical works mix the three stances, and assert by way of tone and emphasis rather than polemical announcement. For a sample of position 1, see Cecilia Tichi, "Spiritual Biography and the 'Lord's Remembrancers,'" in *The American Puritan Imagination: Essays in Revaluation*, ed. Sacvan Bercovitch (Cambridge: Cambridge University Press, 1974), pp. 56–76: "Indeed, neglect by subsequent generations of a form once so popular as to be anthologized probably indicates how little attuned have been post-seventeenth-century sensibilities to the rigid formula of spiritual biography. But aesthetic alienation ought not to prevent an intellectual understanding of the generic grounds from which the 'Lord's remembrancers' worked, albeit unconsciously'" (p. 69). In an essay in the same volume, after several concessive gestures to position 3, David Minter, echoing the last page of *The Great Gatsby*, concludes with position 2: "In their own way, however, the latter-day Puritans were true, though very imperfect and partial, poets: they followed, if not to the bottom, at least into the darkness of their night, there to order words of themselves and of their origins, there to seek a basis of renewal; in their tales of pleasing woe, they sang, as best they could, 'of human unsuccess / In a rapture of distress.' Their characteristic decision was, to be sure, rather to skirt than fully to explore the incongruity first between the intent of the design and the result of the actions of their fathers, and second between the purposes to which they had been dedicated as children and the causes to which they were giving themselves as men. But in their jeremiads they acknowledge and, in their most interesting moments, attempt even to master these incongruities: they attempt, that is, to reconcile, by proclaiming them one, the intent and the achievement of their fathers and they attempt, while going about their business, to remain loyal to the purposes to which their fathers had dedicated them" (p. 55). Or see Mason I. Lowance, Jr., *The Language of Canaan: Metaphor and Symbol in New England from the Puritans to the Transcendentalists* (Cambridge: Harvard University Press, 1980), p. 295: "The secular transformations of the eighteenth and nineteenth centuries have given new meaning to terms like 'type' and 'fulfillment,' but the original organizing principle of the language of Canaan remains clear. America's deepest rhetorical impulse has always been the expression of future promise, an articulation of imminent fulfillment that will no doubt characterize the literature throughout the centuries to come." For a systematic statement of position 3, see Ann Kibbey, *The Interpretation of Material Shapes in Puritanism: A Study of Rhetoric, Prejudice, and Violence* (Cambridge: Cambridge University Press, 1986), which fuses ethnohistory, women's studies, and literary theory to mark out an important new area in Early American studies.

19. Miller's position is most succinctly stated in "The Marrow of Puritan Divinity," *Errand into the Wilderness* (Cambridge: Harvard University Press, 1956), pp. 48–98. On Miller's relation to negative theology, see Donald Weber's introduction to Miller's *Jonathan Edwards* (Amherst: University of Massachusetts Press, 1981), pp. v–xxix. On Miller's challenge to what was in his time the dominant view of Puritanism, see Russel L. Reising, *The Unusable Past: Theory and the Study of American Literature* (London: Methuen, 1986), pp. 53–57.

20. Karl Barth, *The Epistle to the Romans,* trans. Edwyn C. Hoskyns (Oxford: Oxford University Press, 1933), p. 29.

21. Miller, "Marrow of Puritan Divinity," p. 53.

22. Barth, *Epistle to the Romans,* pp. 27–28.

23. One might speculate about the personal and historical motivations for Miller's bleak faith. And also ascertain its political consequences: on the one hand, such an aloof negativity would probably always involve a distaste for the fundamentalist jingoism that so often grips American politics; on the other hand, the decision to confine divinity to the status of an irrevocably remote *Ding-an-sich* effectively removes the question of ought from social deliberations and tends to relinquish the field to pure pragmatism. I am here drawing on Lukács' critique of twentieth-century German neo-Kantianism in *History and Class Consciousness: Studies in Marxist Dialectics,* trans. Rodney Livingstone (Cambridge: MIT Press, 1971), pp. 132–40, 160–68), and on Carolyn Porter, "Are We Being Historical Yet?" in *The States of "Theory": History, Art, and Critical Discourse,* ed. David Carroll (New York: Columbia University Press, 1989), pp. 27–62.

24. Nathaniel Ward, *The Simple Cobler of Aggawam in America,* ed. P. M. Zall (Lincoln: University of Nebraska Press, 1969), pp. 7–8.

25. G. W. F. Hegel, "The ethical world. Human and Divine Law: Man and Woman," section C (BB) VI. A. a. of *The Phenomenology of Spirit,* pp. 267–79. I will cite this chapter only when I use specific quotations from it. My argument draws most heavily on paragraphs 449–52, 455, 460, and 462–63.

26. John Bossy, *Christianity in the West, 1400–1700* (Oxford: Oxford University Press, 1987), p. 27. Thanks to Anne Middleton for bringing this book to my attention.

27. Philippe Ariès, *The Hour of Our Death,* trans. Helen Weaver (New York: Vintage, 1982).

28. Henry Sussman, *The Hegelian Aftermath: Readings in Hegel, Kierkegaard, Freud, Proust, and James* (Baltimore: Johns Hopkins University Press, 1982). Sussman is for the most part concerned with the first half of *The Phenomenology of Spirit,* whereas my argument in this essay concentrates on the reading of *Antigone* that begins the second half. Consequently, he focuses on questions of a less directly social nature, and sees "a world whose only principles are indeterminacy and linguistic copulation" as the major source of inner resistance to Hegel's design, whereas I will emphasize a specifically *social* form of resistance. Despite this difference, I agree with Sussman's general judgment that "Hegel may place his forced twists and leanings at the service of a smooth-running machine of logic and abstraction, but the blunt force involved in this application points in the direction of another, less domesticated realm . . . (p. 2)—though, of course, Antigone's threat to Creon originates in a *more* domesticated realm.

29. Jacques Derrida, *Glas,* trans. John P. Leavey, Jr., and Richard Rand (Lincoln: University of Nebraska Press, 1986), throughout, but pp. 29–30 especially, in the left columns. I became aware of the theoretical importance of the topic of exemplification through conversations with and essays by Jonathan Elmer and David Lloyd.

30. On autochthony in Greek mythology, see Claude Lévi-Strauss, "The Structural Study of Myth," *Structural Anthropology,* trans. Claire Jacobson and Brooke Grundfest Schoepf (Garden City, N.Y.: Doubleday, 1963), pp. 202–28, and Page duBois, *Sowing the*

Body: Psychoanalysis and the Ancient Representations of Women (Chicago: University of Chicago Press, 1988).

31. Cf. "Independence and dependence of self-consciousness: Lordship and Bondage," *Phenomenology of Spirit*, pp. 111-19, and Aléxandre Kojève's revisionary explication in *Introduction to the Reading of Hegel: Lectures on the Phenomenology of Spirit*, trans. James H. Nichols, Jr., ed. Allan Bloom (New York: Basic Books, 1969). See also Georg Lukács, "Reification and the Consciousness of the Proletariat," *History and Class Consciousness: Studies in Marxist Dialectics*, trans. Rodney Livingstone (Cambridge: MIT Press, 1971), p. 166: "Thus for the worker the reified character of the immediate manifestations of capitalist society receives the most extreme definition possible. It is true: for the capitalist also there is the same doubling of personality, the same splitting up of man into an element of the movement of commodities and an (objective and impotent) observer of that movement. But for his consciousness it necessarily appears as an activity (albeit this activity is objectively an illusion) in which effects emanate from himself. This illusion blinds him to the true state of affairs, whereas the worker, who is denied the scope for such illusory activity, perceives the split in his being preserved in the brutal form of what is in its whole tendency a slavery without limits." Hegel, Kojève and Lukács do not argue that those consigned to the slave position are better off, but that they are more likely loci of insight because they are denied participation in fantasias of mastery as well as basic social and material rights. In the consignment of stereotyped mourning to women, the purpose is presumably to effect a specular localization in one gender of the powerlessness that mourning necessarily implies, so that the other gender can enjoy a deluded feel of final competence. The Slave's lucidity is however not inevitable, because exclusion can prompt an intensely energetic quest to secure mastery, or access to the heavenly heart of whiteness, as in *The Great Gatsby* or *Native Son* before Bigger's imprisonment.

32. Derrida, *Glas*, p. 103, left column.

33. The fact that Antigone's remembrance, however different from Creon's, is aimed at constructing a representation that will be judged for adequacy and put to use, and is thus teleological, may account for Derrida's decision to contend that biological decay, rather than Antigone's opposition to decay, is Hegel's greatest nightmare. Whatever dread Antigone may inspire in Creon pales for Derrida before a certain inability that matter prompts in Hegel. As a result, the tension between Creon and Antigone tends to wane as an important topic in the relevant sections of *Glas*. This waning seems to me to be a specimen of the way in which the abstraction of Derrida's thought, like that of Adorno, tends toward superseding distinctions such as Creon/Antigone on the ground that, for all of the parties' apparent antagonism, they are in the last instance engaged in analogous pursuits, in this case teleological memory. I will throughout this book simply bracket Derrida's argument because his search for what Hegel finds unassimilable by spirit tends to dwarf differences within modes of spirit, between forms of ethics, whereas I am using Hegel to define the consequences of the difference between Rowlandson and Puritan ideology, and thus need to keep Antigone/Creon at the center of focus. Luce Irigaray's reading of Hegel's *Antigone* ("The Eternal Irony of the Community," *Speculum of the Other Woman*, trans. Gillian C. Gill (Ithaca: Cornell University Press, 1985), pp. 214-27) is closer to my own in that it concentrates on the battle between Creon and

Antigone. However, Irigaray's feminist-deconstructive suspicion of the notion of law leads her to characterize Antigone's commitment as a "passion of the red blood," thereby neglecting Antigone's high moral tone, recasting it as a primitive compulsion or nature, and favoring the melancholic derangement of mourning that is produced by Creon's violence over Antigone's *argument*. Irigaray thus accepts Creon's description of the difference between himself and Antigone as a difference between law and nature, but reverses Creon's valorization of the former—in effect, she takes the alterity-to-ethics that Derrida locates in matter, and relocates it (with a certain elation) in Antigone. In both Derrida's and Irigaray's arguments, the locus of a rigorous critique cannot be an ethics (cannot in fact even be a locus) because it would in that case circle back into complicity with what it opposes, but the effect of this vigilance toward complicity is liable to be a derogation of positive ethical stances as mystified or crude, and a vaunting of the sort of attributes Creon uses to insult Antigone. My own position is closest to that of Page duBois: "The Greeks saw women not as castrated, nor as exemplifying absence, or the ethically abnormal, but represented them as inseparable from political and economic struggle. They are presented and used ideologically in the theater, to speculate about contesting forms of law and justice . . . " ("Antigone and the Feminist Critic, *Genre*, 19 (Winter 1986), 371–83.) All of the things that duBois says the Greeks did not see women as were of course in effect by Hegel's time: but *Antigone* seems to have helped him to imagine *an*other *ethic,* rather than what is now called The Other. If the exclusion of alternate formations from discourse results in a certain conspicuous but powerful silence, then castration, absence, and ethical abnormality may be taken as effects of silencing, rather than intrinsic traits; if derangement *is* taken to be an intrinsic trait rather than an effect of repression, the repression is liable to be inadvertently perpetuated by a failure to imagine or remember the object of its violence. Cf. Carolyn Porter, "Are We Being Historical Yet?" and Carlo Ginzberg, *The Cheese and the Worms: The Cosmos of a Sixteenth Century Miller,* trans. John and Anne Tedeschi (Baltimore: Johns Hopkins University Press, 1980), pp. xiii-xxvi.

34. Those familiar with Hegel's reading will notice that I am ignoring Hegel's emphasis on the special status of a sister's grief for a brother as the essential form of mourning. Hegel contends that this relation is a love that bridges the gender line but does not involve subordination (father/daughter) or heterosexual desire (husband/wife). In a moment of rare dismissiveness, Jean Hyppolite calls this argument merely ingenious; Irigaray accepts it as a mystified explanation of the affinity of the red blood; Derrida ruminates over Hegel's letters to his sister Christianne; and George Steiner points to a general fixation on the brother/sister relation in European romanticism. My own opinion is that Hegel's valorization of the brother/sister relation depends upon a misreading of one of Antigone's speeches. In itself, this is not for me a flaw, because his revision of Sophocles is what makes him relevant to the Protestant objection to mourning. In this case, however, the misreading is worthy of note, because Hegel's emphasis on Antigone as sister arises from a speech in which she delivers a chilling and withering ironic indictment of Creon's assumptions. Hegel can believe in her apparent emphasis on the brother/sister bond only by missing the irony—and missing the irony may be his mission here. In a confused and violent passage that comes near the end of the chapter (quoted on my p. 47), he will announce that the suppression of women and mourning condemns them to irony as their

sole discursive mode; his failure to consider this speech as irony, therefore, seems to me more a matter of deliberate avoidance than tone deafness, a possibility enhanced by the fact that *as irony* the speech would be an intransigent, inescapable, and utterly unanswerable denunciation of the assumptions Hegel considers necessary if spiritual history is to commence and progress. Hegel desires that Antigone be ingenuous rather than ironic:

> Polyneices knows the price I pay
> for doing final service to his corpse.
> And yet the wise will know my choice is right.
> Had I children or their father dead,
> I'd let them moulder. I should not have chosen
> In such a case to cross a state's decree.
> What is the law that lies behind these words?
> One husband gone, I might have found another,
> or a child from a new man in the first child's place,
> but with my parents hid away in death,
> no brother, ever, could spring up for me.
> Such was the law by which I honored you.
>
> (902–13)

(*Antigone,* trans. Elizabeth Wyckoff, in *Sophocles I: Three Tragedies,* ed. David Grene and Richmond Lattimore (Chicago: University of Chicago Press, 1954), p. 190.) These are shocking lines, displaying a blithe acceptance of the substitutability of loves that outdoes Creon for coldness. Many readers have been appalled by this passage, and it has been periodically suggested that it is a post-Sophoclean interpolation. But we should take the near echo of Creon seriously, and consider the possibility that Antigone is voicing a bitterly acerbic parody of Creon's inclination to reduce persons to exemplary functions. Earlier, when Ismene asked Creon if condemning Antigone would not also destroy his son's marital happiness, Creon replied, in a line that duBois cites as the essence of his callousness, "there are other furrows for his plow" (569). When Antigone speaks her cold lines, she is unaware that Haemon has separated himself from his father's expediency. If, then, she believes Haemon to be complicit, her assertion that "one husband gone, I might have found another" seems more like a vindictively sarcastic rejoinder than a credo of intrinsic attitude. Ismene having deferred to Creon's authority at the beginning of the play, the Antigone of lines 902–13 considers herself completely alone in her commitment, and her contention that "the wise will know my choice is right" expresses the depth of her experience of betrayal and isolation. She does not hope to communicate with anyone on the basis of a shared commitment to the obligation of mourning. Standing alone and inert in the midst of what discourse is permitted, her only ways to speak are silence or acid mimicry of the attitudes that govern Thebes. We can only follow Hegel in taking these lines at face value by failing to notice that elsewhere in the speech Antigone expresses multiple griefs that are by no means limited to Polyneices: "I come as dear friend to my dear father, / to you, my mother, and my brother too." (898–99); "No marriage bed, no marriage-song for me, / and since no wedding, so no child to rear" (917–18). Such griefs, however, she thinks, are expressed to no hearing ears: "I go, without a friend, struck down by fate, / live to the hollow chambers of the dead" (919–20). Unable to speak and be heard on her terms, she can only speak his brutality pushed to an extremity where the brutality is put on view—but again, with no one to hear, though, in their shock, readers have heard, often without realizing she is showing them Creon. The utter suppression of her speech so corrupts discourse that she can only participate in the circulation of utterance through introducing ironic perturbation into the heart of ethical prevarication. I would like to add one more observation, that even taking the passage at face value we cannot accept Hegel's explication of the primacy of the brother/sister bond: Antigone asserts Polyneices' uniqueness not for the reasons Hegel puts forward, but because the parents are dead. In Antigone's ironic lampooning of Creon's commodification of love, Polyneices is rare in the way that a commodity manufactured from since-depleted raw materials is rare, but a commodity nevertheless. Though Hegel may have wished to impose the brother/sister bond on this passage owing to its allure for him, he may also have devised that cumbersome apparatus in order to *bury* the truth of the passage, its unrestrained assault on the reduction of persons to the convenience of function. But again, there are two Hegels here, one telling the other that he will have to go to great length if he is to get past this. (See *Philosophy of Right*, pp. 101–3, for Hegel's denunciation of irony that does not give way to an expression of truth.)

35. Sigmund Freud, "Mourning and Melancholia," *Complete Works,* trans. James Strachey, Vol. 14, pp. 239–58, esp. p. 236. My reading of Hegel is heavily influenced by Jacques Lacan's revisionary fusion of the Hegelian and Freudian theories of mourning in "L'éclat d'Antigone," *L'éthique de la psychanalyse, Le séminaire,* book 7 (Paris: Editions du Seuil, 1986), pp. 285–333, and by Stuart Schneiderman, *Jacques Lacan: The Death of an Intellectual Hero* (Cambridge: Harvard University Press, 1983). See also Jacques Lacan, "Desire and the Interpretation of Desire in *Hamlet,*" trans. James Hulbert, in *Literature and Psychoanalysis: The Question of Reading: Otherwise, Yale French Studies,* nos. 55/56 (1977), 11–52, and Melanie Klein, "Mourning and Its Relation to Manic-Depressive States," *Love, Guilt, and Reparation and Other Works, The Writings of Melanie Klein,* Vol. 1 (New York: Macmillan Free Press, 1975), pp. 344–69.

36. *Phenomenology of Spirit,* p. 270.

37. Jean Hyppolite, *Genesis and Structure of Hegel's Phenomenology of Spirit,* trans. Samuel Cherniak and John Heckman (Evanston: Northwestern University Press, 1974), p. 343.

38. Schneiderman, *Jacques Lacan: The Death of an Intellectual Hero,* p. 152.

39. Lacan, "L'eclat d'Antigone," p. 302.

40. Klein, "Mourning and Its Relation to Manic-Depressive States," p. 352.

41. Lacan, "L'eclat d'Antigone," p. 325.

42. See Judith Butler, *Subjects of Desire: Hegelian Reflections in Twentieth-Century France* (New York: Columbia University Press, 1987), p. 8: "In being reflected in and by that piece of the world, the subject learns that it shares a common structure with that piece of the world, that a prior and constituting relation conditions the possibility of reflection, and that the object of reflection is nothing other than the relation itself. Hence, the subject that encounters an object or Other, or some feature of the world as external and ontologically disparate, is not identical with the subject that discovers itself

reflected in and by those ostensibly external phenomena. In other words, before medi-
ated self-reflection is achieved, the subject knows itself to be a more limited, less autonomous being than it potentially is. In discovering that reflection is possible, and that every
reflection reveals a relation constitutive of the subject, a way in which it is integrally
related to the world that it previously did not understand, the subject cultivates a more
expanded conception of its place. Importantly, the Hegelian subject is not a self-identical
subject who travels smugly from one ontological place to another; it *is* its travels, and *is*
every place in which it finds itself." Though, as Rowlandson implies, mourning is less a
grand tour than a forced march, its repeated encounters with alien objects, the surging
memories, compel transformations of the image of the dead, and with them correspond-
ing transformations of the survivor's understanding of her structuring relation to the
dead. If at the end the mourner does not discover herself to be an "adventurer of the
Spirit who turns out, after a series of surprises, to *be* all that he encounters along his
dialectical way" (6), but rather a wanderer *aware* of what she was and how little she is, the
metamorphoses of her knowledge are nonetheless more dialectical than the exemplifica-
tions of Creon, who is, until his final anagnorisis, "a self-identical subject who travels
smugly from one ontological place to another." Hence both his apparently greater
efficacy and alacrity and her greater reflectivity; hence also, perhaps, the deepest reason
why Hegel is so disturbed by his renunciation of Antigone in favor of the historical
sequence Creon begins, and why he promises that the end of history will allow Antigone
back into the light, into the Spirit "who turns out, after a series of surprises, to *be* all that
he encounters along his dialectical way"—turns out to be even mourning, at some
promised future point.

    43. Freud perhaps comes closest to Hegel's idea in *Totem and Taboo* when he has the
rival sons repress the knowledge of their murder of their father and dedicate themselves
to service to his memory. This opposition between oedipal homicide and sentimental
preservation does not, however, take note that sentimental preservation would also have
to repress the sort of mournful memory Freud would describe five years later in "Mourning and Melancholia." Freud would have approximated Hegel's theory if he had included the insight of *Totem and Taboo* in "Mourning and Melancholia" by suggesting
that the construction of socially utilitarian memories of the dead preempts and deranges
the course of ordinary mourning, resulting in melancholia (or depression). His argument
that this derangement originates in a certain fixated or intransigent incorporation of the
dead seems to me to invite supplementation by Hegel's theory: if mourning ceases
prematurely owing to an incorporation of an image of the dead advanced by a scheme of
social exemplarity, the residue of undone work becomes melancholia. The missing factor
in Freud's theory is a consideration of the preemptive intrusion of ideology into the
course of mourning, an absence he attempts to remedy with the incomplete thesis that
fond memory is used to shield against aggressional memory, rather than that exemplaristic memory is used to shield against full memory. In his introduction to the work of
Nicolas Abraham and Maria Torok, Derrida claims that for Freud mourning accom-
plishes an *introjection* of the dead whereas melancholia is stalled by having *incorporated*
the dead: introjection brings the image of the dead into full assimilation with the self, but
incorporation assimilates the dead as an alien presence, a *crypt* in the midst of the self
with which the self does not communicate. This distinction is useful, but also does not

seem to me complete: in the case of the sort of prolonged and intimate contact that exists between family members, the dead does not need to be *introjected* into the self because that self is in large measure already determined by the history of the relation. The task is not to bring the dead in, but to convert the dead from being an element of life *taken for granted* to being an object of representation, to being an inner image with which the self can communicate to the limit of all the messages that memory proposes. Derrida, Abraham, and Torok's concept of melancholia and incorporation might therefore also be enriched by a consideration of ideological intrusion into mourning: if the mourner takes in an image of the dead that *seems* adequate, but that in fact only *simulates* the dead, then that image will not communicate adequately with memory, but will remain as an encrypted alien body, like the apple embedded in Gregor Samsa's flesh in Kafka's *Metamorphosis,* a flesh rendered insectivorid by its unrepresenting alienation from what it surrounds. Derrida's implication that "so-called normal mourning" is a totalizing and therefore repressive process is based on two related assumptions that carry him away from my own view of mourning, first that the self that "introjects" retains its initial character through the process, and second that the dead is elementally other to the self, and thus can be "introjected" only at the price of a Creonic reduction-to-measure. For Derrida, then, again, "normal" mourning does not escape the curse of exemplarism. If mourning is thus also encrypted, what remains, and where is a credible notion of recovery to be found? Derrida, *"Fors:* The Anglish Words of Nicolas Abraham and Maria Torok," in Abraham and Torok, *The Wolf Man's Magic Word,* Derrida trans. by Barbara Johnson, Abraham and Torok trans. by Nicholas Rand (Minneapolis: University of Minnesota Press, 1986), pp. xiv–xxi.

44. *Phenomenology of Spirit,* pp. 272–73.

45. The continuing utility of the sublimation of grief is manifest in Ronald Reagan's speech after the *Challenger* disaster, which constructed the exemplarity of the victims in such a way as to fortify a national commitment to the renewed militarization of space *so that their deaths would not have been in vain.* On October 2, 1988, Rick Hauck, commander of the first manned space mission after the disaster, responded to Reagan's speech in a manner that displayed a full comprehension of the technique of sublimating mourning through emulative exemplification: "Today, up here where the blue sky turns to black, we can say at long last, to Dick, Mike, Judy, to Ron and El, and to Christa and Greg: Dear friends, we have resumed the journey that we promised to continue for you; dear friends, your loss has meant that we could confidently begin anew; dear friends, your spirit and your dream are still alive in our hearts." *San Francisco Chronicle,* October 3, 1988, pp. A1 and A18. Hauck implies that the *Challenger* mission was *Christic* (Christa): that the debility of the O-rings was a lurking danger or dark necessity that the earlier mission brought forward and thereby purged, enabling a confident new beginning; that this is how we are to remember them, as those who died for us; and that the proper form of remembrance is emulation of what are designated as their values, which ensures that *they are not really dead—only the vehicle has dropped away.* It has since been reported that NASA may have suppressed evidence that the *Challenger* victims survived for some minutes after the explosion, the thought of which would tend to impede an easy passage into symbolic remembrance. The American public's abiding desire to know about those awful moments may betoken a survival of mourning, as may

the curious decision to name the next space shuttle *Atlantis,* after the splendid civilization that disappeared beneath the ocean. One might follow Robert Jay Lifton's comments on post-Vietnam America in his preface to Alexander and Margerite Mitscherlich's diagnosis of the psychological stagnation of Germany after World War II (*The Inability to Mourn,* trans. Beverley R. Placzek [New York: Grove Press, 1975], p. vii-xiv) to consider whether Reaganism in toto may have been a sublimation of grief, a deployment of vigorous images in place of mourning's severe appraisal of those persons, self-conceptions, and ideas that have perished during the last twenty-six years of U.S. history. This speculation is supported by George Bush's inaugural address, which identified Vietnam as the destruction of a whole America, and called for an end to rumination over that event in the interest of moving on, something that the persistent concern over M.I.A. remains suggests that Americans are not yet willing to do. Though he does not discuss mournfulness, Stuart Hall engages quite persuasively with the question of desirable ideology in "The Toad in the Garden: Thatcherism among the Theorists," in *Marxism and the Interpretation of Culture,* ed. Cary Nelson and Lawrence Grossberg (Urbana and Chicago: University of Illinois Press, 1988), pp. 58–74.

46. *Phenomenology of Spirit,* p. 280.

47. *Phenomenology of Spirit,* pp. 288 and 282.

48. Paul Zweig, *Walt Whitman: The Making of a Poet* (New York: Basic Books, 1984), p. 8.

49. Hegel's theory supplements the explanation of the connection between simulative ideology and intransigent unresponsiveness in Jean Baudrillard, *In the Shadow of the Silent Majorities . . . Or the End of the Social,* trans. Paul Foss, Paul Patton, and John Johnston (New York: Semiotext(e), 1983). "The mass absorbs all the social energy, but no longer refracts it. It absorbs every sign and every meaning, but no longer reflects them. It absorbs all messages and digests them. For every question put to it, it sends back a tautological and circular response. It never participates. Inundated by flows or tests, it forms a mass or *earth . . .*" (p. 28). Baudrillard acknowledges the connection between this nonparticipation and Hegel's description of melancholia, bur shows little interest in the etiology of melancholia, in describing what melancholia is a deranged form of: "There would thus be a fantastic irony about 'matter,' and every object of science, just as there is a fantastic irony about the masses in their muteness, or in their statistical discourse so conforming to the questions put to them, akin to the eternal irony of femininity of which Hegel speaks—the irony of a false fidelity, of an excessive fidelity to the law, an ultimately impenetrable simulation of passivity and obedience, and which annuls in return the law governing them, in accordance with the immortal example of the Soldier Schweick" (p. 33; the quotation from Hegel to which Baudrillard refers appears in the text below).

50. *Phenomenology of Spirit,* p. 288.

51. *Phenomenology of Spirit,* p. 16.

52. *Philosophy of Right,* pp. 105–22. This discussion of *Antigone* was brought to my attention by Joseph Kronick.

53. Harry S. Stout, *The New England Soul: Preaching and Religious Culture in Colonial New England* (Oxford: Oxford University Press, 1986), pp. 32 and 4. My debt to Stout's book is not limited to these quotations.

54. This use of minutiae to fortify authority is nowhere more evident than in the careful note that Puritan writers from Winthrop through Cotton Mather took of reports that Anne Hutchinson and her friend Mary Dyer conceived deformed fetuses, and in their imaginative exegeses of the isomorphism between the details of the deformities and the tenets of the heresies that they had entertained before and during the pregnancies. The fetuses, therefore, were *emblems* of the two women's invisible spiritual states; their bodies *told an exemplary truth* that their mouths were laboring to disguise, but *the truth will out.* Cf. Thomas Weld, preface to John Winthrop, *A Short Story of the Rise, reign, and ruine of the Antinomians, Familists & Libertines,* in *The Antinomian Controversy, 1636–1638,* ed. David D. Hall (Middlebury, Conn.: Wesleyan University Press, 1968), pp. 214–15: *"for look as she had vented mishapen opinions, so she must bring forth deformed monsters; and as about 30. Opinions in number, so many monsters; and as those were publike, and not in a corner mentioned, so this is now come to be knowne and famous over all these Churches, and a great part of the world."* This intrusion of divinely composed exemplification, *"as clearly as if he had pointed with his finger,"* must have gratified Weld, Winthrop, and others in part because the antinomians had denied that the emulation of examples was of any worth to the soul: *"Error* 6: The example of Christs life, is not a patterne according to which men ought to act" (p. 220).

55. Sacvan Bercovitch, *The American Jeremiad* (Madison: University of Wisconsin Press, 1978), p. 42, and *The Puritan Origins of the American Self* (New Haven: Yale University Press, 1975), pp. 5, 9, 15, 8. My view of American Puritanism has been substantially shaped by Bercovitch's work, which, by virtue of bringing together the aesthetic formalism of typology exegesis, the sociopolitical analysis of Puritan theory, and the analysis of the structure of conversion psychology, enables a serious and rigorous break from Perry Miller's work and provides a key foundation for contemporary elaboration.

56. David Hall, "Toward a History of Popular Religion in America," *William and Mary Quarterly,* 41.1 (January 1984), 49–55.

57. Because of Puritanism's attention to the small, triviality may be the only concept with less prominence in Puritan theory than humor, however much the attention someone such as Cotton Mather devoted to what we might call the trivial constitutes the essence of what we might find humorous about him: the readiness of all phenomena to bear meaning tended to problematize judgments concerning the triviality of anything. The fact that we continue to find Mather's hyperzealous vigilance, like his earnest extravagance in general, funny, suggests to me that it is for us either *liberating,* freeing us from a certain bondage to putatively self-evident discriminations between the important and the trivial, or *vicariously anxiogenic,* staging in a distanced and embarrassingly unabashed form our abiding latent worry over what may lie beneath the next stone we happen to kick over. *Or both:* if the temperate reasonableness with which the age of Franklin replaces the age of Mather amounts to a modernization rather than an easing of constraint, then Mather's "neurotically" exuberant excessiveness explodes in advance Enlightenment protocols that lie historically between him and us, freeing us to romp about in a golden age of repression, of an *innocent* unfreedom that did not know better than to say its name.

58. T. H. Breen, "The Right and the Wrong Stuff," *American Scholar,* 55.2 (Spring 1986), 279–83.

59. See Paul Boyer and Stephen Nissebaum, *Salem Possessed: The Social Origins of Witchcraft* (Cambridge: Harvard University Press, 1974).

60. Bercovitch, *American Jeremiad,* pp. xv, xii, xiv, 28; *Puritan Origins of the American Self,* p. 20.

61. My discussion of representations of death, funeral sermons, and funerary practices in American Puritan society in the following paragraphs is drawn from: Bercovitch, *Puritan Origins of the American Self,* p. 6; Gordon E.Geddes, *Welcome Joy: Death in Puritan New England* (Ann Arbor: UMI Research Press, 1981); David E. Stannard, *The Puritan Way of Death: A Study in Religion, Culture, and Social Change* (Oxford: Oxford University Press, 1977); David H. Watters, *"With Bodilie Eyes": Eschatological Themes in Puritan Literature and Gravestone Art* (Ann Arbor: UMI Research Press, 1981); Allan I. Ludwig, *Graven Images: New England Stonecarving and Its Symbols, 1650–1815* (Middletown, Conn.: Wesleyan University Press, 1966); and Ronald A. Bosco, ed., *New England Funeral Sermons,* vol. 4 of *The Puritan Sermon in America* (Delmar, N.Y.: Scholar's Facsimiles and Reprints), especially Bosco's introduction. In a recent work on Melville and mourning in antebellum America, Neal L. Tolchin has identified the centrality of a blocking and channeling of mourning in genteel culture, and the consequent production of an underground melancholia (*Mourning, Gender, and Creativity in the Art of Herman Melville* [New Haven: Yale University Press, 1988]). Tolchin's extensive and perspicacious investigation of Melville's America suggests to me that sentimentalism is a reappearance of the Puritan sublimation of mourning, promoting quite different social values, but availing itself of Puritanism's legacy of social technique.

62. See Perry Miller and Thomas Johnson, *The Puritans: A Sourcebook of Their Writings* (New York: Harper and Row, 1963), Vol. 1, pp. 150–51 (Edward Johnson) and Vol. 2, pp. 474–75 (Thomas Shepard).

63. *New England Funeral Sermons,* p. xx.

64. Stout, *New England Soul,* pp. 122–23.

65. Andreas Hyperius, *The Practise of preaching, otherwise called the Pathway to the Pulpit: Conteyning an excellent Method how to frame Divine Sermons, & to interpret the holy Scriptures according to the capacitie of the vulgar people. First written in Latin by the learned pastor of Christes Church, D. Andreas Hyperius: and now lately (to the profit of the same Church) Englished by John Ludham, vicar of Wetherfield. Whereunto is added an* Oration *concerning the lyfe and death of the same Hyperius; which may serve for a president to all the learned men of his calling in our tyme* (London: Thomas East, 1577). All of the quotations I use in the paragraphs below are from pp. 170–75. My attention was brought to Hyperius by Bercovitch's *Puritan Origins,* where it is mentioned on p. 207.

66. Hamlet's implication that there is an objectively proper period violated by Claudius' and Gertrude's practice, however, represents his attempt to posit a contrary "manliness," rather than attention to the demands of grieving. He believes that, but for lust and ambition, there would be a time that is in joint, and he is therefore incompetent to see the anomalous time of the grieving as other than delay—cowardice and indecision, "womanliness." Grief itself, therefore, is extruded as melancholia—as Ophelia—because Hamlet reaches the wrong conclusion about the meaning of his objection to Claudius' mandatory alacrities, because his insuperable allegiance to patrilinearity entails a duty to

act that requires him to swerve from the lesson. See Lacan, "Desire and the Interpretation of Desire in *Hamlet*," on time.

67. Willard, THE HIGH ESTEEM Which God hath of the Death of his SAINTS, in Bosco, *Puritan Funeral Sermons*, p. 4.

68. Joseph Rowlandson, *The Possibility of Gods Forsaking a people* (Boston, 1682), p. 15.

69. Geddes, *Welcome Joy*, pp. 155–68.

70. James Fitch, *Peace the End of the Perfect and Upright* (Cambridge, 1672).

71. John Owen King, *The Iron of Melancholy: Structures of Spiritual Conversion from the Puritan Conscience to Victorian Neurosis* (Middletown: Wesleyan University Press, 1983), p. 49.

72. Stannard, *Puritan Way of Death*, pp. 38–39.

73. Rowlandson, *Possibility of Gods Forsaking a people*, pp. 10–11.

3. Lot's Wife: Looking Back

1. John Calvin, *Commentaries on the First Book of Moses Called Genesis* (Edinburgh: Calvin Translation Society, 1847), pp. 514–15.

2. My discussion of Rowlandson's contradictory velocities in this chapter is derived from Kristin Ross's analysis of adolescent velocities in *The Emergence of Social Space: Rimbaud and the Paris Commune* (Minneapolis: University of Minnesota Press, 1988). Citing Lukács and Sartre, Ross claims that a regulated subjective calm is a generic trait of voice in the bourgeois novel, and then argues that "what distinguishes the adolescent body, then, as it is figured in Rimbaud's work, is a particular corporeal relation to speed: the body is both too slow and too fast. Periods of apparent lulls are broken by violent, spasmodically unbridled explosions, but even this is something of an optical illusion: the heavy torpor or seeming somnambulance of the body qualified by *paresse* hides a body that is in fact moving too fast . . . Laziness for Rimbaud is a kind of absolute motion, absolute speed that escapes the pull of gravity" (p. 54). I am not claiming here that Rowlandson is an adolescent, but rather borrowing Ross's startling phenomenological insight first that dissidence or disaffection can express itself as the *pace* of subjectivity—rather than simply as the *contents* of consciousness—and second her suggestion that the seeming paradox of high velocity and inaction may be an optical illusion, the way a dissidence appears within an ideologically specific definition of *proper pace*.

3. Susan Howe, "The Captivity and Restoration of Mrs. Mary Rowlandson," *Tremblor*, no. 2 (1985), 115.

4. Elaine Scarry, *The Body in Pain: The Making and Unmaking of the World* (New York: Oxford University Press, 1985), p. 35.

5. Sigmund Freud, *Beyond the Pleasure Principle*, trans. James Strachey (New York: Norton, 1961), pp. 6–7.

6. Melanie Klein, "Mourning and Its Relation to Manic-Depressive States," *Love, Guilt, and Reparation and Other Works, The Writings of Melanie Klein*, Vol. 1 (New York: Macmillan Free Press, 1975), p. 344.

7. I recall a *New Yorker* cartoon taped on the office door of my friend Jerry Cavanaugh in which Satan, watching various other devils chiseling "Abandon all hope ye who enter here" on one of the walls of the inferno, says, "It just occurred to me that it would be even *more* hellish if we left them a little hope."

8. Howe, "Captivity and Restoration of Mrs. Mary Rowlandson," p. 116.

9. Herman Melville, "Nightgown," chapter 11 of *Moby-Dick*. Ishmael here first theorizes the phenomenal reversibility he will notice throughout the voyage: the whale's prick reversed to become the cassock, Queequeg's coffin reversed to become the life buoy. For a long while I wondered whether Melville named the whale after Moebius' strip, but I was unable to find evidence.

10. Increase Mather, *Brief History of the WARR With the INDIANS in New England*, in *So Dreadfull a Judgment: Puritan Responses to King Philip's War, 1676–1677*, ed. Richard Slotkin and James K. Folsom (Middletown, Conn.: Wesleyan University Press, 1978), p. 134.

11. Increase Mather, *An Earnest EXHORTATION of the Inhabitants of New England, To hearken to the voice of God in his late and present DISPENSATIONS*, in *So Dreadfull a Judgment*.

12. See Carolyn Dinshaw, *Chaucer's Sexual Poetics* (Madison: University of Wisconsin Press, 1990), pp. 3–27.

13. I take the concept of plausibility here from a lecture by Alan Sinnfield.

14. Milton R. Stern and Seymour L. Gross, *American Literature Survey: Colonial and Federal to 1800* (New York: Penguin, 1975), p. 74.

15. Jane Tomkins, "'Indians': Textualism, Morality, and the Problem of History," in *Race, Writing, and Difference*, ed. Henry Louis Gates (Chicago: University of Chicago Press, 1985), pp. 69–71.

16. Ibid., p. 69.

17. This conclusion entirely depends on the assumption that the ideological formation of Rowlandson's "seventeenth century English Separatist background" so completely dominated the consciousnesses of those under its purview that those consciousnesses were without other content, that social and political life were not a diverse array of attitudes, commitments, and practices. If this assumption is correct, then major proponents of Congregationalism such as Increase Mather were just misguided in the feeling that their cause required them to be discursively agonistic. They had always already won, and they should have relaxed.

18. David Downing, "'Streams of Scripture Comfort': Mary Rowlandson's Typological Use of the Bible," *Early American Literature*, 15.3 (1980), 252.

19. M. M. Bakhtin, "Discourse in the Novel," *The Dialogical Imagination*, trans. and ed. Caryl Emerson and Michael Holquist (Austin: University of Texas Press, 1981), p. 343. When I was a boy, some of the other children in my Sunday school classes had Bibles in which everything spoken by Jesus was printed with red ink.

20. Ann Kibbey, *The Interpretation of Material Shapes in Puritanism: A Study of Rhetoric, Prejudice, and Violence* (Cambridge: Cambridge University Press, 1986), chap. 4.

21. Downing, "'Streams of Scripture Comfort,'" p. 255.

22. Walter Benjamin, "Theses on the Philosophy of History," *Illuminations: Essays*

and Reflections, ed. Hannah Arendt, trans. Harry Zohn (New York: Schocken, 1969), p. 255.

23. Erich Auerbach, *Mimesis: The Representation of Reality in Western Literature,* trans. Willard R. Trask (Princeton: Princeton University Press, 1953), pp. 12 and 19.

24. Howe, "Captivity and Restoration of Mrs. Mary Rowlandson," p. 117.

25. Ibid., 116.

26. Martin Luther, *Lectures on Genesis, Chapters 15–20,* ed. Jaroslav Pelikan (St. Louis: Concordia, 1961), pp. 299, 300.

27. Max Horkheimer and Theodor Adorno, *Dialectic of Enlightenment,* trans. John Cumming (New York: Herder and Herder, 1972), pp. 79–80.

28. Samuel Whiting, *Abraham's Humble Intercession for Sodom* (Cambridge: Samuel Green, 1666), pp. 7–8.

29. Cotton Mather, "Biblia Americana," unpublished MS, n.p., Massachusetts Historical Society. This passage was transcribed for me by Ric Ferguson from a microfilm at the Huntington Library. It reveals Mather's hermeneutic and omnivorous curiosity with special clarity, his attempt to bring together the new science, Scripture, Apocrypha, and mythology, to serve the purpose of indicting excessive grief. Along with the transcription. Ric included a very Matherian article from the *Weekly World News* (October 4, 1988), "Biblical Greenhouse Effect Turned Lot's Wife into Salt":

"A gigantic biblical 'greenhouse effect' caused by the destruction of wicked Sodom and Gomorrah is what turned Lot's wife into a pillar of 'salt,' claims an American scientist.

"The fire and brimstone that God rained down on the two Old Testament red-light districts caused the surrounding atmosphere to overheat tremendously, triggering a bizarre chemical reaction in Mrs. Lot's body when she turned to look back at the raging inferno, said Northwestern University professor I. M. Klotz. Actually, the unlucky lady was turned into a solid block of calcium carbonate, he explained, but the ancient Hebrews used the word 'salt' to describe any mineral with a salt-like taste . . .

"When she turned to look back at the disaster, Mrs. Lot was exposed to an enormous dose of super-heated air with a high carbon dioxide content. This reacted with the natural calcium in her body—and, instantaneously, she became a statue."

Among the several new considerations that Klotz introduces into the story of Mrs. Lot is the possibility that those who survived her *tasted* her.

Once when I was three or four I went with my father to visit a friend of his who was a farmer. I think I remember that the man had lost two fingers below the first joint in an accident with a thresher or some other machine. This sort of mishap is still, I believe, rather common and treated as worthy of only ordinary remark, midway between legend and gossip. While the three of us walked around the farm, I noticed a cubical stone in the bottom of a slight ravine, in the shade of some trees, next to a creek. When I asked my father what the block was for, he told me it was a salt lick for cattle, an assertion that, Doubting Thomas, I verified when his attention was turned away from me a couple of minutes later.

30. See my *Cotton Mather and Benjamin Franklin: The Price of Representative Personality* (Cambridge: Cambridge University Press, 1984), chap. 1–5.

31. Jacques Derrida, "Le facteur de la vérité," *The Post Card: From Socrates to Freud and Beyond,* trans. Alan Bass (Chicago: University of Chicago Press, 1987), p. 489.

32. Marilynne Robinson, *Housekeeping* (New York: Bantam, 1982), p. 194.

33. Howe, "Captivity and Restoration of Mrs. Mary Rowlandson," p. 116.

34. Once in a conversation with me in the San Francisco Mission district, Susan Howe pointed out that the hoof and the fawn fetus are the sorts of food that are prohibited in Leviticus, and called my attention to "The Semiotics of Biblical Abomination," by Julia Kristeva (in *Powers of Horror: An Essay on Abjection,* trans. Leon S. Roudiez [New York: Columbia University Press, 1982], pp. 90–112). Such foods, according to Kristeva, are in the Bible linked with childbirth, shit, blood, corpses, and leprosy as specimens of an abjection or pollution that, like the body of the leviathan in *Moby-Dick,* threatens the absolute with an antemonotheistic confusion, with an insufficient distinction between the real and the good (or, for Kristeva, between the body of the mother and the abstract moral ego), and that is therefore connected with idolatry. But a violation of such dietary prohibitions does not, according to Kristeva's reading, amount to an *identification* with this antemonotheistic X, because killing and eating, *like* prohibition, reify a distinction between the eater and the food. Killing and eating differ from prohibition in being *riskier:* the commingling between the bodies of the eater and the eaten poses the danger of the erasure of the eater's supremacy, of reducing her to the status of the eaten, rather than establishing her clear mastery over the eaten. This is why prohibition *replaces* sacrifice: avoiding the zone of the abject body altogether, the prohibition expels both the low *and* the danger implicit in overcoming the low through dietary contact. Rowlandson's eating of vile food, therefore, *is* a regression, but to an earlier mode of mastery over nature rather than to the sort of oneness with nature that might be suggested by contemporary schools of romantic or primitivistic feminism. I would conjecture that the semiotic advantage of this stance for Rowlandson is that the threatening possibility of identification between the eater and the eaten emphasizes the originating or creative violence of the separation performed, the construction of a subject position rather than the mere acceptance of a culturally stipulated subject position. The subject position constructed in this way transcends nature without simply obeying Puritan prohibitions, and thus *adumbrates* the way in which mourning's nonaligned ethicality challenges Puritan binarity by opposing nature without affirming the order of types.

35. David E. Stannard, *The Puritan Way of Death: A Study in Religion, Culture, and Social Change* (New York: Oxford University Press, 1977), p. 58.

36. *Thomas Shepard's Confessions, Publications of the Colonial Society of Massachusetts,* ed. George Selement and Bruce C. Woolley (Boston: The Colonial Society of Massachusetts, 1981), Vol. 57, pp. 192–97.

37. Anne Bradstreet, *Works in Prose and Verse,* ed. John Harvard Ellis (Gloucester, Mass.: Peter Smith, 1962), p. 41.

38. Kathryn Zabelle Derounian, "Puritan Orthodoxy and the 'Survivor Syndrome' in Mary White Rowlandson's Indian Captivity Narrative," *Early American Literature,* 22.1 (Spring 1987), 82–93.

4. The Strangers

1. Stephen Saunders Webb, *1676: The End of American Independence* (Cambridge: Harvard University Press, 1985), pp. 242–44.

2. Richard Slotkin, *Regeneration through Violence: The Mythology of the American Frontier, 1600–1860* (Middlebury: Wesleyan University Press, 1973), pp. 106–7.

3. I am at this point and in the following paragraphs characterizing the Puritans' ideological attitude, rather than arguing that the Puritans *were* constant in their treaties and negotiations with the Indians. Francis Jennings presents a great deal of evidence that suggests that they were not (*The Invasion of America: Indians, Colonialism, and the Cant of Conquest* [New York: Norton, 1976]).

4. James Axtell, *The European and the Indian: Essays in the Ethnohistory of Colonial North America* (Oxford: Oxford University Press, 1981), p. 41.

5. Ibid., p. 42.

6. Ibid., p. 68. See also Jennings, *Invasion of America,* p. 57.

7. Edmund Leites, *The Puritan Conscience and Modern Sexuality* (New Haven: Yale University Press, 1986), p. 1.

8. Michael Walzer, *The Revolution of the Saints: A Study in the Origins of Radical Politics* (New York: Atheneum, 1973), pp. 3–4.

9. For a careful comparison of European and Indian economic systems that exposes the ideological underpinnings of the opposition between wandering and stability, see Jennings, *Invasion of America* pp. 58–84. It would be very interesting to study Puritan responses to the berdaches, male Indians who occupied a mixture of male and female social and economic positions, who either were celibate or who coupled with (even married) nonberdache males, and who were treated as a third gender rather than as a deviation from either of the other two. Walker L. Williams connects the position of the berdache with taboo systems. Though he believes that we "cannot assume that the berdaches were completely absent from any Native American culture, and we need to question statements that suggest its nonexistence," he has found no evidence of berdaches among the tribes of the Northeast. *The Spirit and the Flesh: Sexual Diversity in American Indian Culture* (Boston: Beacon Press, 1986).

10. Douglas Edward Leach, *Flintlock and Tomahawk: New England in King Philip's War* (New York: Norton, 1966), p. 200. See also Axtell, *European and the Indian,* pp. 261–62. In *1676: The End of American Independence,* Stephen Saunders Webb attributes the failure of the Algonquian war effort to the hostility of the Iroquois nations, located to the west in New York. The Iroquois, led by Daniel Garacontié, in alliance with the New York British, led by Sir Edmund Andros, according to Webb, concluded that an Algonquian failure would be an expedient part of a larger design to reassert monarchical power throughout the North American colonies, a conclusion Webb considers correct. However, the Iroquois Mohicans did not vent their hostility only by actively attacking Philip's forces, but also by withholding support when his supplies were disastrously low. They allowed his defeat to happen, and Webb's thesis can therefore stand alongside Leach's, though there might be some disagreement about the relative importances of Iroquois attacking and withholding. Philip led a startling and wide-ranging campaign that succeeded by way of surprising hit-and-run attacks (hence the incessant movement

of which Rowlandson complains) . . . but which was not congenial to the maintenance of long-term supply networks (hence the scarcities of which she complains, and the eventual need to appeal to the culturally very different Mohawks for support). Webb contends, by the way, that the Massachusetts English had warnings of the attack on Lancaster two weeks before it took place, but failed to heed them (p. 239).

11. Axtell, *European and the Indian*, pp. 74–75.

12. Michael Taussig, *The Devil and Commodity Fetishism in South America* (Chapel Hill: University of North Carolina Press, 1980).

13. Axtell, *European and the Indian*, p. 116.

14. Laurel Thatcher Ulrich, *Good Wives: Image and Reality in the Lives of Women in Northern New England, 1650–1750* (Oxford: Oxford University Press, 1982).

15. Lyle Koehler, *A Search for Power: The "Weaker Sex" in Seventeenth Century New England* (Urbana: University of Illinois Press, 1980).

16. Axtell, *European and the Indian*, pp. 168–206.

17. William Simmons, "Cultural Bias in the New England Puritans' Perception of Indians," *William and Mary Quarterly*, 3d ser., 38.1 (June, 1979), 69.

18. Renato Rosaldo, "Grief and a Headhunter's Rage: On the Cultural Force of Emotions," in *Text, Play, and Story: The Construction and Reconstruction of Self and Society,* ed. Edward M. Bruner (Washington, D.C.: American Ethnological Society, 1984), pp. 178–95.

19. Marcel Mauss, *The Gift: Forms and Functions of Exchange in Archaic Societies,* trans. Ian Cunnison (New York: Norton, 1967), pp. 45, 70, 3, 31.

20. Fredric Jameson, *The Political Unconscious: Narrative as a Socially Symbolic Act* (Ithaca; Cornell University Press, 1981); Jacques Lacan, *The Four Fundamental Concepts of Psychoanalysis,* trans. Alan Sheridan (New York: Norton, 1978), pp. 55, 56, 60.

21. Cf. Dorothy Gale after the disappearance of Glinda from the land of the Munchkins in the movie version of *The Wizard of Oz:* "People come and go so quickly here!"— here in the anomalous zone of the tornado, the vessel in which all the contents of the familiar world are dislocated, disunited, and incessantly circulated, in the wind that L. Frank Baum imprinted on her as her name, as the law of her being: *There* is (a) no-place (that has shown itself to be uncannily) like home. A mournful movie, and one very concerned with the problem of the strangers who appear here where home was.

22. Axtell, *European and the Indian*, pp. 217–19, 264.

23. According to William Simmons, the Narragansetts accounted for the technological superiority of the English plow and other devices by asserting that they contained *manitou,* not a childish or superstitious explanation but rather an attempt to assimilate the alien tool without damaging the integrity of their conceptual system. *Cautantowwit's House: An Indian Burial Ground on the Island of Conanicut in Narragansett Bay* (Providence: Brown University Press, 1970), p. 51.

24. Neal Salisbury, *Manitou and Providence: Indians, Europeans, and the Making of New England, 1500–1643* (Oxford, Oxford University Press, 1982), pp. 42–49.

25. Ernst Bloch, "Nonsynchronism and the Obligation to Its Dialectics," trans. Mark Ritter, *New German Critique,* no. 11 (Spring 1977), 22–38. The quotation above opens the essay.

26. The most illustrative counterpoint here would be Benjamin Church's *Entertain-*

ing Passages Relating to Philip's War (1716), in *So Dreadfull a Judgement: Puritan Responses to King Philip's War, 1676-1677,* ed. Richard Slotkin and James K. Folsom (Middletown, Conn.: Wesleyan University Press, 1978), pp. 393-470. Church was an irascible and extraordinarily successful officer in the Plymouth forces who contributed significantly to the English victory by studying and adopting Indian strategies for forest warfare. He was treated with considerable suspicion owing to his preference for independent and unorthodox techniques, and his narrative seems to have been composed to vent his resentment against the ingratitude of Plymouth's Protestant power elite. In Church's view, the early English defeats resulted from an irrational inability to see the true nature of the Indian and the land, and a consequent failure to fight well. Religion attempts to impose meaning, and so flounders: ingenuity sees what is there, and wins. In keeping with his general polemical intent, Church's representation of the enemies dediabolizes them by presenting them as protobourgeois: when confronted by a white man who is reasonable, rather than riddled by prejudice, they recognize the main chance, abandon their cause, and sign on with Church to help end the war. Indians are reasonable beings when presented with reasonable options. Church's disaffection, like Franklin's and unlike Rowlandson's, fractures Puritan paradigms in order to introduce the benign reign of reason, a new clarity whose intactness is signaled by the exclusion of any strangeness or deep cultural difference from his representations of his ingenious red allies, with one exception, which is wondrous, like Ishmael's glimpse of the center of the great armada: "Proceeding in their March, they crossed another River, and opened a great Bay, where they might see many Miles along shore, where were Sands and Flats; and hearing a great noise below them towards the Sea. They dismounted their Horses, left them and crep'd among the bushes, until they came near the bank, and saw a vast company of *Indians,* of all Ages and Sexs, some on Horse-back running races, some at Foot-ball, some catching Eels & Flat-fish in the water, some Clamming, &c. but which way with safety to find out what *Indians* they were, they were at a loss" (p. 431).

27. Axtell, *European and the Indian,* pp. 245-71.

28. Jennings contends that the absence of herds was the major difference between Indian and European economic activity in North America, with the result that textiles became, along with guns and liquor, a highly prized commodity that had to be gotten from the Europeans and that therefore fostered dependency. *Invasion of America,* p. 18.

29. Mauss, *The Gift,* throughout, but esp. pp. 22, 43, 44, and 71 on the personality of money. In *Cautantowwit's House,* Simmons reports that the "belief that objects had souls has been convincingly attested among seventeenth century Algonquians of eastern Canada" (p. 57). On the significance of *mana,* which has many affinities with *manitou* as Simmons describes it (though I assume that the resemblance between the words is coincidental), see Lévi-Strauss's long introduction to the French edition of Mauss's *Sociologie et Anthropologie* (Paris, 1950), an essay that has had considerable influence on French theory, especially Lacan (Jeffrey Mehlman, "The Floating Signifier: From Lévi-Strauss to Lacan," *French Freud: Structural Studies of Psychoanalysis, Yale French Studies,* 48 [1972], 10-37). On the warding-off of bourgeois fungibility, see Taussig, *Devil and Commodity Fetishism.*

30. See Axtell, *European and the Indian,* pp. 110-31, and Simmons, *Cautantowwit's House,* 50-62: "When death occurred, it was an occasion not only for grief, but for fear

and circumspect behavior. Women blackened their faces when one of the family suffered illness, and everyone smeared his face with black paint at death. The wigwam in which the death occurred was abandoned; after the death of his son, the great sachem Canonicus burned his house and all the property within. During the mourning period, which lasted from three months to perhaps over one year, the grievers refrained from play, cosmetics, and angry words . . . The Narragansetts forbade the mention of the name of a dead person, and anyone bearing such a name was obliged to adopt another. To utter names of the dead was so heinously profane that 'the naming of their dead *Sachims,* is one ground of their warres.' In 1665, King Philip arrived in Nantucket with a number of warriors to kill an Indian known as John Gibbs who had mentioned the name of Massasoit, Philip's late father. Fortunately in this case, the English inhabitants of the island, through bribery and a show of force, managed to rescue the talkative John Gibbs" (p. 58; Simmons' citations omitted). "A sympathetic connection might be assumed between a person's name and his soul, and one who pronounced a dead man's name risked coaxing the soul back from the portals of death to cause mischief. The manifest function of a proper burial was probably to usher the soul from the dead body to its new sanctuary, where it remained apart from human affairs. The soul of a dead man who was not buried or who was impiously mourned might wander unhappily among the living and perhaps endanger them" (p. 59). "A taboo on sexual relations after childbirth is widespread throughout the world and is usually accompanied by the belief that any infraction will threaten the infant's health. Mourning taboos may likewise be seen as precautions to ensure that the soul of the recently departed maintain its course away from the living. In both instances the abstentions protect thresholds that have only lately and warily been crossed . . . Fear of the unburied dead and improperly mourned could . . . indicate an underlying sense of . . . power in indeterminate states of being, in that which is betwixt and between" (p. 62). "Among the Indians of eastern Canada, the corpse was never carried through the door, but was carried through the wall to which the sick person had turned when he died" (p. 67; Simmons' citations omitted).

31. John Bossy, *Christianity in the West, 1400–1700* (Oxford: Oxford University Press, 1987).

32. Axtell, *European and the Indian,* pp. 272–316.

33. Jennings, *Invasion of America,* pp. 21–31.

34. Simmons, *Cautantowwit's House,* p. 51.

35. Jennings notes that daily washing was ritualized among the Algonquians of Virginia and the Carolinas (*Invasion of America,* p. 50).

36. Jennings, *Invasion of America,* p. 12.

37. Simmons, "Cultural Bias in the New England Puritans' Perception of Indians," p. 68.

38. Gilles Deleuze, "Michel Tournier and the World without Others," trans. Graham Burchell, *Economy and Society,* 13.1 (1984), 56.

39. Annette Kolodny, *The Land before Her: Fantasy and Experience of the American Frontier, 1630–1860* (Chapel Hill: University of North Carolina Press, 1984), p. 33.

40. Bercovitch, *American Jeremiad,* 1–131.

41. John Winthrop, *Winthrop's Journal: "History of New England," 1630–1649,* ed. James Kendall Hosmer (New York: Scribners, 1908), Vol. 2, pp. 238–39.

42. See Axtell, *European and the Indian*, pp. 62–72; Neal Salisbury, "Red Puritans: The 'Praying Indians' of Massachusetts Bay and John Eliot," *William and Mary Quarterly*, 31 (1974), 27–54; William S. Simmons, "Conversion from Indian to Puritan," *New England Quarterly*, 52.2 (June 1979), 197–218; James Holstun, "John Eliot's Empirical Millenarianism," *Representations*, 4 (Fall 1983), 128–53; Jennings, *Invasion of America*, pp. 228–53.

43. Perry Miller, *Roger Williams: His Contribution to the American Tradition* (New York: Atheneum, 1970), p. 53–54.

44. Salisbury, "Red Puritans," p. 46.

45. Axtell, *European and the Indian*, pp. 168–206.

46. Quoted in Jennings, *Invasion of America*, p. 249.

47. Rowlandson mentions another Praying Indian, James the Printer, on p. 357, briefly and without judgment. According to Kathryn Zabelle Derounian, James Printer "was accused of participating in the Lancaster raid, and although acquitted, he ran away to join the Indians: he even acted as an Indian scribe during Rowlandson's ransom negotiations. Taking advantage of an amnesty offer, James the Printer returned to his old trade, probably working in Boston until about 1680 and then rejoining Green, Sr., in Cambridge on the second edition of the Indian Bible from 1680 to 1685. He was therefore definitely in Cambridge when Green, Sr., published the second and third editions of Rowlandson's book. George Parker Winship argues that one of the typesetters 'had an undeveloped phonetic sense that governed his spelling,' and he strongly suspects the Indian. Diebold cites numerous examples of phonetic misspellings throughout the first Cambridge edition and concludes that while English spelling was not standardized at this time, an unusually large number of errors appears in this—and even the next— Cambridge imprint. Therefore, the misspelling of 'Addition' [rather than 'Edition'] on the title page of the second edition, added to the other errors, points to James the Printer as the culprit." "The Publication, Promotion, and Distribution of Mary White Rowlandson's Captivity Narrative in the Seventeenth Century," *Early American Literature*, 23. 3 (1988), 245.

48. In the early 1980s, Norman Grabo presented a lecture to the Berkeley English department in which he argued that at the end of the narrative Rowlandson's alienation survives. At the time, I thought the narrative was a typical specimen of Puritan discourse, unusual only for its content rather than for its form or attitude. Obviously, I've come to see things Grabo's way, though I think that there are differences between the ways we explain the narrative. To the best of my knowledge, Grabo has not published his lecture as a chapter or essay.

49. Marilynne Robinson, *Housekeeping* (New York: Bantam, 1982), p. 153.

5. Afterword: Rowlandson's Future

1. Kathryn Zabelle Derounian, "The Publication, Promotion, and Distribution of Mary White Rowlandson's Captivity Narrative in the Seventeenth Century," *Early American Literature*, 2. 3 (1988), 240.

2. Edmund Morgan, *Visible Saints: The History of a Puritan Idea* (Ithaca: Cornell University Press, 1963), pp. 64–113.

3. Norman Pettit, *The Heart Prepared: Grace and Conversion in Puritan Spiritual Life* (New Haven: Yale University Press, 1966), p. 17.

4. David L. Greene, "New Light on Mary Rowlandson," *Early American Literature,* 20. 1 (Spring 1985), 32.

5. Ibid., pp. 32–33.

6. Ibid., pp. 33–34.

Index

The Wisconsin Project on American Writers

A series edited by Frank Lentricchia

DATE DUE			
FEB 01 '93			
DEC 9 '96			